MODERN
UTOPIAN FICTIONS

from H. G. Wells to Iris Murdoch

MODERN
UTOPIAN FICTIONS

from H. G. Wells to Iris Murdoch

PETER EDGERLY FIRCHOW

The Catholic University of America Press
Washington, D.C.

LIBRARY OF CONGRESS CATALOGING-IN-PUBLICATION DATA

Firchow, Peter Edgerly, 1937–
Modern utopian fictions from H.G. Wells to Iris Murdoch / by Peter
Edgerly Firchow.
p. cm.
Includes bibliographical references and index.
ISBN-13: 978-0-8132-1477-1 (alk. paper)
ISBN-10: 0-8132-1477-7 (alk. paper)
1. English fiction—20th century—History and criticism.
2. Utopias in literature.
3. Dystopias in literature.   I. Title.
PR888.U7F57 2007
823′.9109372—dc22
2006009565

FOR PAMINA

"Dies Bildnis ist bezaubernd schön"

CONTENTS

ACKNOWLEDGMENTS

I am grateful to the editors of the *Midwest Quarterly* and of *Literary Imagination* for allowing me to reprint, as Chapters 1 and 3 of this book, respectively, the following revised essays, "H. G. Wells's Time Machine: In Search of Time Future—and Time Past" (45, no. 2 [winter 2004]: 123–36), and "Huxley, Fukuyama, Marcuse, and the End of History" (4 [2002]: 237–62). The former essay was awarded the Victor Emmett prize for the best essay to appear in the *Midwest Quarterly* in 2004. My thanks also go to the Graduate School of the University of Minnesota for a Grant in Aid which allowed me to hire the very able Alex Mueller as my research assistant for a year. His expertise in bibliographical matters was a great help. I would also like to express my gratitude to the lively group of undergraduate seniors in my utopian seminar at the University of Minnesota in spring 2005. We shared ideas, some of which have found a place in this book.

It's also a pleasure to thank James Sexton and, especially, Christoph Irmscher, both of whom read the book and whose suggestions helped me avoid a variety of blunders. I want to thank, too, Martin Löschnigg and David Haley for reading and commenting on some of the chapters. Suzanne Wolk edited the book and thereby also reduced the number of errors I would otherwise have committed— though for any that remain I am of course solely responsible.

Finally, as always, I want to thank my wife, Evelyn S. Firchow, for her tireless support—and for giving me a taste of what utopia might be like.

PREFACE

Titles of books, at least of discursive books like this one, need to be justified or explained. Even a title like "Modern Utopian Fictions," where each constituent element should be familiar to readers of literary criticism, requires some preliminary discussion. Let me therefore begin with "utopia" and proceed almost immediately to "fiction," a concept with which utopia has become intimately and, I think, inexorably linked.

Utopia—or at least the study of utopia—is notoriously one of those places where the literary imagination and the social scientific imagination intersect. By "social science" I do not so much mean history, that art that is sometimes referred to as a science. History is always present in utopia, since the future is always a function of the past as well as of the present. I mean rather that most presumptively scientific of the social sciences, political science, the "science" which seeks to tell us what good government is or at least ought to be. Utopia may be a no place—that is, it is a fictional place—but it is always a no place with good government.

This intersection of different types of imagination, for which perhaps "opposition" would be a better word, begins at the very beginning of the hypothetical establishment of utopia, with Plato's *Republic*. Since, however, in Plato's day the social sciences had not yet been invented, or at least had not been differentiated and named— Aristotle, to be sure, did write a *Politics,* but then he also wrote a *Poetics*—Plato thought he was practicing philosophy and so posited a Philosopher King for his utopia rather than a social scientific monarch (or academic dean?). But Plato was also a failed poet who nevertheless produced in *The Republic* a work of poetry (with "poetry" broadly defined to include all the imaginative literary arts, as, say, the German word *Dichtung* does). Even so, he specifically and rather paradoxically excluded poets from his utopian state because, in his view, poets told lies. Creating "lies" or fictions, which is what poets (again broadly defined) do, was, to Plato's mind, the same thing as telling lies plain and simple. In his view, such fictions were at two removes from "true" reality rather than merely one, as "ordinary" reality supposedly is. Of course, though Plato did not mention it, by this criterion his own *Republic* stands self-condemned as a twice-told lie, since it too is obviously not "real" but "merely" a fiction.

But the same is also true for just about all subsequent attempts to depict utopia. They too are "lies"; they too are fictional. Perhaps therefore it would be better and surely less self-contradictory to approach utopian fictions from a less harshly Platonic perspective. Perhaps the "fiction" in "utopian fictions" is just as important as the "utopia," and, at least as far as modern utopias are concerned, very likely even more so. This supposition would help to explain why just about all utopias—notably of course those dealt with in this book—have tended to be produced by strictly literary people, with only an occasional social scientist like B. F. Skinner mixed in. At a minimum, placing the fictional element of utopia at an equal or superior level of importance with the social scientific element—i.e., answers to the question as to what constitutes the ideal state—means that human nature and human psychology must be introduced into the study of utopia. In other words, the literary notion of character must be introduced. Doing so means that the "literal truth" of the ideal state (that is, the social scientific truth) is always tested by and against the truth of our own lived experience (the literary truth). There is, then, more than one truth, and a realistic utopia (as well as studies of such utopias) must take account of their competing claims.

In this book I have sought to do justice to those competing claims, though perhaps not always in an entirely objective manner. I have tried to show how, in different ways and to different degrees, the depiction of utopia (and dystopia) in the modern period has become increasingly literary, so that what is utopian about these fictions must always be viewed, and interpreted, from the literary perspective. This increasingly important literary component is often evident in what strikes the reader as the peculiar and even contradictory ways in which the plot is developed or the scene and characters described. In Wells's *Time Machine,* for example, we need to understand—and explain—the paradox that as the Traveller voyages into the future he also voyages into the past. Or in Orwell's two anti-utopian narratives, how and why Soviet "reality" (history) is transformed into fictional guises. Or in Golding's *Lord of the Flies,* why two groups of boys of different but still prepubescent ages come to crash-land on a tropical island without suffering the least injury. This process of "fictionalizing" utopia culminates in Iris Murdoch's *The Bell.* With Murdoch the utopian element becomes once and for all subordinate to the fictional one; or, put another way, with Murdoch utopia is absorbed into the genre of the novel. It becomes triumphantly fictional, even though Plato would have denounced it as a lie.

This is true, despite the fact that *The Bell* was written by a philosopher/novelist who was also a lifelong admirer of Plato. Murdoch can remain of Plato's party, while at the same time seeming to oppose it, because she persuades us of the truth of her utopian possibilities (or fictions) by "testing" those possibilities against the hypothesized experience of a series of variegated and often extraordinarily complex characters. For her the good community can only be one in which truly real or at least realistic (though of course nevertheless fictional) characters are able to live and even flourish. Compare this procedure with that of Francis Fukuyama, a social scientist who not long ago caused dismay among his colleagues because he dared to find fault with a conception of human nature that was limited to economic interest alone as a motive force for action. Turning back to Plato, Fukuyama argued for a more complex conception of human nature, one that would at least add the thymotic motive to provide for a fuller and more persuasive understanding of why humans act as they do.

This is not to say that writers of utopian fictions are lacking in social scientific imagination. H. G. Wells was an international celebrity in his day not only because of his fiction (including of course also his utopian and dystopian fiction), but also for having written or co-written books as different as *The Outline of History*—probably the best-selling book of history ever—and *The Science of Life* (together with Julian Huxley and his son G. P. Wells), which sought to explain the biological sciences to a whole generation of readers. So too Aldous Huxley, who along with his novels and stories wrote books on psychedelic drugs, on the art of seeing, on history, and on religion. As for George Orwell, one could view him as a social scientist even before he became a novelist, since his first published book, *Down and Out in Paris and London,* is really more of a social study of the *Lumpenproletariat* than it is a novel. A little later he followed up this precedent with fascinating studies of the industrial poor in *The Road to Wigan Pier* and of the Spanish Civil War in *Homage to Catalonia.* Shaw's plays were from the very outset, as in *Widowers' Houses* and *Mrs. Warren's Profession,* close examinations of acute social problems, and, given his lifelong suspicion that his audiences might not be sufficiently intelligent to grasp what he was saying in his plays, he supplemented them with long prefaces to ensure that they did. Iris Murdoch, of course, was a professional philosopher before she became a novelist, and even William Golding taught philosophy and English before he was able to make a living out of his writing.

Still, one must not forget that it is for aesthetic reasons that we keep reading Wells's *Time Machine* after more than a hundred years, and not for social scientific ones—not that I mean to imply that those reasons have ceased to be relevant. And it is surely significant too that, after some two and a half millennia, what is remembered most vividly from *The Republic* is its most imaginative and poetic part, namely the Allegory of the Cave. Judging the novels I deal with here on an admittedly informal aesthetic/social scientific scale, Iris Murdoch's *The Bell* is, I think, the most literary, and George Orwell's *Animal Farm* and *Nineteen Eighty-Four,* dealing as they both do with thinly veiled versions of the Soviet Union, are probably the least. Nevertheless both of Orwell's fictions have survived the year 1984 (and also the year 1989) without becoming dated, a survival they owe far more to the continuing literary power and complexity with which they challenge the imagination than to their confrontation with a Soviet system that no longer exists. Here too I want to make it clear that for me one of the most important links among all the often variegated chapters of this book is the conviction that if utopia (along with dystopia) is to be effective, it must be at least as effective aesthetically as it is substantively.

Finally, what about the word "modern" in the title? In the most obvious sense, the word is appropriate because all of the utopias I consider in this book belong to the modern period, which, as far as literary history is concerned, usually refers to the years from about 1890 to 1960. *The Time Machine* was first published in 1895 and *The Bell* in 1958. But they are modern too in another sense, that is, in the sense that, even at their most optimistic, as in Shaw's *Major Barbara*, they remain suspicious of utopia. For all of these writers, in other words, utopia has in an important sense ceased to be utopian. This may be because, as in Shaw, it has become mixed up with death and destruction, or, as in Murdoch, it may not be a habitable place for the sorts of people who need it most, particularly those people who possess complex characters and active imaginations. For others, notably for Huxley, Orwell, and Golding, utopia has assumed what for them is its characteristic modern form, namely, dystopia. As far as they are concerned, there is no more good place. There are only different kinds of bad places. This may not be an especially encouraging prospect for those of us who have kept alive the hope for a better world, if not exactly for a utopia, but then we too are moderns—or even postmoderns—and must take our fictions with the proverbial grain of ironic salt.[1]

---

1. Bernard Crick, the author of one of the best-known biographies of Orwell, is not primarily a man of letters but is rather (or was until recently) professor of political science at Edinburgh University. In the Preface to his collection of *Essays on Politics and Literature* (1989), he complains of the cultural divide between practitioners of literary and political analysis, and hopes for a more tolerant and interdisciplinary analysis and discussion of fictional texts (vi–vii).

MODERN
UTOPIAN FICTIONS

from H. G. Wells to Iris Murdoch

INTRODUCTION

Very few utopias stand out as great works of literature. . . . The
didactic purpose overwhelms any literary aspiration.

Krishan Kumar

Nearly twenty years ago I published an essay entitled "Utopia, Eutopia, Youdopia: The Technology of Happiness." I make mention
of this obscure bibliographical fact not primarily to blow into my
own scholarly horn, but merely to prove that I have been thinking
and writing about utopian subjects for quite some time, as well as
to demonstrate that the word "utopia" can mean, and has meant,
different things to different people at different times—including of
course to myself. Back when I wrote the above-mentioned essay I
was thinking about how the usual meanings of the "u" word—"no
place" and "good place," utopia and eutopia, a pun originated by
that archetypal utopianist, Sir Thomas More—related to the drug
culture of the 1960s, especially in such technologically advanced and
quasi-utopian places as California. So, basking a little in the august
tradition of Sir Thomas, I ventured to add a pun of my own, not,
however—let me make the disclaimer at once—based on anything
more than a vague familiarity with ancient Greek.

At least until relatively recently, the good place and the no place,
eutopia and utopia (and, more surprisingly, perhaps even the bad
place and the no place, depending on how we define dystopia), have
often, as in More's case (e.g., the contrasting Books I and II of *Utopia*),
accompanied one another, since the one has tended to gain in emotional force by being opposed to the other, just as heaven needs hell to
ensure its attractiveness. That is not to say, however, that the good no-
place has not haunted the imagination of humanity for just about as

long as humanity remembers. The Garden of Eden and the Blessed
Isles provide ample testimony for the enduring appeal of the good
no-place, which, admittedly, was for many people until not too long
ago a not altogether imaginary someplace. For some of us it still is.

More recently, the good someplace has been occasionally identified with an actual geographical locality, even a very specific one,
such as, say, Athens in the fourth century BC, or Byzantium in the
sixth century AD. (See W. B. Yeats's *A Vision* for more on these and
other quasi-utopian places and moments.) Ford Madox Ford, in
those halcyon (or should one say utopian?) pre-1914 days when—in
memory at least—the sun was always shining and he was still generally known as Ford Madox Hueffer, even discovered utopia (along
with eutopia) in the now seemingly unlikely, peaceful, and prosperous town of Giessen in central Germany (Hueffer 1911, 456). Other, better-known and more widely persuasive twentieth-century examples include Margaret Mead's *Growing Up in Samoa* and some of
the literature written about the Soviet Union in the 1920s and 1930s,
notably Sidney and Beatrice Webb's *Soviet Communism: A New Civili-
sation?* Even today, at the beginning of the twenty-first century, after
the disillusionment following the collapse of the Soviet utopian experiment, remnants of utopian social thinking continue to exist in
some of the neo-hippie communes in California and, though admittedly for very different reasons and in very different ways, in the neo-
conservative think tanks of Washington, D.C.[1]

And, of course, during the latter half of the nineteenth century,

1. Many contemporary writers on utopia assume that utopia must be "progressive," that is, largely sympathetic to Marxist or neo-Marxist views and causes. This is
clearly the case with a contemporary critical overview like Russell Jacoby's *The End of
Utopia*. While it's probably true that left-wing utopias and dystopias outnumber right-
wing ones, there seems no necessary reason why this should be so. As Krishan Kumar
remarks somewhat caustically, "Marxism may be a very good way of analysing past
and present societies. But it has no more hold on the future than any other theory, utopian or otherwise" (1987, 53). Still, as a matter of statistics, of the writers discussed in
this book, we should note that both Shaw and Wells were at one time leading members of the (socialist) Fabian Society. Iris Murdoch was for a short time a card-carrying
member of the Communist Party of Great Britain. George Orwell initially wanted to

the United States of America was strewn—one might perhaps more appropriately say littered—with examples of mostly failed attempts at utopia, of which the Oneida community is only the best known. These were typically inspired by a mixture of religious motives and elements drawn from that celebrated and influential trio of French utopian thinkers of the early to mid-nineteenth century, Henri Saint-Simon, Auguste Comte, and Charles Fourier. (New) "Harmony"— the name of numerous small towns in the United States, including one in my home state of Minnesota—is a vestige of this once powerful utopian movement.

Over the last hundred years or so, utopia has come to seem a more realistic and even real place. As the prospect of utopia's becoming a social reality has grown ever closer, a strong reaction has set in, one that on the surface may seem surprising and even paradoxical. The Russian religious philosopher Nicholas Berdyaev was, I think, the first to make the reasons for this reaction against utopia explicit, and therefore he is appropriately acknowledged in an epigraph at the beginning of Aldous Huxley's *Brave New World*. But the idea is already implicit in Alexis de Tocqueville's *Democracy in America*. Americans might think they were free and happy, so Tocqueville concluded, but it was only a freedom qualified by and made subject to the tyranny of the majority. American happiness, he concluded, was delusory, a happiness more or less indistinguishable from smug self-satisfaction. Nor was Tocqueville by any means alone. His contemporary the German poet Heine confessed ironically that he sometimes thought of sailing to America, "that pig-pen of freedom / Inhabited by boors living in equality." And his fellow German and approximate contemporary Nietzsche, along with many other nineteenth-century

join the Spanish War as a member of the Communist International Brigade, and only chose the POUM (United Marxist Workers' Party) in Barcelona when he couldn't. Aldous Huxley early joined the 1917 Club (a club named in honor of the 1917 Bolshevik Revolution in Russia) and later described himself as a Fabian socialist. Only William Golding could be thought of as at all inclined toward sympathizing with conservative political views, though even he joined the Communist-sympathizing Left Book Club in 1938 (Carver 2002, 386).

European intellectuals, was convinced that Americans were hopeless-
ly given over to the dubious and hardly utopian pleasures of money
grubbing—"fumbling in a greasy till," as a disillusioned William Butler Yeats would a little later describe his own countrymen, many of
whom had already emigrated to the United States or were in the process of doing so.[2] In short, utopia in its American manifestations was
seen to foster a uniform and often sham egalitarianism rather than a
genuine liberty. (It undoubtedly did foster a genuine commercialism
and consumerism, however.) Utopia in the Western world, as a consequence, became increasingly something to be dreaded rather than
looked forward to.

These on the whole new and largely negative visions of utopia are generally referred to as "dystopias," or more rarely as "caco-
topias," and sometimes more obviously as "anti-utopias." (These
names for negative utopias are, however, not always treated as synonymous.) They are, as all of these designations suggest, "bad" places, though they are always bad in very special ways. In other words,
they are not just some random ugly and unhealthy place—such
as, say, Gary, Indiana—but bad places that were once and perhaps
still are considered to be "good" places, though only by a relatively
small number of adherents. Put another way, dystopias still retain
traces of their utopian origin. Indeed dystopias may once have been
widely accepted as utopias, as, for example, Plato's *Republic* once
was thought of as archetypically utopian. (Wells's *Time Machine* in
fact explicitly depicts a dystopia that once was a utopia.) Nowadays,
however, it is usually viewed negatively because of its strongly (and
perhaps even inherently) racist and antidemocratic tendencies. Behind Huxley's dystopian New World State there is the failed dream
of an American utopia, just as behind Orwell's dystopian Oceania
there is the failed dream of a Soviet utopia.

Deliberately conceived dystopias, such as Huxley's and Orwell's,

2. See my entry on the United States in the forthcoming *Imagology: A Handbook
of the Literary Representation of National Characters,* edited by Joep Leerssen and Manfred Beller, for more on European views of the American utopian experiment.

however, differ from most utopias that have merely become dystopias over time in that they are usually satirical. To be sure, this may also hold true for certain aspects of positive utopias, as it does to a degree, for example, for Sir Thomas More's *Utopia*, especially for those sections dealing with property and money. So too with the fourth book of Swift's *Gulliver's Travels*, where the satire of contemporaneous (British) humanity is even more obvious. This tendency for utopia to turn into or to be replaced by dystopia, and for dystopia to be primarily a vehicle for satire of existing social conditions, is by no means universal. Nonsatirical utopias continue to be written, such as B. F. Skinner's *Walden II* or Ernest Callanbach's *Ecotopia*. This is even true of Margaret Atwood's *A Handmaid's Tale*, where the satirical elements are outweighed by her intensely feminist concerns. Indeed, in the cases of two of the most notable and more or less recent writers on utopian subjects, H. G. Wells and Aldous Huxley, negative utopias are eventually replaced by positive ones. Significant too in this connection is the fact that the famously sardonic George Orwell reveals unmistakable utopian impulses in *Burmese Days*, *Homage to Catalonia*, and *Coming Up for Air.* And even *Animal Farm* and *Nineteen Eighty-Four* contain elements, such as the brief period following the overthrow of the humans in the former novel and the mysteriously beautiful "Golden Country" in the latter, that are clearly utopian (Firchow 1992, 17–38). Not that the utopian impulses in the writings of Wells, Orwell, and Huxley are by any means identical. In *A Modern Utopia* Wells embraces a utopia of technological sophistication, whereas Huxley's *Island* is (with certain important qualifications) moderately opposed to technological development, and Orwell's "Golden Country" is implacably antitechnological, as is also the Oceanic state, at least insofar as nonmilitary technology is concerned.

Despite these admittedly somewhat ambiguous but on the whole positive elements (or, possibly, even because of them), most of the memorable utopian fictions of our time are largely pessimistic—not of course about the future, but really about the present. What after all would be the point of attacking the future? As Samuel Hynes points out, primarily but not exclusively with Orwell in mind, "Utopias do not predict the future; they judge the present. The best modern examples of the genre of *1984*—H. G. Wells's *Time Machine,* Huxley's *Brave New World,* Golding's *Lord of the Flies*—use future time in similar ways, to isolate and emphasize certain aspects of the human situation in order to focus attention on them; the intention is admonitory, not prophetic" (Hynes 1971, 15).

Technology, or, more commonly, the opposition to technology, is undoubtedly an important recurrent theme in much utopian and dystopian fiction. This tendency is even more obvious in a literary genre that often overlaps with utopian/dystopian literature, namely, science fiction, a genre which should perhaps be more appropriately termed "technology fiction." Not surprisingly, therefore, there are obvious utopian elements in the writings of the acknowledged inventor of science fiction, Jules Verne, especially in his *20,000 Leagues Under the Sea,* just as there are obvious technological elements in the fiction of that most utopian of modern novelists, H. G. Wells. Such technification, to coin a word, of modern utopian fiction is amplified in a number of immensely popular movies and TV series, among them *Star Wars, Dr. Who,* and *Star Trek,* though most of these are also indebted to the long tradition of books of imaginary voyages, especially those dealing with traveling to the moon. Technology, of course, is the modern equivalent of what in earlier ages used to be called magic. But modern technology is magic that really works, bringing with it not only the prospect of an earthly paradise but also the suddenly daunting prospect—as with just about all modern utopias—of actually having to inhabit it.[3]

One of the great fears of the anti-utopians with respect to tech-

3. Science fiction also partakes of another quasi-utopian area of sociological study (or of sociological speculation, at any rate) called "futurology"—again the *scientification* of an older concept, here that of the prophet. Like the prophet, the futurologist foretells the coming of the promised land—of utopia—or of its opposite, apocalypse, that is, dystopia.

nological progress is that it will ultimately deprive all but a tiny minority of people—or perhaps even everyone—of anything "useful" to do; it will, in other words, substitute itself for actual lived life.[4] This is a fear, it should be noted, that precedes by many decades the current denigration of "virtual" or computer-generated reality. It is, for example, clearly expressed in E. M. Forster's anti-utopian short story "The Machine Stops." Humanity is now faced with a problem for which humanity is utterly unprepared because hitherto it had never presented itself as a problem. Previously it had, in fact, been a desirable end. The new and unanticipated problem is what to do with a life in which work is no longer required—is, in fact, no longer even possible. In a world where leisure is compulsory, utopian existence suddenly seems horrifying precisely because it is "utopian," because it is so easy and comfortable and, paradoxically, so unproblematic. Utopia, it turns out, delivers for most of its inhabitants not intellectual and emotional challenges but only an animalistic hedonism and, what is perhaps even worse, boredom. Aldous Huxley's *Brave New World* is the classic example of a future society in which technology has—magically and ironically—provided humanity with all it had thought it desired.[5]

Not that the growth of technology is the only or perhaps even

4. That is not, however, what the author of *The Book of the Machines* fears in Samuel Butler's *Erewhon*. There it is the distant prospect of the evolution of machinery into conscious entities that will be "superior" to humans that so disturbs him that he demands that all machines less than 271 years old must be destroyed. The issue here is not so much that that the machines will supplant man or become harsh taskmasters. "[T]here is no occasion for anxiety," the author of *The Book of the Machines* assures his readers, "about the future happiness of mankind so long as he continues to be in any way profitable to the machines." The real problem is that human pride will be irreparably damaged. The idea that humans could be intellectually inferior to some other entity is as repugnant to this professor of the Colleges of Unreason as is the idea that "even at the remotest period my ancestors were other than human beings." If he really believed that, he would "take no further pleasure or interest in life" (Butler 1985, 222).

5. Huxley's dystopia, however, does provide for work (or at least a kind of makework), so that that the inhabitants of the New World State at least feel as if they are making a contribution. This is true even of the lowest orders of workers, of epsilons like the, technologically speaking, quite unnecessary elevator operator.

the primary reason why there is so powerful a reaction against utopia in the twentieth century. In an important sense the reaction was
to be expected, was in fact inevitable, given the pendulum swings
characteristic of prior literary and intellectual history. Besides, there
is—and always has been—a fundamental disagreement among writers on utopian subjects (both for and against) with respect to the
answers to the two essential questions to which all utopian societies—and perhaps all societies as such—must find answers, namely:
(1) what constitutes the good life? (ethics); and (2) what is human nature really like? (biology and/or psychology).

To ethics first: in the West there have been, almost from the very
beginning, two opposing and perhaps incompatible assumptions
about ethics, that is, first, an assumption based on a version of the
utilitarian calculus, which, of course, was not always called such but
formerly usually went under the name of hedonism. Essentially, the
assumption here was that one could (should) evaluate human experience in terms of the greater or lesser amount of happiness that an
experience provided. (Crucial here, of course, are the definitions of
happiness and unhappiness.) In this view, an experience is good to
the degree that happiness outweighs unhappiness, and a good life is
thought of as one in which good experiences (as defined above) outnumber bad ones.

The second type of ethics also operates on a kind of calculus,
though most of its adherents would be reluctant to admit it. Here
the measurement is of the intensity (or depth or quality) of an experience rather than the quantity of happiness it brings with it. This
sort of ethics applies primarily to religious experience, but insofar as
aesthetic experience is also ethical experience, it belongs to this category. After seeing a particularly good performance of *Hamlet* or *Lear*,
we do not feel happy; we feel moved. We do not measure our happiness or lack of it but rather the intensity of our response, and we
seek to inquire into the reasons for it, as Aristotle long ago pointed
out. In terms of a good life, this second type of ethics often values
a brief and even tragic life as superior to a long and happy one—the

martyred saints are to be preferred over those who were unmartyred, just as the lives of Romeo and Juliet are superior to those of Baucis and Philemon.

How does this difference in ethics relate to the utopia/dystopia distinction? Generally speaking, the answer to this important question is that utopias tend to operate in accordance with the first type of ethics, dystopias in accordance with the second.[6]

As for the second essential concept on which utopian/dystopian writers agree or disagree—that is, the nature of human nature—it would seem that underlying all utopian societies, from Plato's on down, there is a more or less systematic psychology, as well as a more or less systematic counterpsychology, for keeping citizens under control, with the aim of producing socially predictable and socially acceptable (stable) results. The citizens, however, may as a consequence no longer be what we, as members of a diverse and on the whole liberal society, would recognize as "human."

Put another way, the question is whether human nature is essentially good, so that what needs to be developed is a social structure—ideally of minimal complexity—where that goodness will be free to express itself fully. (Rousseau is the best-known exponent of this view.) Or is human nature essentially (or at least statistically) bad, so that what is needed is a structure that will assure complete control of such "bad" impulses as aggression, sexual libido, or the desire for power, as described, say, in Golding's *Lord of the Flies* or Orwell's *Nineteen Eighty-Four.* Or is humanity not easily classifiable under either category? As Joseph Wood Krutch remarks, after the behaviorist revolution, it would seem that "'human nature' does not exist in the sense which the phrase implies. Whatever desires, tastes, preferences, and tendencies have been so general and so persistent as to create the assumption that they are innate or 'natural' must be, as

---

6. This distinction also raises the related question about the way(s) in which utopias and dystopias resemble each other, or differ, in terms of the aesthetic or "literary" experience they provide. Christian Enzensberger, for example, argues that only dystopias possess any sort of literary merit (Biesterfeld 1982, 15).

a matter of fact, merely the most ancient and deeply graven of the conditionings to which the human animal has been subjected." "Human nature," in other words, is just another way of describing human social conditioning, whether systematic and deliberate or unsystematic and seemingly random.

Is it therefore inevitable that humans will become malleable at the hands of a seemingly or ironically benevolent authority, as in Huxley's *Brave New World,* for example, or even in Skinner's *Walden II*? In an important sense, all utopian and dystopian literature is made up of such fictional "experiments" in which human nature is put to the test. Indeed this may be true, though less obviously so, of all realistic fiction. The question posed is, ultimately, always the same, though it may look superficially different, namely, given certain social conditions, how would human beings react, change, develop?

This "experimental" aspect of utopias and dystopias is especially evident in Huxley's *Brave New World* and *Island,* but it also figures importantly in Shaw's *Major Barbara* and Golding's *Lord of the Flies.* In some cases, the dystopian vision represents a more "objective" repetition of the social experiment conducted in the utopia (or vice versa), as, for example, in the case of Wells's utopian novel *Men Like Gods* and Huxley's dystopian satire *Brave New World*. More rarely it also works the other way around, as when the aging Huxley revises the opinions of the youthful Huxley in his utopian fiction *Island* (1962).

Finally, we need to address the important literary question— though it's not merely a literary question, I think—as to whether there is such a thing as a genre of utopian fiction, with definable and predictable characteristics. And, if so, is there a corollary dystopian genre? Can we, for example, define utopia essentially and sociologically, as Lars Gustafson does, as the "depiction of a society outside of historical experience?" (Biesterfeld 1982, 10). Or, as George Kateb does, by adding up all the certifiably utopian characteristics of "peace, abundance, leisure, equality, untroubled virtue" in order to arrive at a definition (1976, 83)? And if that is possible, is utopia nevertheless a genre which, like most other literary genres, flows easily into other literary genres? Orwell's *Animal Farm* is at least as much of a fable as it is an anti-utopia, and the society it depicts is not by any means entirely "outside of historical experience." Golding's *Lord of the Flies* is not only a dystopia but also an adventure story consciously modeled on Ballantyne's *Coral Island*. *The Bell* is fundamentally a very traditional novel, with some other elements mixed in, such as philosophy and magical realism. *Major Barbara* is a highly imaginative retelling of the Faust story, among other things, including an Ibsenist discussion play, a feminist and even Darwinist thesis play—and, of course, "just" a very powerful and effective drama.

It is here, at the intersection of utopia and fiction, that I have tried to locate this book. My principal thesis is that, at roughly the same time as utopia increasingly came to approximate reality, especially in the United States and the former Soviet Union, a number of important writers of fiction—among them some of the ones considered in this book—have sought to show how this approximation has in one way or another failed to achieve its goals. In doing so, their "demonstrations" have stressed the fictional (or, more broadly speaking, the literary) aspects of utopia in order to make those "demonstrations" more persuasive. So, for example, *The Time Machine* is as innovative as a work of fiction as it is as a depiction of a future anti-utopia. Today, more than a hundred years after its initial appearance, it is remembered because of its rich literary resonance and context rather than because of the quasi-scientific jargon about the mathematics of four dimensions on which its theory of time travel rests. It is its symbolic qualities that reverberate in the memory, not its quasi-scientific factoids. *Ars,* as Horace might have said, had he been living today, still remains *longa,* but *technologia* has definitely become *brevis.*

Similarly with Shaw's *Major Barbara.* Shaw, like Wells (or at any rate the Wells of dystopian fictions like the *Time Machine*), is still an immensely popular writer, though less so within the groves of academe than on the stages of (off) Broadway and the West End. The

striking and, to my mind, shameful neglect of Shaw on the part of
the universities is probably—and paradoxically—due to his overt didacticism rather than to his overt socialist politics. It is for literary
rather than political reasons that he is no longer taught or even read
in the academic world. His "message," in other words, is thought
to be too obvious to require the interpretive services of an established literary priest-class. Even to contemporaries—Yeats, for example—he seemed as unpoetic as a sewing machine, in which guise he
once, so Yeats claimed, manifested himself in a nightmare. Yet, despite the long history of academic neglect of Shaw the literary artist, some of his best plays, *Major Barbara* among them, continue to
puzzle and fascinate the general public—along with a few unfash-
ionable academic critics. It is precisely the "poetic," antimechanical
aspects of *Major Barbara* that have kept it alive since its first performance precisely one hundred years ago. Not, however, that its paradoxical message of salvation through destruction has lost any of its
relevance in the chaotic world of today.

As for Huxley's *Brave New World*, its title, along with the world
of dreadful joy that it so powerfully depicts, has by now passed into
the language as a "household" concept. Huxley's ironies about the
"brave new world" have triumphed even over Shakespeare's, and
his literary insight into how that world would (and will) develop
has proved far more illuminating than the merely sociological insights of eminent contemporary social critics and philosophers like
Fukuyama and Marcuse. Much the same could and should be (and
is here) said for George Orwell's two influential anti-utopian fictions, *Animal Farm* and *Nineteen Eighty-Four*. Though both of these
fictions are intimately related to the political developments of the
first half of the twentieth century, they have retained their reader-
ship (at least in the West) not primarily because of their politics but
because of their artfulness. *Animal Farm*, we have come to realize,
is one of the most perfect satires written in our time, and *Nineteen
Eighty-Four* turns out to be far more complex in its literary makeup
than most readers have hitherto recognized. That is why *Nineteen*

Eighty-Four is still read even after the year 1984 and the Soviet Union itself have long passed into history. Otto Friedrich is wrong to say that *"1984* is a good book despite the fact that it is a bad novel" (1984, 99). The book's lasting appeal is not merely or even primarily due, as he claims, to its "political insight." It is due much more—not only after the passing of 1984 and the Soviet Union, but certainly also after those events—to its specifically literary qualities, such as its complexity and ambiguity. As for its alleged lack of fully realized characters, that is an absence that is directly caused by the kind of world the Oceanic future represents. "The book cannot be understood," so Irving Howe maintains, "nor can it be properly valued, simply by resorting to the usual literary categories, for it posits a situation in which these categories are no longer significant" (Howe 1971, 43).

William Golding's *Lord of the Flies,* like Orwell's two anti-utopias, reflects the prevalent pessimism of its time, but what has sustained it for readers over the decades is the paradoxical vitality with which that pessimism is presented. Even though the premises on which Golding's anti-utopian vision is based have largely vanished—there is, for the moment at least, no more cold war heating up into nuclear war, and there are no more "remote" islands unobservable by satellite and unlocatable by global positioning systems—still his exploration of the depths of the human psyche has remained relevant some fifty years after the book's publication. If anything, this is even more true of Iris Murdoch's *The Bell,* which deals with a world in which the most up-to-date technology is a mechanical tiller. Murdoch's novel is the most novelistic of all the utopias that I deal with in this book. One of its aims, indeed, seems to be to test the extent to which utopia and fiction can be reconciled; that is, it seeks to answer the question as to whether the vast variety of human beings, as we encounter them in life as well as in the great novels and dramas of the past, can be accommodated in the necessarily much narrower confines of utopia.

Utopian as well as anti-utopian impulses, then, have in recent years come to manifest themselves increasingly in aesthetic and not merely sociological ways. Utopia must now be redefined not simply as "the depiction of a society outside of history" but as the depiction of believable characters confronted with the problem of how to create and live in an often ironically "ideal" society while still retaining their humanity. The question which even the dystopians among these writers seek to answer is how to devise an ideal or near-ideal society in which actual human beings can live, not how to adapt or condition or genetically engineer human beings so that they will be able to live in an "ideal" society that has been more or less arbitrarily conceived. The social shoe, in other words, must be made to fit the human foot, not the other way around. It is for this reason, I believe, that modern utopian and dystopian fictions do not always find a local habitation within easily identifiable literary categories.

On the whole, it is probably safe to say that all utopian and anti-utopian fictions share the strengths and weaknesses of the novel (or play) of ideas. That is, in this "genre" the intellectual element tends to outweigh the emotional one. Talk tends to dominate over action, with talk sometimes unfortunately degenerating into sermonizing. Still, the impulse to imagine utopia, along with dystopia, is probably archetypal and related to the basic human need to ask and answer eschatological questions. That need will probably only cease to be felt when humanity either ceases to be recognizable as consisting of individual humans (at least in the view of those of us living at the beginning of the twenty-first century), or when humanity actually enters utopia (or dystopia). And when that happens, "mere" literature won't matter anymore.

It is in its emphasis on the literary aspects of modern utopia that my study differs from most previous studies of the subject. Not that such previous studies have ignored the fact that utopias are fictions or that they may and probably do possess an aesthetic dimension. One of the most notable recent students of utopia, Krishan Kumar, for example, shows his awareness of the issue by openly admitting that he has "not been much concerned with the specifically literary quality of the works" that he deals with. Though he knows very well that all of these works are literary fictions, he acknowledges that as a social historian he does not "feel particularly competent to analyse" them. Nevertheless he does feel competent and confident enough to venture on a vast generalization regarding the possible results of such literary analysis, even when conducted competently, namely, "that not much is to be gained in doing so." In his view only Sir Thomas More's *Utopia* and William Morris's *News from Nowhere* possess any real literary merit, by which Kumar seems to mean that their "prose" is a pleasure to read; but even so, their literary quality in no way affects their merit as utopias (1987, 25). Implicitly, it seems, Kumar thinks of literary criticism as consisting of a series of primarily subjective and impressionistic responses to texts, differing radically in this way from the supposedly logical and considered analyses practiced by the social and political "sciences." As for the utopias of Butler and Huxley and Orwell, they are apparently the products of mere literary hacks.

That is why Kumar considers utopias not in literary terms but "chiefly as contributions to social thought," and that is also why his book, so formidable in its historical and sociological dimensions and learning, turns out to be so disappointing in its analyses of particular works of fiction, notably Aldous Huxley's *Brave New World* and George Orwell's *Nineteen Eighty-Four*. He fails to see that Huxley's satire of the future Fordian utopia is based on a deliberate impoverishment of human nature when contrasted with the wealth of human experience as displayed in the great literature of the past (i.e., John Savage's Shakespeare). His analysis of *Brave New World,* in other words, is inadequate because it lacks a literary dimension, lacks even the insight to recognize that *Brave New World* is, literarily speaking, one of the greatest anti-utopian satires ever written. So too with Orwell, where Kumar fails to see that the whole thrust of *Nineteen Eighty-Four* is utterly changed once one perceives that Orwell has provided the book with two plots, one overt and the other covert. He fails, in other words, to see the point of this important difference to an understanding of the book because it is a difference based on a

literary not a sociological insight. That is also why, when one finish-
es reading Kumar's otherwise informative book, one is left wonder-
ing why he chose to deal with literary fictions by writers like Huxley
and Orwell in the first place, given his admission that he possesses
no appreciation of their specifically literary qualities or of the relevance of those qualities to a fuller understanding of the nature of
utopia.

That Kumar is fully aware of the considerable gap between literature and sociology in the discussion and analysis of utopia does
not by any means remedy the situation.[7] In a later essay on Wells
and sociology, he confesses that "[w]hat perhaps [*sic*] we rather need
to remind ourselves [of] is that most of Wells's utopias are in the
form of novels." And, beyond such possible reminders, Kumar even
admits that "[u]topias are by definition fictions" (206). Still, that admission does not mean that Kumar bothers to subject Wells's utopian fictions to a specifically literary analysis, one that would take
into account, say, *The Time Machine*'s "subtlety, its allusiveness, its satirical edge and its frequent shifts of mood" (207). It's not enough
to pay pious lip service to a literary rather than a sociological understanding of utopian fiction. The proof, as always, is in the actual
consumption of the pudding, not in grand generalizations about its
hypothetical tastiness. Ultimately, even utopia must stand (and with-
stand) the test of reality.

This rather lamentable situation is not helped, of course, by literary critics—or literary *theoreticians*, to be precise—who argue that
there is no such thing as literary theory or even literary criticism.
This is a position most notably (or notoriously) taken up by Terry
Eagleton, whose vastly popular *Literary Theory: An Introduction* concludes paradoxically that there is no literary theory but only political theory. Clearly relishing his role as the aging *enfant terrible* of the
fashionable theory circuit, Eagleton maintains that "[t]he final logi-

7. This distinction is not really identical, as is sometimes claimed (e.g., by Frederick Karl), with the one between literature and (hard) science, that is, the supposed
gulf between the "two cultures" posited by C. P. Snow.

cal move in a process which began by recognizing that literature is an illusion is to recognize that literary theory is an illusion too." What deluded literary folks like ourselves, in other words, have in the past (mis)taken for literary analysis, is nothing more than "a branch of social ideologies" (204). It would seem that for some people, as Kingsley Amis once said, reality consists of a mixture of politics and sports. For a select few like Eagleton, however, it's just politics plain and simple. So circumscribed, reality becomes boring, like listening to Fidel Castro's seven-hour political monologues or, for that matter, watching an interminable cricket game. Reality must encompass illusions, especially literary illusions—if indeed they are illusions, since for most people (and not just for Don Quixote or Emma Bovary) their illusions *are* what constitute their reality—and that is finally what imagining utopia is all about.[8]

8. That reality must include what are usually thought of as illusions is persuasively argued by Joseph Wood Krutch: "We may doubt the conclusions of our logic, the premises of our philosophy, and even the evidence of our eyes, but we cannot doubt these emotions and these desires, since they are for us the only ultimate realities" (1956, 114).

CHAPTER I

H. G. WELLS'S *TIME MACHINE* AND THE END OF UTOPIA

God damn you all: I told you so.
                    H. G. Wells

*Whatever else it is—and it is many things—The Time Machine is
certainly an exercise in that curious literary subtype called utopian
fiction.*
                    Frank McConnell

Realist of the Fantastic

Although sometimes dismissed as a facile work of scientific fantasy
and the progenitor of a seemingly endless series of literary as well as
cinematic clones, the real significance of H. G. Wells's *Time Machine*
(1895) lies in its extraordinary innovativeness, an innovativeness that
is as literary as it is scientific. Without wishing to seem paradoxical,
it does seem fair to say that *The Time Machine* looks forward as much
to *À la recherche du temps perdu* as it does to *Dr. Who*—which is why,
more than a century after it first appeared, it still fascinates new generations of readers.[1] If it was nevertheless the scientific dimension

---

1. In later years, Wells notoriously professed to be a journalist rather than an artist, but it's clear that initially at least—that is, before he became established as a writer—he was determined to be counted among the generation of remarkable narrative artists who were beginning their careers in the nineties, notably Joseph Conrad.
That he had considerable reservations about Conrad et al. is evident, however, from

that initially attracted most attention—almost an inevitability during an age when science came to matter more than literature—it is its enduring literary power that has kept it alive after its original scientific basis has either eroded or faded into reality.

The literary and scientific innovation of the novel begins with the title itself. For the first time in a work of fiction Wells provided an up-to-date, technologically and scientifically grounded rationale for doing something that had hitherto been justified as occurring either by means of magic or through some sort of dream vision. (Indeed, faint traces of such earlier modes of time travel are suggested, first at the beginning and then again at the close of Wells's novel, but both are mentioned only to provide an opportunity to reject them.) Even the idea of *traveling* in time is new and original with Wells. Other, more or less contemporaneous narratives that deal with confrontations of the future and the present, such as Edward Bellamy's *Looking Backward* (1888), or the present and the past, notably Mark Twain's *A Connecticut Yankee in King Arthur's Court* (1889), do not bother to treat the actual journey in any realistic detail. On the contrary, they seem almost embarrassed by it, viewing time travel as more of an obstacle to be gotten over than as an integral part of their narratives. Their methods of travel are therefore no more credible to a skeptical, scientifically trained mind like Wells's than Rip Van Winkle's long sleep would have been. (Though, to be sure, in *When the Sleeper Wakes* [1899] Wells does transport his protagonist into the year 2100 by means of a very old-fashioned trance of more than Vanwinklean proportions.)

In another, related respect too Wells is innovative. In *The Time*

---

his subsequent remarks about them in *Experiment in Autobiography*, where he censures them for being "uneducated." "Instead of being based on a central philosophy," Wells the "scientist" writes, "they started off at a dozen points; they were impulsive, uncoordinated, wilful. Conrad, you see, I count uneducated, Stephen Crane, Henry James, and the larger part of literary artistry" (quoted in Karl 1973, 1049). Wells himself, on the other hand, not only was a proud graduate of the Normal School of Science, but his first published book was *A Textbook of Biology* (1891) and he reviewed regularly for the well-known scientific journal *Nature*.

Machine he not only appeals to a recently created audience which, like himself, expected its fictions to be at least as technologically sophisticated as the articles on technology and science in its newspapers. He also appeals to an audience that, like himself, had been nourished on a rich fare of travel literature, especially travel to exotic places and often—as with Livingstone and Stanley—under conditions of extreme hardship and danger. It is in this context that we should understand the striking differences in the treatment of time travel between Wells and his contemporaries. As Wells was conceiving and writing the various drafts of *The Time Machine,* he was also experiencing, along with his prospective readers, the ambiguously triumphant close of the last great age of British imperial exploration and expansion. This momentous and often violent activity has left clear traces on Wells's fantasy, as, for example, when the Traveller describes his initial difficulties with learning the language of the Eloi—an aspect of their encounters with new peoples that many contemporaneous explorers stressed. Suggestively, only four years after the publication of *The Time Machine,* another sometime professional traveler and would-be explorer, Joseph Conrad (also an early and enthusiastic reader of *The Time Machine*), wrote a celebrated account of a journey up the Congo River which, for his narrator Marlow at least, is also explicitly a journey back into the distant past.

The unusual title—for a work of fiction, that is—of Wells's novel calls immediate attention to the issues of technology and scientific credibility, as does the introductory frame narrative with its lengthy disquisition on mathematics and the nature of the fourth dimension.[2] This technological and scientific emphasis also helps to explain why Wells deliberately avoids providing a name for the Time Traveller in the final version of the novel, whereas his earlier, more conventional drafts had referred to him by such exotic names as "Bayliss" and "Dr. Moses Nebogipfel." The reader, so Wells apparently

2. According to Roslynn Haynes, Wells was the first notable thinker to conceive of time as a fourth dimension. What is more, his discussion of it "not only predates any other, but proceeds with meticulous clarity and accuracy" (1980, 54).

felt when he revised those earlier drafts, must not be sidetracked by extraneous details from the principal issue at hand, namely, the technological issue of travel by means of a time machine. Besides, there is the additional and by no means negligible consequence that in referring to the Time Traveller by his function rather than by a given name from the very outset of the narrative (indeed, "The Time Traveller" are its first words), the narrator is shown implicitly to accept the *truth* of the Time Traveller's story, and to thereby encourage us to accept it too.

In fact, the very existence of a distinct narrator and a frame narrative provides an innovative and believable context for the Time Traveller's seemingly fantastic story, a context to which we as readers can refer to check his veracity. Similarly, the Time Traveller's guests—all of them to a greater or lesser degree skeptical—serve in a variety of ways as surrogates for our readerly skepticism, anticipating our most obvious doubts and objections. In several cases, the professions of the guests are specified, as in the cases of the Medical Man and the Psychologist, as well as later on the Editor and the Journalist. It is surely significant that these are professions that particularly qualify their practitioners, both by training and experience, to observe any sort of chicanery on the part of the Time Traveller. Though no such chicanery is ever discovered—and here Wells is brilliantly realistic—they retain their skepticism nevertheless. They are, as it were, professional skeptics. Even the unnamed narrator is a scientist of some description, as we learn indirectly when he informs us that he is a member of the prestigious—and quite real—Linnaean Society. And he too was, so he tells us, initially skeptical. It is in fact to some extent his claim that he was only gradually persuaded of the truth of the Traveller's tale that helps us to believe it as well. Only the skepticism of the "sillier" guests, who lack scientific qualifications, is wholly discounted.

The relaxed "gentlemen's clubroom" atmosphere of the frame narrative, with its pipes and slippers and cozy fire, is also designed to lull readers into suspending their natural inclination toward disbelief. It all seems so perfectly ordinary and real. In this way Wells is able to domesticate the mostly wildly fantastic elements of his narrative—most notably the "fact" of time travel—by first embedding them in familiar and mundane surroundings. As the narrator remarks of the Time Traveller's tale, "The story was so fantastic and incredible, the telling so credible and sober" (89). It is this aspect of Wells's technique that caused Joseph Conrad to address him admiringly as "O Realist of the Fantastic!" Hence, it is no accident that Wells's literary strategy conforms so closely to a principle enunciated memorably in the preface to his *Seven Famous Novels,* namely, that the secret of writing successful fantasy fiction is *not* to make all things indeterminate and possible, but to alter only a single, isolated aspect of reality (viii). In other words, to be believable in producing this kind of fantasy one may write a "what-if-pigs-could-fly" kind of story, but one needs to limit it exclusively to flying pigs. Introducing flying human beings, for example, would be to break the rules. It is really this deliberate, self-imposed constraint that distinguishes the scientific fantasy as developed and practiced by Wells from other sorts of fantasy. His aim is not so much to astound his readers with strange fictions as it is to work out logically and coherently how life would differ, given a single significant change. That is why time, and time alone, has become permeable in this story, and our understanding of the whole of life has utterly changed because of it.

Our natural skepticism is further reduced by Wells's innovative technique of rendering the future world of AD 802,701 realistically and experientially. The Time Traveller is made to enter an utterly strange world without the assistance of any guide to help explain things to him, such as is often the case in earlier—and, for that matter, later—utopian fictions. He himself feels the absence of a "convenient cicerone" (63). But the very absence of such an intermediary makes the story much more realistic, for it forces readers to confront the strange new world precisely as the Time Traveller does, only gradually realizing along with him how this world is constituted and why. It is very much the kind of impressionistic technique, but here on a much larger scale, that Ian Watt ascribes to Joseph Conrad and calls "delayed decoding." The very lack of precise information is in this way turned to advantage by Wells, by having his fictional Traveller comment ironically—and paradoxically—on how in some "visions of Utopias and coming times which I have read, there is a vast amount of detail about building, and social arrangements, and so forth. But while such details are easy enough to obtain when the whole world is contained in one's imagination, they are altogether inaccessible to a real traveller amid such realities as I found here" (57).[3]

The Time Traveller's understanding of the future is solely based on his deductions, which—no matter how persuasive they may seem to us—remain mere hypotheses to the very end. It is surely not by chance that this method of deduction from empirical evidence is identical with the one famously described by Wells's old and much admired teacher at the Normal School of Science, T. H. Huxley, in "How a Scientist Thinks" (1866). It is also the method used by the Time Traveller's even more celebrated fictional contemporary, Sherlock Holmes, to solve his variegated mysteries.[4]

The Mystery of Humanity

But fascinating as all this is, there is also something else here, something that makes this logical, scientific process emotionally powerful and that helps transform a series of cold scientific hypotheses

3. Generically speaking, *The Time Machine* is obviously an anti-utopia, or negative utopia, rather than a positive one. Patrick Parrinder calls it an "ironic" utopia. Wells was later to become uncomfortable with whole idea of utopia (both positive and negative) with which he had become so inextricably identified. By way of avoiding the label, he stated his preference in a 1939 radio broadcast on the subject for the term "anticipatory tale," which in his view was distinguishable from utopian fictions by its greater realism as well as its propensity to "foretell [the likely future]—more often than not, with warnings and forebodings" (quoted in Parrinder 1985, 115).

4. In an 1894 contribution to *Nature* Wells even mentions Conan Doyle along with Edgar Allen Poe's "Murders in the Rue Morgue" as relevant to his own writing (quoted in Rainwater 1995, 75).

into a compelling work of art. For here the mystery is not merely an abstractly scientific one, or even one in which the mystery has been caused by some criminal act. Here the mystery lies deeper. Here the mystery resides in humanity itself, as well as in that curious and extraordinary specimen of humanity named H. G. Wells.

It is a mystery that manifests itself in two strikingly ingenious and related ways: namely, first, in the sense that the Time Traveller's personal safety—and, eventually, also that of his friend Weena—depends on his ability to grasp what is really going on in the world of the Eloi and the Morlocks. But, second, it also manifests itself in another more personal—and even more subtle—sense, as the story explores the individual psyche of its author. So, when the Time Traveller notes the existence of "certain circular wells, several, as it seemed to me, of very great depth" (56), the attentive reader is immediately alerted to the possibility that these wells will reveal some mystery connected not only with the future world but also with Wells's own psyche. And so it turns out to be. It is only by facing up to the horrors of the lower depths that the Time Traveller—along with Wells himself—can understand who, as a human being, he is. For the future schism of humanity into the creatures of light (the Eloi) and the creatures of darkness (the Morlocks) is not merely social but also psychological. In a way that would surely have pleased Wells's contemporary, Sigmund Freud, Wells confirms the existence of ego and id, the conscious and unconscious levels of human perception. Descending into one of the wells, Wells's Time Traveller also descends into his and his author's unconscious self, discovering in the process that he is—and both are—not merely the representative(s) of the gentle, beautiful creatures of the upper world but also of the hideous, cruel ones of the lower. Wells has descended into the wells of his being, as it were.[5]

5. That Wells's psyche is profoundly implicated in this depiction of a future schism of present-day humanity along class lines is also evident in his otherwise inexplicable preference for the Eloi over the Morlocks. Given the Traveller's hypothesis, evidently shared by Wells himself, that the Eloi are the descendants in the remote

More profoundly, however, than in probing the mystery of the Time Traveller's psyche, or even Wells's own, the mystery of *The Time Machine* focuses on the ultimate destiny of the human race, or, put differently, on trying to provide a credible answer to the question of the meaning of human life and development. Since this question is not a merely or strictly "scientific" one but rather a profoundly human question—indeed, one of the most profound—it cannot be asked (or answered) logically, but only symbolically. In this respect, *The Time Machine* is not only an innovative but also very much a representative work of the late nineteenth century, a period often designated as the Age of Symbolism. It is perhaps here too that the influence of Hawthorne shows itself most strongly, whose *The Scarlet Letter* Wells claimed to have been reading just before he began writing *The Time Machine*.

That it is a profoundly symbolical narrative becomes apparent no later than the moment when the Time Traveller regains consciousness after tumbling head over heels from his machine into the world of AD 802,701. What he at first perceives only indistinctly through the sheets of hail falling all around him turns out to be an immense figure "of white marble, in the shape something like a sphinx, but the wings, instead of being carried vertically at the sides, were spread so that it seemed to hover. The pedestal, it appeared to me, was of bronze, and was thick with verdigris. It chanced that the face was towards me; the sightless eyes seemed to watch me; there

---

future of the leisure class and the Morlocks of the working class, the socialist Wells's sympathies should have been with the latter rather than the former. Yet he clearly prefers the inhabitants of upstairs to the inhabitants of downstairs, not only aesthetically but also emotionally, as in the case of his "girlfriend," Weena. (According to Peter Kemp this preference for upstairs over downstairs is rooted in Wells's childhood upbringing [1982, 14].) Evidently Wells's unconscious takes precedence here over his conscious. The conflict between Wells's rational and irrational selves can also be analyzed in Jungian terms. Michael Draper, for example, argues that "[t]he eccentrics who dominate Wells's [early] fiction are certainly obsessive, often beyond the point of irresponsibility. They find themselves in conflict with everyday reality on behalf of a more fantastic, colourful and sometimes dangerous world, their rebellions powered by rebellious energy and directed by irrational imagination" (1987, 442).

was the faint shadow of a smile on its lips. It was greatly weather-worn, and that imparted an unpleasant suggestion of disease. . . . At last I tore my eyes from it for a moment, and saw that the hail curtain had worn threadbare, and that the sky was lightening with the promise of the sun" (43–44).

Before turning to the mystery of the Sphinx itself, however, we first need to ask ourselves what the meaning might be of the curtain of hail that initially impedes the Time Traveller's sight. The answer to this question is really quite simple, though to the best of my knowledge it is a question that has never even been asked by previous critics of the novel. The answer is that the curtain of hail is explicitly an indication that we are dealing here with an (the?) Apocalypse, for the word "apocalypse" is in fact derived from two Greek words that in combination literally mean an "unveiling, or a drawing aside of a curtain." Significantly, it is also a Greek rather than an Egyptian Sphinx which the Traveller sees, as is clear from its possession of wings, though the Greek Sphinx was never depicted, as the Traveller knows full well and even tells us, with wings outspread. Why the wings should be carried in this unusual position is puzzling, at least at first, but the question as to why the Sphinx is Greek rather than Egyptian is not difficult to answer. It is because the Greek Sphinx notoriously asked a riddle to which the answer was "Man"; and all those travelers on the road to Thebes who were unable to solve this riddle were killed. The Sphinx's wan, Mona Lisa–like smile seems occasioned by its suspicion that this is a riddle which the Time Traveller—along with the rest of humanity—has not been and will never be able to answer satisfactorily. It is a suspicion that this story, full as it is of ingenious hypotheses, does nothing to dispel. As for the outspread wings, these may allude either to the angels who, with wings extended and bearing swords of fire, expelled Adam and Eve from the Garden of Eden, or else and perhaps more likely to the fact that, as the cliché has it, "time flies." (There may also be a hint that this particular sphinx was meant to be associated with the statue of "winged Victory," thereby suggesting that its makers had once mistakenly thought they had triumphed over time.)

The Sphinx itself is weather-beaten and shows signs of decay that are reminiscent of disease. So too with the buildings the Traveller visits, which, when they are not in a wholly ruinous state, reveal signs of decay and disarray. The glass in some of the windows is shattered, the tables cracked, the slabs on the floors worn thin in places, even the decorations are "very badly broken and weatherworn" (46). It is these and other related phenomena that lead the Traveller to conclude that he has "happened upon humanity upon the wane" (50). Though the Traveller later develops and refines this hypothesis as he learns more about the world of nearly one million years in the future, he never changes his mind that it is a world in which humanity has degenerated.

Humanity on the Wane

As critics such as Bernard Bergonzi have often pointed out, Wells's decision to portray a humanity on the wane rather than one on the rise is related to the widely shared, late nineteenth-century apocalyptic mood of pessimism. But Wells's pessimism differs in important ways from that of most of his contemporaries in that, for him, things are destined in the relatively long term—something like a hundred thousand years—to get a lot better before they get a lot worse. He also differs in asserting paradoxically that things will get worse precisely because they will have first gotten better.[6]

---

6. Wells later became more optimistic about the long-term future of humanity, as and possibly because his own personal fortunes improved. In *The Science of Life*, which he co-authored with Julian Huxley and his own son, G. P. Wells, he argued that there is "much in life that may make intelligent men impatient, but it is not reasonable to let impatience degenerate into pessimism. . . . The progressive development of the scientific mind may survive all the blundering wars, social disorganization, misconceptions and suppressions that still seem to lie before mankind. Until in due course the heir comes to full strength and takes possession" (1474).

In this sense, too, Wells is a radical innovator. He is the first writer of utopian fiction to argue that the achievement of utopia will inevitably lead to stagnation and degeneration. He is the first major novelist to make this claim because he is also the first to be fully informed of and convinced by Darwin's theory of evolution. The driving force behind Darwin's theory is, as is well known, the struggle for the survival of the fittest. What is less well known is that a concomitant aspect of Darwin's theory posits that once this struggle ceases—or is artificially brought to a close, i.e., by human agency—the fittest will no longer survive but must inexorably degenerate into ever more hopeless states of unfitness. That is why the splendid utopian conditions whose natural and human remnants the Traveller encounters in the remote future cannot endure. The very elimination of harmful insects and of disease, of predatory animals and of overt cruelty, and especially of the need to work for one's food and shelter: all of these apparent blessings are really a curse. For, as the Time Traveller states: "What, unless biological science is a mass of errors, is the cause of human intelligence and vigour? Hardship and freedom" (51). The point here seems to be that, while one may be able to change undesirable aspects of nature, one cannot change the inexorable laws of nature themselves.[7]

Utopia, in other words, is and must ever be a condition of stasis. It represents, almost by definition, a state of perfection, but perfection, in its root meaning, as Wells knew perfectly well, refers to something that is *finished* or *ended*. "An animal perfectly in harmony with its environment," so the Time Traveller affirms emphatically, "is a perfect mechanism. . . . There is no intelligence where there is no change and no need of change. Only those animals partake of intelligence that have to meet a huge variety of needs and dangers"

7. According to David Hughes, the Eloi and Morlocks "are entangled in an evolutionary mechanism that, ironically, is the residual force . . . that man built hoping to stop the evolutionary clock" (1977, 59). In Wells's later utopia, *Men Like Gods*, the elimination of bothersome insects and animals is, however, viewed as a positive development (91).

(81–82). Evolution, on the other hand, when not manipulated by humanity, is always linked to time and to change. It will not tolerate perfection because evolution is only finished when time has reached an end. There will come a time, of course, when time must have a stop, and it is precisely this desperate knowledge that the Time Traveller acquires when he escapes the Morlocks and travels into a future thirty million years hence. While this second voyage is much less fully rendered than the first one to AD 802,701, it is amply apparent that the processes of degeneration and simplification posited by the law of entropy have continued apace. The monstrous crab-like creatures that attack the Traveller are undoubtedly the symbolic progeny of the Morlocks (and possibly are even intended to be thought of as their "real" progeny), just as the only other visible, living "thing like a huge white butterfly" is a symbolic descendant of the Eloi. The dialectic of evolution, and the struggle of good and evil, continue, though in a necessarily altered and less complex form. At the Traveller's very last stop in the future, however, only one form of animate life survives—a tentacled, hopping "football"-like creature—suggesting that at last the dialectic of evolutionary life has played itself out. Evolution has become devolution, and this wretched descendant of a once triumphant humanity has, as it were, survived only to be "kicked" like a football into oblivion. The earth has stopped rotating on its axis and is drawing ever nearer to the "huge red-hot dome of the sun." Like the Morlocks, whom the Traveller once watched horrified as they were drawn helplessly toward a fiery destruction, the earth itself will soon plunge into the sun, and life will have committed suicide.

The Machine of Time

It is by means of a time machine that the Time Traveller manages to gain answers to the eternal questions that have plagued the curiosity of mankind from the dawn of consciousness. What will happen to humanity? What is the meaning of human existence?

How will the world end? Significantly, these are questions—and answers—that have been traditionally associated more with literature than with the social sciences. Not that the Time Traveller's answers are particularly encouraging. But it is surely significant that, discouraging though they may be, these answers do not discourage the Traveller himself from seeking to make further voyages in time. He is a committed adventurer and heroic explorer, for whom the time machine, as a symbolic representation of human ingenuity, takes precedence over other, more spiritual matters. That is perhaps why, although the Traveller's actual machine looks and functions something like a bicycle, the small model that he shows his assembled guests is explicitly described as resembling a clock. "The thing the Time Traveller held in his hand," so the narrator informs us near the beginning of the story, "was a glittering metallic framework, scarcely larger than a small clock, and very delicately made" (34–35). The original meaning of "time machine" is, of course, a machine for telling time, a meaning Wells is fully aware of. The implication is that we are *all* of us "time travelers," equipped with time machines that measure our temporal progress. The principal difference between our travel and that of the Time Traveller is merely our inferior speed, not the fact of time travel itself.

Once one is alerted to the symbolic significance of clocks in *The Time Machine,* one has a new sense of what Wells is implying when he has the Morlocks hide the time machine inside the pediment of an ironically smiling sphinx. The mystery of time, it would seem, is contained within the greater mystery of what it means to be human. As Jorge Luis Borges long ago pointed out, Wells's early novels don't just "tell an ingenious story . . . they tell a story symbolic of all processes that are somehow inherent in all human destinies" (1964, 87).

Time Future Is Time Past

An even more striking and ominous feature of the distant future depicted in Wells's novel is its remarkable resemblance to the equally remote past. That is why, when the Time Traveller tells his skeptical friends and acquaintances before undertaking his first adventure into time that he doesn't know if the machine will take him into the future or into the past, he speaks more truly than he knows himself. Only part of the temporal paradox, however, is evident in the extraordinary fact that both the Time Traveller and the narrator refer to his experiences of the very distant future in the past tense, with the curious result that the latter is able to conclude in the Epilogue to the story—without any apparent trace of irony—that for him "the future is still black and blank—is a vast ignorance, lit at a few casual places by the memory [*sic!*] of his [the Time Traveller's] story" (90).

There are also other, less obviously paradoxical indications that the Traveller's voyage into the future is to be understood as a simultaneous voyage into the past. So the decorations he sees in the building where the Eloi eat and sleep remind him of Phoenecian writing. The Sphinx itself is a creature associated with a time that, viewed from the perspective of the late nineteenth century, was the distant past. Both the Eloi and the Morlocks evoke—apparently quite deliberately—mythical and real aspects of the human past.[8] The vegetarian Eloi dwell in a kind of Garden of Eden belonging to the innocent childhood of the human race, whereas the Morlocks are primitive, carnivorous "cave" dwellers, who hunt and kill for their food.[9]

8. The Eloi, however, though perhaps not the Morlocks, are evidently also intended to evoke the contemporaneous present, given their close resemblance to the "useless" and "degenerate" flower people associated with Oscar Wilde and satirized by Robert Hitchens in *The Green Carnation*. I do not agree, however, with Frank McConnell that Aubrey Beardsley's 1894 engraving, "A Snare of Vintage," is "an obvious source for Wells's invention of the Eloi" (1981, 79).

9. If another of Wells's quasi-scientific fantasies is any indication, then the Morlocks seem to have been wise not to make a meal of the Time Traveller, despite nib-

Symbolic too—perhaps even overly symbolic—of the pastness of the future is the Time Traveller's trip to the building that he calls the Palace of Green Porcelain, a massive and only partly ruined structure that he discovers was a museum rather like a combination of the Museum of History, the Museum of Science, and the British Museum of his own time. It houses the decayed remnants of past life and art, including even the huge skeleton of a dinosaur, along with rusting machinery and fragments of what can still be recognized as books. The Time Traveller himself makes the connection explicit by remarking that "[c]learly we stood among the ruins of some latter-day South Kensington!" (73). In this building he not only quite literally finds the past contained in the future, but he also begins himself to revert to a far earlier and much more primitive state of human social evolution—going, as it were, back from the future without the aid of a time machine—by divesting himself of his shoes along with other bits of his clothing, and then arming himself with a club, so as to do battle with the villainous Morlocks. Later, after barely managing to escape from his primitive enemies, he travels further into the past by paradoxically traveling further into the future, finally reaching back—or is it forward?—to the ends and origins of life.

But first let us pause to ask ourselves what Wells's intention might be in fusing, and even confusing, time past with time future. His primary intention, I believe, is parabolic, but parabolic in both senses of the word. To begin with, he means us to think of it as parabolic in the customary sense of being a parable. That is, he means his story to be read as a parable about what may happen to humanity if it fails to embrace egalitarian social policy and opts instead for class

---

bling at him on at least one occasion. In *The War of the Worlds*, the Martians who have, as is also the case in the world of 802,701, eliminated the known causes of disease, ironically succumb to the infections communicated to them by drinking the infected blood of a primitive humanity, of which the Time Traveller is of course also a part. At the end of *The Time Machine* the Time Traveller journeys into the past—or at least proclaims his intention to do so—but is never heard of again. In "A Story of the Stone Age" (1897), however, Wells depicts the kind of world that the Time Traveller may have encountered.

division and enmity.[10] But it is also parabolic in the (I think, more profound) sense of being a "parabola." That is, the Time Traveller's experience is quite literally parabolic, for it demonstrates that what goes up one side (namely, the past) must come down, with precise symmetry, on the other side (or the future). This is a notion Wells probably picked up from T. H. Huxley, his much admired teacher at the Normal School of Science. Six years after publishing *The Time Machine,* Wells wrote of Huxley that, as a student, he believed Huxley was "the greatest man I was likely to meet, and I believe that all the more firmly today." Huxley uses the image of a parabola in his essay "The Struggle for Existence in Human Society" (1888), by arguing that "the course of life on the surface of the earth was like the trajectory of 'a ball fired from a mortar,' and 'the sinking half of that course is as much a part of the general process of evolution as the rising'" (quoted in Hillegas 1974, 19–21). Decay, then—or degeneration or waning or whatever name one wants to use for human decline—is inevitable and not simply a consequence of perpetuating the error of class division since the close of the nineteenth century.

Though the Time Traveller's journey begins at a point on the evolutionary parabola when human history has not yet reached its

10. That Wells the socialist believed that this literal division into two groups, one living aboveground, the other below, was an ominous sign of what might happen is evident from his making it a feature of another future fantasy, "A Story of the Days to Come," where the "prosperous people lived in the upper storeys and halls of the city fabric" but "the industrial population dwelt in the beneath in the tremendous ground floor and basement, so to speak, of the place" (1900, 162). In *When the Sleeper Wakes* (1899), the distinction is also very clearly drawn, though not spatially: "Here was no Utopia, no Socialistic state. He had already seen enough to realize that the ancient antithesis of luxury, waste and sensuality on the one hand and abject poverty on the other, still persisted" (69). Aldous Huxley's division of the population of his future New World State into two biologically distinct castes seems to be indebted to Wells's prediction in *The Time Machine*. Huxley's alphas and betas are genetically the result of the union of a single fertilized egg, whereas the gammas, deltas, and epsilons are genetically multiplied and altered by subjecting the egg to chemical and other treatments. It should be noted, however, that Wells's socialism was Fabian rather than orthodox Marxist. Late in life, he remarked that he had "always had a peculiar contempt and dislike for the mind and character of Karl Marx, a contempt and dislike that have deepened with the years" (1942, 66).

full potential, it is nevertheless located, in spatial terms, very close to that point. That is why he is able to feel contempt for the Eloi's apparently childish fears of the dark and the Morlocks that come out of it. After all he emerges fearlessly, as he puts it with something of the arrogance of the nineteenth-century imperialist, "out of this age of ours, this ripe prime of the human race" (68).[11]

But not only the image of the parabola is central to the novel. Even more important is the image of the clock—of the time machine. The largest clock of which we humans have immediate knowledge and experience is the sun, which is why the dials on the time machine are set to record only days or multiples of days. How basic the identification of time and sun is for the Time Traveller is evident from his attempt to express the concept of time to the Eloi, almost immediately after he has met them for the first time, by pointing toward the sun. Significantly, when the Time Traveller reaches the furthest point in his voyage into the future, some thirty million years hence, he finds that the sun has increased immensely in size, turned red, and apparently stopped moving. The cosmic clock has nearly come to rest and we are, paradoxically, back at the beginning of time—Darwinian time, at any rate—with the only moving, living thing anywhere to be seen a football-shaped creature trailing tentacles and hopping about among the shallows of what is still (or again?) the blood-dimmed tide—out of which we all emerged eons ago and back to which we are all destined to return.

---

11. The Time Traveller, it should be remembered, is able to shed some light on both the nocturnal and subterranean darkness by means of his supply of aptly named "safety matches." I disagree, however, with John Huntington, who sees in these matches the symbol of the Time Traveller's "intellectual dominance" over the creatures of the future by means of his use of "present-day technology" (1982, 49). Like his iron club, the Time Traveller's (accidental) use of fire to destroy his enemies is symbolic rather of his reversion to the past.

CHAPTER 2

SHAW'S *MAJOR BARBARA*

What Price Utopia?

You know, the creature is really a sort of poet in his way.
George Bernard Shaw

"Major" Barbara

In late November 1905, when *Major Barbara* was first staged in London, the title of the play must have struck at least some of those attending the opening night as odd and puzzling. A woman's name preceded by a military title? How could that be? Was this a play about a modern Amazon? Of course, once the initial audience had seen the play, they would have understood why Shaw had entitled his play as he did, or at least they would have understood some part of the reason. Major Barbara, of course, isn't *really* a major, not at any rate in the sense of being an officer in the "real" army. She's "just" a major in the Salvation Army, which isn't really an army at all. It's a play on words, "just" another one of those verbal tricks put over on the gullible English by that brilliant but incorrigible Irish jester, George Bernard Shaw.

As for the Barbara part, those original playgoers would undoubtedly, and quite rightly, have linked her to the contemporaneous struggle for the enfranchisement of women (and for women's rights generally), which was much in the news at the time. So too was, although admittedly to a much lesser degree and within a much more limited context, the author's well-known sympathy for that struggle, as expressed, say, in such earlier plays as *The Philanderer* and *Mrs. Warren's Profession* or a book like *The Quintessence of Ibsenism*.

Knowledge of Shaw's feminist sympathies would have provided an answer for many of the questions that the audience who saw the play for the first time would have had, but not for all of those questions. For, despite Shaw's widely known sympathies for the plight of women, there would still have remained the question as to why Shaw had named his play after a female character when it was so clearly centered on that Shavian alter ego and real protagonist, Andrew Undershaft. Why, then, did Shaw choose Barbara for the title? Wasn't it amply apparent, by the end of the play, that Andrew Undershaft had triumphed over his daughter? Wouldn't the play, therefore, have been more appropriately entitled *Andrew Undershaft?* Or even *Unashamed?*[1]

Perhaps so, but one good reason why the play's title singles out Barbara is because Barbara has a pivotal role in the play in a way that Undershaft does not. She is the only "major" character, with the possible exception of Adolphus Cusins—who isn't really major anyway—who changes or develops, who is kinetic. Powerful and prominent though he is, Andrew Undershaft remains essentially static throughout the course of the play, the only change being that he is said to "fall in love" with his daughter somewhere along the way and therefore resolves to set aside his commitment to his Armorer's "foundling" tradition, though apparently not his Armorer's faith (to sell to all comers), in her favor. He arranges for his future son-in-law, the nominal and rather feeble "foundling" Adolphus Cusins, to assume his name and manage the works at Perivale St. Andrews, but it is his daughter Barbara who will assume his spiritual inheritance. It is she who will manage what is even more important than the works,

1. In fact, Shaw told his biographer Archibald Henderson that "Andrew Undershaft's Profession" might have been a more appropriate title if he hadn't already used similar titles before (Wisenthal 1974a, 58).

namely, the salvation of the employees of those works and, by implication, assist in the spiritual salvation of humanity at large.

Bill Walker and Adolphus Cusins

Lurking behind the ethical and philosophical substance of this play, as Shaw tries to make clear in his Preface, are a number of largely forgotten nineteenth-century English and Irish influences, such as Charles Lever, Ernest Belfort Bax, and Captain Wilson. Not named, but probably even more influential, is Thomas Carlyle, whose observations about Captains of Industry and the "One Institution" in *Past and Present* are, as we shall see, at least as relevant to the play as anything written or said by Lever, Bax, or Wilson. Unnamed too is the German poet, playwright, and universal genius, Johann Wolfgang von Goethe, for whom both Carlyle and Shaw professed great admiration. Goethe's influence is discernible in a number of ways, not least in the way his celebrated but morally ambiguous magus, Faust, figures variously and importantly, though not explicitly, in establishing the ethical framework of the play. If nothing else, the frequent references to Mephistopheles and the sale of souls should alert the reader to the relevance of Goethe's philosophical verse drama, *Faust*. "It is not the sale of my soul that troubles me," Cusins remarks when facing up to Undershaft's offer to take over the management of the armaments business at Perivale St. Andrews:

> I have sold it too often to care about that. I have sold it for a professorship. I have sold it for an income. I have sold it to escape being imprisoned for refusing to pay taxes for hangmen's ropes and unjust wars and things that I abhor. What is all human conduct but the daily and hourly sale of our souls for trifles? What I am now selling it for is neither money nor position nor comfort, but for reality and for power. (149)[2]

2. It would appear, however, that Cusins is actually selling his soul for the "reality" of money and position, since, as Barbara tells him bluntly, he "will have no power," just as Undershaft "has none" (129).

In fact—and this is perhaps an early indication of Cusins's business acumen—he has at this point sold his already somewhat oversold soul to Undershaft (not to mention the prior sale to Barbara herself, as Lady Britomart intimates [134]), for as he informs Barbara after having spent a night in drink and conversation with her father, the latter has now completed "the wreck of my moral basis, the rout of my convictions, the purchase of my soul" (116).

As in *Faust*, there is also a wager in this play, with Undershaft expressing his willingness to subject himself to the "temptations" of the West Ham Salvation Army shelter if Barbara will agree to do the same for his ideal city, the site of his armaments plant, Perivale St. Andrews, on the following day (72). The wager here, though again not explicitly stated, is for Barbara's or Undershaft's soul. This becomes apparent in the second act when the conflict between them is worked out in terms of Undershaft's surrogate, Bill Walker. When Bill returns to the shelter after having been humiliated by his former girlfriend's new boyfriend, he offers to make up for having hurt Barbara's assistant, Jenny Hill, by contributing a pound (the equivalent in today's money of something like $100) to the Salvation Army. Barbara, however, refuses, saying, "No: the Army is not to be bought. We want your soul, Bill, and we will take nothing less" (103).

Barbara of course turns out to be dead wrong. Not only does she not get Bill's soul, not only is she forced to witness the "selling off" of the Salvation Army's "soul" to her father, but she implicitly acknowledges the loss of her own soul when she exchanges her Salvation Army uniform for ordinary everyday dress. Not that Bill isn't willing to sell his soul too. (Undershaft seems to be the only character in the play who is unwilling to sell his soul, though he is willing to wager it.) It's just that he objects to selling it to Barbara and the Salvation Army. When Peter Shirley tells Walker that the latter would "sell [himself] to the devil for a pint of beer; only there aint no devil to make the offer," Bill enthusiastically agrees in his somewhat exaggerated cockney accent that he would: "[*unashamed*] 'Sao Aw would, mite, and often ev, cheerful. But she cawnt baw me.' [*Ap-*

proaching Barbara] 'You wanted maw saoul, did you? Well, you aint got it'" (112).[3]

It's quite true. She doesn't have it, but one reason why she doesn't have it is that Bill Walker's soul is so very closely allied to (if not identical with) her father's. One obvious clue to the link between the two is Shaw's stage direction, as cited above: "*unashamed*." Does anyone need to be reminded that this adjective also succinctly describes Undershaft's faith as an armorer, i.e., that it defines his soul?

Like Bill Walker, Undershaft is, as he openly and a little boastfully admits himself, the product of poverty and ignorance. He may be a millionaire now but his origins were very 'umble. "*I* was an east ender," he proclaims emphatically (143). He *was* an East Ender but he clearly no longer is.[4] The reason why he no longer is an East Ender, no longer poor and starving, he goes on to say, is because he resolved while still very young to become "a full-fed free man at all costs," even if those costs included going against the prevailing Christian morality as promulgated by such institutions as the Salvation Army.[5] Echoing Nietzsche—though Shaw denies it in his Preface (13)—he tells his family that he "would rather be a thief than a pauper. I had rather be a murderer than a slave. I dont want to be either; but if you force the alternative on me, then, by Heaven, I'll choose the braver and more moral one" (143). No slave morality for Undershaft, it would seem. Like Bill, he unapologetically resorts to violence to gain his ends, or at least he says he has done so in the

3. It is odd and surely significant that Peter Shirley, whose social origins seem to be much the same as Bill Walker's, speaks almost perfect standard English.

4. Though Shaw, who was born in Dublin, was no East Ender, he did experience at second hand some of the urban poverty that Undershaft describes. While working as cashier for a Dublin land agent, Shaw was responsible for collecting the rents in a very poor part of the city. It was this experience, according to Donald Brook, that first "aroused his interest in social problems" (1944, 129).

5. Undershaft does not go into details, perhaps because then he would have to admit that he, like his prior namesakes and owners of the armaments business, was actually chosen for the job primarily because he was an impoverished East End foundling.

past and, given the wrong circumstances, would do so again; and like Bill he offers to make up for his violence by paying for it. Money talks in this play, and it does so chiefly through Shaw's mouthpiece, Andrew Undershaft.

It is surely significant that Bill Walker fits Undershaft's requirements for a foundling rather better than does that foundling in name only, Adolphus Cusins. The presumably original justification for insisting on a foundling to succeed to the Undershaft business—the idea of bringing "fresh blood" and socially unconditioned (or unspoiled) brains into it—is not going to be satisfied by introducing a man who admits to chronic physical weakness and an inability to figure out whether three-fifths is more than one-half. Though Bill may actually be legitimate in the technically legal sense—i.e., not a foundling—he is presented as being without any outside support, unlike Barbara and even Cusins. Certainly we know nothing about his parentage. We do know, however, that he is utterly self-reliant and not particularly mindful of the prevailing mores of English society. These are character traits that surely fit him rather better for managing a large business enterprise, especially an armaments factory, than does Cusins's knowledge of ancient Greek. Like Undershaft—and unlike Cusins—Bill is aggressive and argumentative, surely qualities that suit an armaments manufacturer. On the other hand, Cusins's knowledge of a "hypothetical language" like ancient Greek (as it is referred to in *Erewhon*) fits him primarily for employment in a College of Unreason, which is where he appears to have previously had a job. It would not have impressed Samuel Butler, whom Shaw claims in his Preface to have admired enormously.

Undershaft is either being very obtuse or else scheming to flatter Barbara's husband into a job when he says of Cusins that he is "exactly the sort of fresh blood that is wanted in English business" (134). Bill's determination, on the other hand, to demonstrate his power over his sometime girlfriend, Mog Habbijam, by violent means if necessary, shows how indifferent he is to the moral outlook of his surroundings. He is as determined to win Mog back as Undershaft is

determined to gain the soul of his daughter. That Undershaft succeeds and Bill does not is less a function of Mog's new boyfriend
Todger Fairmile's strength than of Shaw's failure to grasp the significance of his own creation.[6] Though he may be afraid to assault
the granddaughter of the Earl of Stevenage physically, Bill does not
hesitate to do violence to Jenny Hill and Rummy Mitchens, and he
won't hide his contempt for "Dolly's" (i.e., Cusins's) puppet-like de-
pendence on Barbara's good will. Bill's nonconformist and politically
very incorrect behavior—so obviously reminiscent not only of Undershaft's own past condition as an upstart East Ender but also of
his current, more "respectable" but still violent occupation as a producer of weapons of mass destruction—makes it all the more surprising that Undershaft does not even consider Bill a possible candi-
date for the job of taking over the management of his armaments
factory. Or, for that matter, that Shaw himself dismisses Bill in the
Preface as "a common English character" whom "[w]e meet everywhere" (35).

Is the reason, perhaps, for this odd and rather contradictory behavior on the part of Andrew Undershaft (and behind Undershaft,
of course, of George Bernard Shaw) that he—along with Shaw himself—has become the representative of another, even more "common English character," namely, a snob? To Cusins Undershaft expresses his contempt for "the common mob of slaves and idolaters."
However, lest we should be tempted to think that Undershaft might
be referring here to the middle or even working classes, Cusins
catches him up immediately by warning him that "Barbara is in love
with the common people. So am I" (97). This retort does not leave
Undershaft (again like his creator) at a loss for words. He is a social
elitist (snob?), Undershaft admits, precisely because he once was a
proletarian himself: "This love of the common people may please

6. This is something Shaw did grasp in *Man and Superman*, where the irreverent
working-class character Henry Straker is shown to be the equal, if not the superior,
of the upper-class characters, including the protagonist Jack Tanner. Still, Straker is
very tame—even a kind of pet of Tanner & Co.—in a way that Bill Walker is not.

an earl's granddaughter and a university professor; but I have been a common man and a poor man; and it has no romance for me. Leave it to the poor that poverty is a blessing: leave it to the coward to make a religion of his cowardice by preaching humility: we know better than that. We three must stand together above the common people: how else can we help their children to climb up beside us?" (97–98).[7] Undershaft, so we are apparently meant to conclude, does not love the common people; but he does love the children of the common people, or, rather, he loves the hope for social and biological improvement that he sees potentially embodied in a future generation. Significantly, Barbara is the child of that sometime "common" person, Andrew Undershaft.

Do "we three" really know better? Does even Undershaft all by himself really know better? Not only does he not help the unrepentant and quite unhumble Bill Walker to "climb up beside us," he does not even help the vain liar and thief—and snob—"Snobby" Bronterre Price to the kind of job at Perivale St. Andrews (as gatekeeper) that he does provide for that very accommodating and rather subservient "common" person, Peter Shirley.[8] (Though Shaw claims in theory not to believe in the existence of the "deserving poor" as opposed to the allegedly "undeserving poor," in practice he rewards the former and dismisses the latter.) As for Cusins, he not only will become a millionaire himself when he in due course turns, at least nominally, into Andrew Undershaft, he will also be marrying the daughter of a millionaire and the granddaughter of an earl—not bad for a foundling who is fated, willy-nilly, to "stand above the common people."

7. Undershaft's unabashedly elitist attitude toward the working classes reminds us that Shaw, though a socialist, was also an elitist. The Fabian Socialist movement, of which he was a lifelong enthusiastic proponent, after all endeavored to change society from the top down, just as Undershaft proposes to do, rather than from the bottom up.

8. Part of the reason, however, why Peter gets this particular job may be because of the link between his Christian name and that of the heavenly gatekeeper, St. Peter. Perivale St. Andrews, after all, resembles nothing more than, as Cusins puts it, "a heavenly city" (129).

Barbara, to be sure, by virtue of being a woman is and will remain subordinate, at least in name, to the patriarchal conditions prevailing in Britain at the beginning of the twentieth century.[9] (See Virginia Woolf's *A Room of My Own* for more details.) Like her mother, she will have to extract such privileges as she may acquire or desire from her male partner, Cusins, despite her superior ability and social status. Not that the patriarchy won't go along with the idea of her managing the business indirectly. Though Undershaft is adamantly opposed to accepting his ultraconventional son Stephen as his successor, he explicitly instructs Lady Britomart that if she wishes "to keep the foundry in the family" she "had better find an eligible foundling and marry him to Barbara."[10] That is precisely what Lady Britomart sets out to do when, a short time later, after having given up all hope of ever overcoming her husband's objections to Stephen, she tells Undershaft that "Barbara has rights as well as Stephen. Why should not Adolphus succeed to the inheritance?" (134).

Adolphus does succeed to the inheritance, though few readers of the play, I think, would agree that he should do so.[11] His excuse for existing seems to be that Undershaft needs him as a means for more or less respectably manipulating Barbara into the succession, as he could not have done if he had married Barbara off to Bill. Cusins doesn't really belong among the "big three" of *Major Barbara*, whereas, potentially and by temperament at least, Bill does. Cusins's technical foundling status, along with his peculiar name, makes him into a comic character, rather like that "foundling" in Oscar Wilde's *Importance of Being Earnest* who was found in a trunk in the left

---

9. Like Bill Walker and Snobby Price, Rummy Mitchins vanishes from the play after the second act and is never considered for employment at Perivale St. Andrews.

10. As Maurice Valency suggests, Shaw may be thinking here (and elsewhere in the play) of Bertha von Krupp's taking over the management of Germany's largest armaments concern in 1902 when her father died, leaving her as the sole heir (1973, 249–50).

11. Among those few are Jerome Wisenthal and Colin Wilson, both of whom see Cusins as the dominant character in the last part of the play (Wisenthal 1974a, 61; Wilson 1969, 192).

luggage department at Victoria Station.[12] "Dolly," one is forced to conclude, has much the same status in the play as his overtly comic rhyming counterpart, "Cholly." (Charles Lomax, the fiancé of Barbara's sister, Sarah.) Cusins is Tweedledee to Lomax's Tweedledum. It's hard to imagine him as the future leader of the greatest private enterprise in Britain, an enterprise which apparently, if one is to believe Undershaft, holds the strings of the parliamentary puppets at Westminster. The official hollow man of the play, Stephen, would have served this purpose just as well, and arguably even better, being already not just the son of the richest man in England but also the grandson of an earl. Undershaft, on the other hand, undoubtedly is, as Shaw reminds us explicitly in the Preface, "the hero" of the play (18), despite his also admittedly rather peculiar name and sometime foundling status. (More on this later.) It's hard to imagine Undershaft being found in a trunk or wheedling his way into a position of power.

Barbara

But if Undershaft is the hero, Barbara is undoubtedly the heroine of the play. Just why this should be so is at times rather puzzling, perhaps never more so than in the great speech she makes at the conclusion of the play. In that speech, a "transfigured" Barbara announces that she has "got rid of the bribe of bread. I have got rid of the bribe of heaven. Let God's work be done for its own sake: the work he had to create us to do because it cannot be done except by living men and women. When I die, let him be in my debt, not I in his; and let me forgive him as becomes a woman of my rank" (152). Among the several puzzling things about this speech is what she means by "woman of my rank." Is she referring to her "rank" of major in the Salvation Army? If so, as she apparently is if one is to

12. Cusins's odd name seems to refer partly to his being his own cousin—i.e., an allusion to his purely legal foundling status—but also to "cozening" Undershaft and Barbara into believing in him as a possible successor to the armaments business.

believe what she says immediately afterward about Major Barbara
dying "with the colors" (153), an assertion confirmed by Shaw's pref-
atory remark that "Barbara's return to the colors may yet provide a
subject for the dramatic historian of the future" (27), then that must
mean she is planning to rejoin the Salvation Army. And if indeed she
is planning to rejoin, what then could she possibly mean by "salvation" as applied to workers who, as her father tells her, are already
"strongly religious" to begin with (126) and who live in a town filled
with churches which an initially skeptical Cusins has pronounced to
be "perfect! wonderful! real!" (129)? If Barbara can't bribe them with
bread or, what seems more to the point, with heaven, what can or
will she bribe them with? With Shaw's plays, perhaps? (Significantly,
we are not told of the existence of a playhouse at Perivale St. Andrews.) If so, the outlook is not promising. What measurable difference to humanity at large—and to the "common people" in particular—has a century of performances of Shaw's plays made? Or is she
implying that she will now be a major (or an officer of even higher
rank) in some other army, possibly that of the Life Force?

The Life Force is never mentioned in *Major Barbara*. Inevitably,
as a self-appointed "dramatic historian of the future," one wonders why not? Is it because it was mentioned so prominently, perhaps even over-mentioned, in Shaw's earlier play, *Man and Superman*?
Could Shaw therefore assume that his audience of largely intellectual and well-read playgoers would make the connection between
that play and this one?[13] There are, it is true, hints here and there
in the play that there is some purpose directing the affairs of the
Undershaft family, both present and prospective, along with that
of humanity in general. Is it too much to call that purpose, as Barbara does at the end of the play, God? Barbara claims, after all, to
have gotten rid of the bribe of heaven, but she still explicitly re-

13. Shaw published *Man and Superman* in 1903 but its single public performance
in London two years later by the Royal Court was not a success. No attentive reader
of the play, however, could possibly have missed the frequent references to the Life
Force, especially in the third and fourth acts.

tains, though not apparently as a bribe, her allegiance to the project of accomplishing "God's work." This God, so it would appear, either does not reside in heaven or, if he does, does not think his residence there sufficiently attractive to potential transfers from Perivale St. Andrews. In any case, heaven is probably unnecessary since it ("the heavenly city") already has been established within driving distance of London, where, at least so far as the principals of this play are concerned, God's work can be carried out more conveniently than in some remote heavenly sphere. God's work, moreover—whatever it may be—requires living human beings, especially extraordinary ones like Barbara and her father rather than merely "common" ones, to get itself accomplished.[14] (Again one thinks of *Faust* in this connection, particularly of his insistence on "ewig streben"—i.e., striving eternally.) Perhaps all she really needs to do is to persuade herself of the worth of her (and God's) work, and the rest will follow on its own.

Doing God's work also means, so Barbara claims, that she will be conferring a favor on God, so much so in fact that when she dies God will be in her debt, rather than the other way around. When that moment comes, she also proposes to "forgive" him, though it's not entirely clear what God needs to be forgiven for, especially after Shaw had already noted in his Preface that "[f]orgiveness, absolution, atonement, are figments" (32). The only thing that is clear is that the Barbara, who, at the end of the second act of the play, had, in imitation of Christ, repeated Christ's words of seeming despair, "My God: why hast thou forsaken me?" (111), now rather proudly, if not arrogantly, in turn promises not to forsake her God but to carry out his work and even forgive him. If indeed Barbara means now to resume her position in the Salvation Army—that is, "return to the colors," in Shaw's words—then it would seem that something has

14. There may be a connection here between Perivale St. Andrews as a utopian city and the contemporaneous, quasi-utopian Garden City movement, founded by Ebenezer Howard. I am indebted to James Sexton for this insight.

happened to radically change not only her relationship to God but also to radically change God himself.

It is probably not accidental that Barbara is named Barbara. The significance of her name would be even more apparent if Shaw had called the play *Saint Barbara* instead of *Major Barbara*. A couple of decades later he would entitle what is arguably his greatest play using the name of a female saint, *Saint Joan,* though he might with equal reason have called it *Major General Joan.* It should not therefore surprise us unduly to learn that the Barbara who was a fourth-century martyr and saint is noted in particular for being the patroness of armorers. Barbara Undershaft's Christian name has, so it would seem, predestined her to assuming the management at Perivale St. Andrews. It may also have another, more ominous significance. Because of her unauthorized conversion to Christianity, and her adamant refusal to forego her new religion, St. Barbara's fanatically pagan father delivered her up to Martian, governor of Nicomedia, who had her subjected to a variety of cruel tortures. When she still refused to yield, her obdurate father decided to decapitate her, but at the last moment was prevented from doing so when a sudden bolt of lightning struck him dead. Are we to surmise from this mythological precedent that Barbara will have to await the demise of her father Undershaft before she too will be beatified for carrying out God's work? And does Undershaft belong to the party of the devil, as he himself claims, or is he too (nevertheless?) engaged in furthering God's work?

Aside from St. Barbara's devotion to a kind of militant Christianity—admittedly somewhat different from Barbara's initial commitment to the Salvation Army—their close connection to their respective fathers is strikingly suggestive. While, on the face of it, Undershaft would seem to be quite unlike St. Barbara's cruel father, he too is very definitely pagan—he may even be a pagan god, Dionysos, if we are to believe the repeated protestations of his future son-in-law, Cusins—who is determined to change his daughter's allegiance to her Christian faith; and indeed he apparently succeeds in doing so, fortunately for him without in the process being struck dead by lightning. But he does, unlike St. Barbara's father, manage to cut off his daughter's head, though only metaphorically, or, to be precise, not her head but her heart. For, in losing her faith, Barbara suffers heartbreak, rather like Ellie Dunn in the later Shaw play that functions as a kind of sequel to this one, *Heartbreak House*. When her fiancé is about to join in the celebrations subsequent to Undershaft's purchase of the Salvation Army, by marching off and beating his drum loudly, she tells him quietly: "Dolly: you are breaking my heart" (109).

Not for long, though. When Barbara accuses her father of having taken "a human soul from me and turn[ed] it into the soul of a wolf" (i.e., Bill Walker's soul), he replies by faulting her for despairing too easily: "Can you strike a man to the heart and leave no mark on him?" It is this remark that reinvigorates Barbara's faith and begins the process of healing her broken heart: "Oh, you are right," she says, "he can never be lost now: where was my faith?" (128). Where indeed? Just waiting, apparently, for another opportunity to go briskly to work, a grand opportunity that her father promises to provide her with at Perivale St. Andrews. Referring again to Bill Walker, Undershaft now tells Barbara that where she failed, he himself would succeed: "you talk of your half-saved ruffian at West Ham: you accuse me of dragging his soul back to perdition. Well, bring him to me here; and I will drag his soul back again to salvation for you. Not by words and dreams; but by thirty-eight shillings a week, a sound house in a handsome street, and a permanent job. In three weeks he will have a fancy waist-coat; in three months a tall hat and a chapel sitting; before the end of a year he will shake hands with a duchess at a Primrose League meeting, and join the Conservative Party" (142). Oddly enough, however, such an invitation to Bill Walker to get his soul saved by Undershaft has not been and will apparently not be extended, though it's doubtful that Bill would accept.

This, then, is "salvation"? By way of Undershaft's Professor Higgins and Bill Walker's Eliza Doolittle? Small wonder that Barbara seems skeptical that Bill's soul would be better off if saved in this way. Or are we to believe that Bill's soul is really Bill's body, just as, according to Undershaft, Barbara's is? Or, for that matter, as the souls of his workers' at Perivale St. Andrews are? By looking "after their drainage" while they "find their own dreams," Undershaft claims to have saved their souls. (This provides a new gloss on Brecht's famous apothegm that "erst kommt das Fressen, dann kommt die Moral." Or "grub first, then ethics," in Auden's translation.) He goes on to inform Barbara that he has saved her soul in much the same way, though evidently only by long distance, not having seen her or apparently even thought about her since she was a child. How did he accomplish this feat? Answer: "I fed you and clothed you and housed you. I took care that you should have money enough to live handsomely—more than enough; so that you could be wasteful, careless, generous. That saved your soul" (141). Evidently, however, Barbara was not fully aware while growing up of the already saved status of her soul, for at some point in her maturation process she must have come to feel that her soul would only flourish if she lived less handsomely and less wastefully by joining the Salvation Army, where she manages to subsist on a pound a day.

What is still unclear about all this, however, is what Barbara's task will be at Perivale St. Andrews if her father has already managed to save all the souls there, along with her own. A little later he tells her that he wants her to try her "hand on my men: their souls are hungry because their bodies are full" (143). Just how their souls could still be hungry if it's true that their souls already have been saved remains unclear. Perhaps souls and bodies are not the same after all. Perhaps it's a little too much to expect metaphysical consistency from an East Ender turned armaments manufacturer; perhaps it's just that Undershaft will twist an argument any which way, so long as it achieves the end he is aiming for. After all, he is not just Mephistopheles or Dionysos, but also Machiavelli. Still, even if we can agree that his workers haven't had their souls saved by Boss Undershaft, it nevertheless remains unclear as to what Barbara will or should be cooking up in order to feed their hungry souls.

Undershaft

Andrew Undershaft claims to be a religious man. It's a little difficult to determine, however, just what his religion actually consists of. Not long after learning that his daughter Barbara is an officer in the Salvation Army, he ventures to say that its motto might be his own: "Blood and Fire" (69). To which his future son-in-law Lomax sensibly, if a little rudely, objects that it must differ from the Salvation Army's Christian variety, alluding fairly obviously to Undershaft's armaments factory and its seemingly satanic (as in "dark satanic mills"), fiery, and bloody underpinnings. Undershaft is not in the least put out by all this. He counters that Christianity, "which enjoins you to resist not evil, and to turn the other cheek, would make me bankrupt." His morality—his religion—he goes on to say, "must have a place for cannons and torpedoes in it" (71).

Undershaft, so much is clear, is not a Christian, whatever else he may be, though he evidently sees a connection between what he does at Perivale St. Andrews and what the Salvation Army—and his daughter—are doing. When, on the following day, as he visits Barbara at the Salvation Army shelter, she introduces him to one of the unemployed workers as a fellow Secularist (i.e., atheist), he immediately objects that he is anything but a Secularist; "on the contrary, [he claims to be] a confirmed mystic." Put out a little by this assertion, Barbara asks just what this might mean in terms of practicing an actual religion. Now, instead of elaborating on his alleged mystical beliefs, Undershaft baldly asserts that "I am a Millionaire. That is my religion" (88). A little later, in response to Cusins's inquiry about whether he possesses a religion, he answers affirmatively that he does and that there are two things necessary to salvation in it, namely, "money and gunpowder" (93). Just what money and gunpowder, or blood and fire for that matter, might have to do with being a confirmed mystic he does not explain. In any case, Cusins seems not to bother his head much with these various and seemingly contradictory assertions about Undershaft's religion. He focuses instead on identifying Undershaft's religion with those religions he knows best—pagan Greek religions—and so arrives at the conclusion that Undershaft's visit to the West Ham shelter is an attempt to convert the "Salvation Army to the worship of Dionysos" (95). Then, immediately after Undershaft has used the money he has earned from making weapons and gunpowder to buy the Salvation Army, Cusins exclaims that "Dionysos Undershaft has descended. I am possessed" (110).

Just what all this is supposed to mean, neither Cusins nor Undershaft (nor Shaw) ever explains. There are hints, though. At the crucial point during the negotiations between Undershaft and Cusins for the succession to the armaments business, the former warns the latter that he should not expect to come to Perivale St. Andrews out of a lust for power, because he won't have any, to which the latter replies, rather boastfully, that he has more power and more will than Undershaft does. The reason for this difference is that, as Cusins notes, Undershaft does not "drive this place," whereas apparently Cusins thinks he will. To Cusins's inquiry as to what does drive the place, Undershaft replies mysteriously, "A will of which I am a part" (139). It is at moments like this that one is forced to agree with Georg Roppen's assessment of Shaw (or at least of Undershaft) as a "mystic and a prophet" (1956, 353).

Andrew Undershaft's religion seems to consist of a fusion of this-worldly and otherworldly elements. What's on the other side remains murky for the most part.[15] As for what's on this side, Under-

---

15. This is a flaw in the play that Shaw was evidently aware of and wished to correct, even more than he had already tried to do in his Preface. That is no doubt why not long after the first production of *Major Barbara* he began giving talks on the "Religion of the Future." This religion is the religion of creative evolution, also apparently Undershaft's "otherworldly" religion, which holds that we "are all experiments in the direction of making God." God, in other words, is a creation of humanity—and ultimately humanity *is* God, and vice versa. "What God is doing is making himself,

shaft insists on his "gospel of money and gunpowder," (96) by which he seems to mean that his religion essentially consists of equating might with right. It's not a simple equation, however, for he seems also to believe in adjusting certain existing mights to correlate better with hitherto neglected rights. It's also clear that his this-worldly religion takes precedence over his otherworldly religion. His first, very practical commandment is that no one must get in the way of his primary goal of being a "full-fed free man." The second, rather more idealistic commandment is that everyone else should be equally full-fed and free, a condition which, if achieved, would bring about "an England worth living in" (143). Undershaft is fully aware that getting to such an England would involve a great deal of violent death. "I hate poverty and slavery worse than any other crimes whatever," he tells his daughter. "And let me tell you this. Poverty and slavery have stood up for centuries to your sermons and leading articles: they will not stand up to my machine guns. Dont preach at them: dont reason with them. Kill them" (143).

Among the curious and still rather shocking things about this speech is what the "them" that are supposed to be killed refers to. According to the traditional rules of English grammar, it seems incontrovertible that "them" must refer to poverty and slavery. However, just how abstractions like poverty and slavery are to be killed with machine guns is unclear. Does Shaw mean us to substitute "poor people" and "slaves" for these euphemistic abstractions? Is he seriously maintaining that we should gun down all the poor and enslaved and thereby arrive at a free and full-fed England? Or is he sug-

---

getting from being a mere powerless will or force. This force has implanted into our minds the idea of God. We are not very successful attempts at God so far, but I believe if we can drive into the heads of men the full consciousness of moral responsibility that comes to men with the knowledge that there will never be a God unless we make one," then perhaps a more "successful" God and a more successful "human" will come into being. This is apparently what Shaw means us to understand when Barbara says that when she dies, God will be in her debt. And it is what Undershaft is referring to when he claims to be a mystic and part of a greater will (quoted in Holroyd 1989, 216).

gesting something less appalling but no less drastic and marginally more appealing, at least to orthodox Marxists, namely, that we
should kill all the rich, full-fed "parasites" and then distribute their
wealth and food equitably among the poor, starving, and enslaved?

That Undershaft is involved in the manufacture of weapons of
mass death is not accidental, but essential to an understanding of
his outlook, in terms of both his own "religion" and the meaning
of the play. There may be a resemblance, as Shaw himself once remarked, between Undershaft and his earlier antiheroic characters,
Cashel Byron, Sartorius, and Mrs. Warren, in that all of them are
"prospering in questionable activities" (1949, 143), but that resemblance, as J. L. Wisenthal points out, is only superficial. There is, as
Wisenthal says, "a crucial distinction between Undershaft's profession and the others: weapons can be a direct instrument of social
change, which slum dwellings, brothels, and whisky are obviously
not. Undershaft defends his gunpowder in a way in which the other
immoralists could not defend their wares" (1974a, 60).

Despite the euphemisms in *Major Barbara*, Shaw usually was not
averse to making public his controversial views on doing away with
those whom he considered "superfluous" or worse. Even in the Preface to the play, he argues that "if we were all as resolute and clear-
sighted as Undershaft, an attempt to live by what is called 'an independent income' would be the shortest way to the lethal chamber"
(19). (It probably did not escape Shaw, who by this time was indepen-
dently wealthy, that this might well include himself.) In *Crude Crimi-
nology* there is a separate section entitled "The Lethal Chamber" in
which Shaw advocates exterminating human "nuisances and monsters" (192). Perhaps the clearest and most chilling statement of this
view occurs in *Everybody's Political What's What*, where Shaw goes so
far as to maintain that the time of useful people should not be wasted
in guarding so-called useless people in jails. "Such freaks," Shaw says,
"should be pitied and painlessly killed without malice as a mad dog is
killed. And so should all who are not worth their salt and are spoiling
the lives of those who are worth their salt and a bit more" (281).

At first Barbara is repelled by Undershaft's relish for killing. Not that he tries to hide it from her—or from us. That relish—and Shaw's determination that his audience should be fully aware of it—is apparent in both the dialogue and the stage directions when Undershaft first comes on stage to greet his family in Perivale St. Andrews. He tells them that he has just received "good news from Manchuria" (where the Russo-Japanese War was being waged at the time Shaw was writing the play), namely, that one of his aerial battleships has succeeded in wiping out a Russian fort with three hundred soldiers in it. After making this announcement, he goes *"striding across to Stephen . . . kicking the prostrate dummy* [soldier] *brutally out of his way"* (130).

How, after such talk and behavior, Undershaft nevertheless manages to retain the admiration and even affection of his family and, what is more important, of his audience and critics, is something of a mystery. Perhaps it is because, as Desmond McCarthy observed after seeing the play, Undershaft talks big about violence, but in fact turns out to be "a good young man" [*sic*] with a desk job. Nicholas Grene too seems to feel that in some ways Shaw has not made Undershaft nasty enough, and that this failure produces an excess of sympathy for him: "Shaw's admiration for Undershaft, his unwillingness to give him any really unpleasant not to mention diabolic traits, produces an imbalance in the play—particularly in the final act" (1984, 94). But is this really fair? Undershaft is a character who faces both ways: in the dark direction of what W. H. Auden would later term "necessary murder" as well as in another and opposite direction leading to a kind of utopia. For Undershaft, after all, being prepared to kill is "the final test of conviction, the only lever strong enough to overturn a social system, the only way of saying Must" (143). Undershaft, whatever his motivations, is really more of an idealist than a realist. Making money out of death is mere sideline for him. What he really wants to make is utopia. He is, as Fukuyama, following Plato, would say, a prime example of the thymotic man, someone, that is, who does not act simply out of self-interest but for the sake of the larger social entity. Why he should want to do so is simply not explicable in terms of the primitive economic psychology of Marxism or even in the more sophisticated terms of Freudian psychology. But then Shaw's own motives for wanting to devote himself altruistically to the cause of a better humanity are also not explicable in those terms. Don Juan perhaps expresses Undershaft's motivation best in the third act of *Man and Superman* when he says that "as long as I can conceive something better than myself I cannot be easy unless I am striving to bring it into existence or clearing the way for it. That is the law of my life" (137). In the end, then, both Barbara and Cusins, who are also with inexplicable altruism looking for a means of overturning what they consider to be an unjust social system, come to share Undershaft's views on killing, or so at least it seems if we are to believe the "mystical" words uttered by both immediately following Barbara's last great speech.

> *Cusins:* Then the way of Life lies through the factory of death?
> *Barbara:* Yes, through the raising of hell to heaven and of man to God, through the unveiling of an eternal light in the Valley of The Shadow. (152)

The eternal light here refers, I think, to the light shed by the Life Force, which, after the apocalypse—the word "apocalypse," as noted in an earlier and different context, means "unveiling" in Greek—will abolish the distinctions between heaven and hell, and man and God. But to reach that point, "we" must first pass through the factory of death, must accept the Darwinian and Undershaftian condition that life progresses only by means of a dialectic with death. Put simply, if paradoxically, the Life Force is also a Death Force. Unfortunately, despite Barbara's transfiguration, all of this remains very vague and cloudy. Or perhaps it's not unfortunate at all. According to his critics, Shaw's aesthetic fault, after all, is that he explains too much, and trusts too little to the intelligence of his audience. That is no doubt why he appeared one night in a dream to his fellow countryman, W. B. Yeats, in the form of a sewing machine, grinning all the while.

What, then, in conclusion, *is* Undershaft's religion? It is, I think, a continuous effort to partake in this process of the unveiling of the light, whatever intermediate darkness that may involve. (Faust's injunction about "ewig streben" seems crucially relevant here.) It is to recognize that one serves the cause of humanity best when one accepts the dialectic of life and death. This is an idea—and a religion?—that remains constant for just about all of Shaw's plays hereafter. That is also why we recognize a deliberate echo of Undershaft when the Serpent tells Adam in *Back to Methuselah* that the voice in the garden is his own voice, to which Adam replies: "It is; and it is not. It is something greater than me: I am only a part of it" (1931, 861). It is the voice of God that Adam hears, which is also the voice of Adam, which is also the voice of Shaw, which is also the voice of the Life Force, the force that will gradually drive humanity out of one garden in the remote past and into another in the remote future, as far as thought can reach. It is also, I think, no accident that Undershaft's name refers to the somewhat obscure but quite real London church of St. Andrew Undershaft. Andrew is both a "saint" in this extraordinary evolutionary religion, a religion that, as Cusins realizes early on, links Undershaft to a fertility cult like that of Dionysos, as is also apparent in his curious surname (undershaft = maypole).

As Julian Kaye points out, Shaw is, however, also alluding in Undershaft's name to Carlyle's Captain of Industry (Carlyle coined the phrase), Plugson of Undershot, a name which Shaw uses intertextually again in a later play about another life-affirming maker of death-dealing weapons, Captain Shotover in *Heartbreak House* (15). In *Past and Present* Carlyle considers a variety of potential "saviors" of England, including Plugson of Undershot, whose respected firm of Plugson, Hunks, and Co. is located, not coincidentally, in the parish of St. Dolly Undershot. Carlyle dismisses him, along with just about all of the other candidates, such as the politician Jabesh Windbag and the aristocrat Pandarus Dogdraught, but not without first saluting him for his hard work: "Plugson, who has indomitably spun cotton merely to gain thousands of pounds, I have yet to call a Bucanier and Chactaw, till there come something better, still more indomitable from him" (192). In the figure of Andrew Undershaft, there does come something better, and certainly something more indomitable.

For, unlike his fellow Captains of Industry, Undershaft does not manufacture cotton, but guns; and unlike them he is not "blind," because he sees that "all human things do require to have an Ideal in them; to have some Soul in them" (189). Still, Carlyle praises Plugson for having been "a Captain of Industry, born member of the Ultimate genuine Aristocracy of this Universe, could he have known it" (192). Undershaft, though a foundling and sometime East Ender, also belongs to that aristocracy; and, despite being at times as greedy for money as Plugson, he knows that money is only a means to an end. Like his daughter, Barbara, he too recognizes that the real answer to the problems facing England—and humanity in general— can only be resolved by Carlyle's "One Institution," i.e., the army though in his case it's not so much the actual army (or, for that matter, the in this respect misnamed Salvation Army) as the coherent organized effort characteristic of armies and of armaments factories. It is only through such an "army" that humanity will find salvation. It may actually be that Shaw has something like Edward Bellamy's "industrial army" in mind (Bellamy 1995, 60–66). Paradoxically, salvation is only possible because an institution organized to achieve violent ends knows how to kill and is prepared to do so, or, as Carlyle puts it: "Strange, interesting, and yet most mournful to reflect on. Was this, then, of all the things mankind had some talent for, the one thing important to learn well, and bring to perfection, this of successfully killing one another?" (262).

Undershaft combines industry with destruction, the creation of life with the creation of death. These are the traits that link him inextricably to a Life Force which is also a Death Force. That is why, as he tells Cusins, he wants to "hand on my torch to my daughter. She shall make my converts and preach my gospel—"

> *Cusins:* What! Money and gunpowder!
> *Undershaft:* Yes, money and gunpowder, Freedom and power.
> Command of life and command of death. (96)

If Shaw had given the last great speech at the end of the play to Undershaft instead of to Barbara, he might very well have let him recite Carlyle's grand paean to the "One Institution": "O Heavens, if we saw an army ninety-thousand strong, maintained and fully equipt, in continual real action and battle against Human Starvation, against Chaos, Necessity, Stupidity, and our 'real natural enemies,' what a business were it!" (263).

In the end, then, as Shaw told his friend Gilbert Murray (on whom Cusins was modeled) when the latter complained about Undershaft's complete "victory" in the final act of the play: "Undershaft is in the right" (quoted in Grene 1984, 94).

Utopia

Perivale is a real place in Middlesex, a part of Greater London that is best known today perhaps for its reasonably priced nine-hole golf course. At the time Shaw wrote the play, it must have consisted mostly of farms and pleasant countryside. Its name means "vale of pears," which, so far as I can tell, has no significance for the play, though it's possible that Shaw was attracted to the name because of its close resemblance to the name "Percivale," of which more later. The Shavian town of Perivale St. Andrews, on the other hand, is entirely fictional, with no connection to any real locality, except for the presence perhaps of two Middlesex hills. Shaw's stage directions describe the town as follows: *"Perivale St. Andrews lies between two Middlesex Hills, half climbing the northern one. It is an almost smokeless town of white walls, roofs of narrow green slates or red tiles, tall trees, domes, campaniles, and slender chimney shafts, beautifully situated and beautiful in itself"* (128–29). The description sounds almost Mediterranean, what with the white walls, red tile roofs, and campaniles. Cusins, who has been touring the place on his own in hopes of finding its seamy side, has been unable to come up with anything discreditable. It only "needs a cathedral," he says, "to be a heavenly city instead of a hellish one" (129). A little later he describes it as "horribly, frightfully, immorally, unanswerably perfect" (130). Stephen and Sarah, who have also been looking over the town with a less negative outlook, wax enthusiastic about the nursing home, the libraries, the schools, the ballroom, the banqueting chamber, the insurance fund, the pension fund, the building society, along with various other "applications of cooperation." The emphasis here on "cooperation" rather than competition suggests that Undershaft's Perivale functions on a basis similar to Edward Bellamy's Boston of the year 2000. Lady Britomart, too, after seeing the town, feels renewed pangs of regret at having forfeited the inheritance. She now insists that the houses, the furniture, the gardens and the orchards must absolutely belong to her family, and threatens to call in a doctor if Undershaft persists in his folly of wishing to leave them all to his successor.

Perivale St. Andrews is evidently a kind of utopia/eutopia, a no place that is also a good place. It contrasts very favorably with Barbara's West Ham Salvation Army shelter, as Undershaft does not hesitate to point out, after Barbara ventures to call his model city a dark and "dreadful place." Even she is forced to admit that it has "beautiful clean workshops, and respectable workmen, and model homes":

> *Undershaft:* Cleanliness and respectability do not need justification, Barbara: they justify themselves. I see no darkness here, no dreadfulness. In your Salvation shelter I saw poverty, misery, cold and hunger. You gave them bread and treacle and dreams of heaven. I give them from thirty shillings a week to twelve thousand a year. (141)

Salvation, so it would appear, means something very different to Undershaft than it did to Barbara while she was still a major in the army. For Undershaft salvation takes place when one has full employment and is full-fed and lives in a place like Perivale St. Andrews; for Major Barbara salvation meant, when it actually happened, conversion to evangelical Christianity, though on the evidence of her converts it really tended to mean only the sort of hypocritical piety displayed by Snobby Price. Essentially, at the end of the play, we are confronted with these two very different conceptions of salvation: Barbara's already failed notion of salvation in heaven, for which the unacceptable price is poverty in the here and now, and Undershaft's salvation as embodied in a seemingly perfect Perivale St. Andrews, for which the apparently acceptable price is that beneath (or inside) its beautiful exterior are vast quantities of explosives and death-dealing weapons. Since Barbara's salvation has already been discredited, there remains only Undershaft's version to be considered.

What evidence is there that Perivale St. Andrews is representative of salvation? Of utopia? We have Undershaft's word for it, and we have the reactions of Barbara, Cusins, and the rest of Undershaft's family. Is that enough? Even if we accept Undershaft's word and credit the responses of the others, are we persuaded? Should we be? Barbara seems persuaded but really isn't. For her, Perivale St. Andrews is only the first step to salvation. Once having seen the place, she feels that she must possess it, rather like her mother, though not because of the houses and gardens but because of "all the human souls to be saved: not weak souls in starved bodies, sobbing with gratitude for a scrap and bread and treacle, but full-fed, quarrelsome, snobbish, uppish creatures, all standing on their little rights and dignities. . . . That is where salvation is really wanted" (152).

Oddly enough, it seems that Undershaft must share his daughter's views on the matter. Why else would he have urged her to try her hand at saving the souls of her workers? Why insist on her coming to Perivale St. Andrews to preach his gospel? By endorsing her missionary activity, he is acting contradictorily and even against his own interest. The contradiction arises from the fact that if his workers are already "saved," there is no need for any further "saving." And if there is no such need, then why bother to make unnecessary trouble for a business which seems to be running very smoothly as it is by giving authority to someone whom his workers will identify as a religious fanatic? Making explosives and weapons requires the greatest calm and discipline, characteristics that neither Barbara nor Cusins seems to possess.

If Perivale St. Andrews is already perfect and a heavenly city, as Cusins suggests it is, then it does not need further change. Changes can only make it worse rather than better. Yet Undershaft seems bent on making such changes by establishing as his successors a woman who is determined to make religious converts and a man who will no doubt ruin the business if he follows his stated intention of selling "cannons to whom I please and refus[ing] them to whom I please" (139). The only logical conclusion one can draw from Undershaft's behavior is that he does not really believe that Perivale St. Andrews is a utopia. Though he and his gospel seem to carry all before them at the end of the play, in reality it is Barbara who wins, though only because Undershaft wants her to win. He wants her to move his seemingly perfect city to yet greater perfection, though he apparently does not know how that will happen or what that greater perfection will look like. He wants, as it were, his daughter to transform Perivale St. Andrews into Percivale St. Andrews, into the truly heavenly city, that is, the City of God which Percivale and Galahad, alone of all of Arthur's knights, are privileged to see at the end of the Grail quest. Undershaft's city, it turns out, is only a stopping place along the way. The quest for utopia must and will continue.

Making Sense of *Major Barbara*

R. J. Minney tells an amusing story about the making of the film version of *Major Barbara*. During the rehearsals for the movie, at which Shaw himself was usually present, Rex Harrison (playing the role of Cusins) and Wendy Hiller (Barbara) were unable to make much sense out of Barbara's great speech at the end of the play. Harrison told the producer, Gabriel Pascal, about their difficulty, and both then approached Shaw about it and asked him to explain it to them. Shaw took the script into a corner and, according to Harrison, "sat with his head in his hands and read it silently. When

he had finished, he said: 'Oh what a terrible scene! Did I write that?'
But he wouldn't alter the scene. He said: 'I have no right to touch
the play—it's a classic'" (Minney 1969, 136).

Minney's (or Harrison's) story implies that the older Shaw had
forgotten what the younger Shaw had originally meant when he
wrote those last pages of the play. That, however, despite the amusing story, does not really seem to have been the case. For when Shaw
finished the first version of *Major Barbara* in early September 1905,
he himself was surprised and dismayed at the ease with which Undershaft had converted his daughter and future son-in-law to his
"gospel." A little later, while reading the play out loud to Murray
and some others, he admitted that he did not "know how to end the
thing." It is not surprising, therefore, that Michael Holroyd should
conclude, after discussing Shaw's continuing doubts about what to
make of the last scene in *Major Barbara*, that it is "perhaps the most
complex and ambiguous that Shaw ever wrote" (1989, 106–9).

It is a conclusion that Alfred Turco had already arrived at some
time earlier. At the beginning of his discussion of *Major Barbara*,
Turco says that it "poses enormous critical difficulties" (1976, 193).
In his view, nearly all of those difficulties spring ultimately from the
complex character of Andrew Undershaft, a view that I can understand but with which I do not entirely agree. Undershaft, complex
and fascinating though he undoubtedly is, is a less problematic character than Barbara. How to explain the paradox of her acceptance,
on the one hand, of her father's shameless gospel of mass destruction in the here and now while still seeking to convert his prosperous workers to a gospel of meek salvation in the future? This is a
hard question to answer, and yet it is one of the principal questions
that the play demands that we do answer. That is why even an as-
tute critic like Colin Wilson is puzzled as to just what "Barbara's and
Cusins's marriage and joint commitment to the Undershaft business
means practically," since "the manufacture of torpedoes and aerial
battleships is hardly likely to benefit the common people, or provide

the means for them to bring the intellectual oligarchy into their service."

There have been numerous attempts to address this problem. Maurice Valency's answer is that Undershaft's principal aim is to overthrow the existing social system by placing the "socially minded" (i.e., Barbara and Cusins) in effective control of the "armed forces [so] that the government can be induced to do what is necessary to secure a good life for all" (1973, 253). Left to their own devices, he argues, the rich would never undertake anything so obviously against their interests.

Unfortunately, though I confess I sympathize with Valency's point of view, there are several obvious flaws in his argument. To begin with, it is self-contradictory. Undershaft, after all, is immensely rich, richer than just about anybody else. Hence, there is no obvious reason why he should act against his own self-interest any more than his fellow millionaires would. There is the further problem that, if indeed his own and his fellow oligarchs' self-destruction is what Undershaft hopes to achieve, there is no need for him to employ Barbara and Cusins to make this happen. He could do it all by himself, probably more efficiently. Finally, there is the obstacle of his and his predecessors' (and presumably successors') true armorer's faith, namely, to "give arms to all men who offer an honest price for them, without respect of persons or principles: to aristocrat and republican, to Nihilist and Tsar, to Capitalist and Socialist, to Protestant and Catholic, to burglar and policeman, to black man, white man and yellow man, to all sorts and conditions, all nationalities and faiths, all follies and all crimes" (138).

This "faith," to be sure, rings rather hollow, when one reflects that it is a good deal more likely that the tsar rather than the nihilist will be able to pay the hefty asking price for Undershaft's weapons, or the white man rather than the black man, not to mention—what seems to be most relevant to the pockets of the supposedly socialist Shaw—the capitalist rather than the socialist. As Anatole France once famously remarked, while everyone is prohibited from begging or sleeping under the bridges of Paris, it is only the poor who habitually defy the law.

With reference to Barbara's task at the close of the play, Valency's argument is that she will teach the workers to value their "freedom" or "spiritual liberation," even though they may not yet realize that they neither need nor want it. Still, the absence of that freedom prevents them from being "completely human" (263). This is an end which, again for reasons Valency leaves unspecified, Undershaft could not achieve on his own but needs Barbara to do for him. Even granting the validity of the objective, however, in "practical" terms it still remains unclear just how Barbara will go about making Undershaft's prosperous workers desire and feel the need for such an ill-defined "freedom."

Another, rather simpler—and also more brutal—way of making sense of the ending of the play would be to argue that Undershaft wants Barbara and Cusins to begin selling arms to "progressive" buyers so as to incite a war. It's true, of course, that such progressive buyers might not have the money to purchase very expensive merchandise, which would then mean that the Undershaft concern would either have to sell the weapons at a loss or even give them away. In the long run such a strategy would, of course, force Barbara and Cusins out of business, but perhaps that would not be a problem since they might not be hoping for a long run. On the other hand, selling to selective buyers might not be a precondition of bringing about a huge war, since just selling weapons to all comers, as Undershaft and his predecessors have apparently been doing for years, would probably achieve the same purpose, especially if those weapons were to be made increasingly destructive. The ultimate aim of such a strategy would be to have the various buyers (i.e., capitalist nations) engage in a catastrophic war that would leave them so exhausted that they would then be extremely vulnerable to social revolution.

The advantage of reading the play in this way is that, in effect, this is pretty much what actually did happen during and after the 1914–18 war. In 1931, when looking back at the war and speculating about what difference it had made to the success of socialism, Shaw concluded that the immense violence of that war "has changed the world more in four years than Fabian constitutional action seem[s] likely to do in four hundred" (1961, 305–6). This way of looking at the ending of the play would also have the advantage that it would agree with Marx's prophecy that the advanced capitalist nations would inevitably destroy each other through internecine war.

According to Isaiah Berlin, Marx was convinced that "the periodic crises due to the absence of planned economies, and unchecked industrial strife, would necessarily grow more frequent and acute. Wars, on a hitherto unprecedented scale, would ravage the civilized world, until finally the Hegelian contradictions of a system, where continuance depends upon more and more destructive conflicts between its constituent parts, would obtain a violent solution. The ever-decreasing group of capitalists in power would be overthrown by the workers whom they themselves would have so efficiently drilled into a compact, disciplined body" (1952, 229). A disadvantage of such a Marxist analysis of the play, however, is that it would make Undershaft out to be something of an ogre, since he would be setting up both his daughter and his son-in-law for destruction. It would also make him out to be something of a fool, though no doubt an idealistic one, since such a colossal international war could also involve his own destruction, or, if already dead, at any rate the destruction of his enterprise and the tradition that goes with it. Perhaps a more realistic objection, however, is that, as with Valency's interpretation, there is no need to introduce either Barbara or Cusins into the business if he wants to achieve this objective.

No: there must be some other motive involved here, one that requires Barbara's active participation—and perhaps Cusins's too.

Enter J. L. Wisenthal, who reads the ending of *Major Barbara* in terms of Shaw's *Perfect Wagnerite*. In his view, the problem with Undershaft is that he is a "less highly evolved" specimen than either

Barbara or Cusins. "He evidently feels," Wisenthal surmises, "that a man is saved if he has been saved from poverty. He cannot see the need for further evolution beyond material well being" (1974a, 68). Barbara, on the other hand, can. She realizes that her father has only provided the crude foundation, and that she will have to build a more sophisticated superstructure on it. She will, in other words, have to "try to convert the men [of Perivale St. Andrews] to something beyond Philistine, bourgeois, snobbish individualism." (This idea, however, fails to take into account the various "applications of cooperation" mentioned earlier in the description of Perivale St. Andrews [130].) Undershaft, Wisenthal goes on to maintain, is in a position analogous to Wotan, who cannot regain the ring from Fafnir without breaking his word to him, just as Undershaft is unable to defeat poverty without violating his oath to preserve the armorer's faith. Wisenthal then quotes a "key" passage from *The Perfect Wagnerite* that further shores up his argument, to the effect that Wotan/Undershaft's "desire is toward a higher and fuller life" and that therefore he longs "in his inmost soul for the advent of that greater power, whose first work, though this he does not see as yet, must be his own undoing" (quoted in Wisenthal 1974a, 75). In other words, Father Undershaft (or Wotan) must sacrifice himself to his heroic progeny if there is to be a return to Valhalla (i.e., utopia). Only humans—at least heroic humans—can actually achieve a future universal well-being that the gods can only foresee. (Wisenthal develops the *Ring/Major Barbara* parallel more fully in his 1974 essay, "The Underside of Undershaft: A Wagnerian Motif in 'Major Barbara.'")

Wisenthal's interpretation is perhaps the one that most satisfactorily explains the puzzling ending of *Major Barbara*. Not that it answers all of our questions. Just how, for example, Undershaft can be described as less "evolved" than Barbara if the play so clearly indicates that in the end he is "right" and she is "wrong" Wisenthal is unable to explain. Also, his reading still does not clarify just what it is that Barbara and Cusins will actually be doing in Perivale St. Andrews to persuade the workers to overcome their "Philistine" prejudices in order to move on to some supposedly higher, "socialist" state. Are Barbara and Cusins perhaps going to hold classes, at which they will explain creative evolution and take attendance? Cusins's background as a professor would at least fit him for the latter activity. (In this connection, one also wonders why Wisenthal is so certain that Underhaft's workers *are* philistines in need of instruction.) I don't want to blame Wisenthal, however, for leaving these matters vague, since the fault lies clearly with Shaw for leaving them vague in the first place. But then again perhaps we should not really think of it as a fault, since his vagueness will allow future generations of critics and playgoers to go on trying to make sense of this extraordinary play.

CHAPTER 3

UTOPIA AND THE END OF HISTORY

Huxley, Fukuyama, Marcuse

*Not until there is a settled and definitive world order can there be
such a thing as a settled and definitive version of human history.*
Aldous Huxley

Fukuyama and the Hegelian End of History

In *Brave New World,* Aldous Huxley's satiric vision of the technologically sophisticated, politically stable, and contented World State
of six centuries hence, one of the principal tenets is Henry Ford's
"beautiful and inspired saying" that "History is bunk" (34). Given the
fact that Ford has become (along with Freud) the *logos* of the future,
this is not a dictum to be taken lightly. That is why we owe it only
to a rare, paradoxical whim of the local World Controller, Mustapha
Mond, that we are provided with a summary of the historical background leading to the foundation of the New World State. How to
explain the oddity of being given a history lesson when history has
been officially abolished? Well, aside from reasons of novelistic necessity, perhaps it is because, even after history has ended, the way
of the world still remains much as it always has been, so that rulers—especially when they are as powerful as Mond—can break the
rules even when they have been promulgated by Our Ford himself.

History, so Mond informs us, has become such bunk in the future that it has ceased to exist altogether. No books published pri-

or to AF 150 (or, in our terms, 2058 AD) have been allowed to survive—outside of Mond's secret booksafe, that is. The museums,
almost as if following Marinetti's directive, have been blown up, the
museum-goers have been massacred, and, of course, history is no
longer taught in schools. But why make such a fuss about history?
The chief reason, I think, is because for Huxley's future rulers the
past is dangerous, just as it is for the rulers of Orwell's Oceania in
Nineteen Eighty-Four. History reminds people that society was not always organized along the same lines as it now is, and that it may
even have once been based on quite different assumptions. Such a realization will set people to thinking that their societies could also be
subject to alteration, possibly through their own agency. The future
world order (Huxley's as much Orwell's) abhors this thought and
will do its utmost to stifle it.

While history has ended for Huxley's New World State primarily because of its awareness that historical consciousness may
undermine its continuing stability, it has ended for seemingly
quite different reasons for those of us who are living in developed,
liberal-democratic societies at the turn of the third millennium. That
is, it has ended for us, if we are to believe Francis Fukuyama's startling
thesis, as put forward in his celebrated—or notorious—essay of 1989,
"The End of History?" first published in the *National Interest* and later expanded into a less tentatively titled book, *The End of History and
the Last Man* (1992). According to Fukuyama, history has ended because "liberal democracy may constitute the end point of mankind's
ideological evolution" and the "final form of human government."
For Fukuyama, this Hegelian notion holds true because history represents a progressive elimination of internal social "contradictions"
or "false consciousnesses," ultimately culminating in the liberal-
democratic society briefly established by the 1789 French Revolution, a society in which there are supposedly no contradictions and in
which true consciousness has finally been made manifest.[1]

---

1. In what follows, I do not wish to address the sometimes hotly debated question as to whether the ideas about history attributed by Fukuyama to Hegel are actu-

It was, of course, no accident that Fukuyama first formulated his controversial thesis exactly two hundred years after the outbreak of the revolution in France, for he was among the first to recognize that 1989 might be quite as epoch-making a date in world history as 1789. With the impending fall of the Soviet Union and soon thereafter with its actual collapse (a historical fact which may also account for the absence of the question mark in Fukuyama's book-length version of his thesis), Fukuyama concluded that "the twin crises of authoritarianism and social planning have left only one competitor standing in the ring as an ideology of potentially universal validity: liberal democracy, the doctrine of individual freedom and popular sovereignty" (1992, 42). Not only, however, was it the only ideology left standing, it was also the only ideology left imaginable. Hence it had ceased, in Hegelian (as well as in Marxist) terms, to be merely an ideology and had become historical truth. "Today," so Fukuyama confidently concludes, "we have trouble imagining a world that is radically better than our own, or a future that is not essentially democratic and capitalist . . . we cannot picture to ourselves a world that is *essentially* different from the present one, and at the same time better" (1992, 46).[2]

---

ally Hegel's, or Hegel's as interpreted by Alexandre Kojève, or Hegel's as interpreted by Kojève and reinterpreted by Allan Bloom—or if they are merely Fukuyama's own eccentric interpretation of all or some of the foregoing. At issue in this chapter is rather the question of whether and to what extent Fukuyama's argument about the end of history and the last man (to whomever indebted) relates to Aldous Huxley's New World State, as rendered in *Brave New World*. Readers should therefore take care not to read my references to Fukuyama's Hegelian ideas as meaning that I believe they are "in fact" Hegelian. For specialist Hegelian reactions to Fukuyama, see the section on "The Myth of the End of History," in *The Hegel Myths and Legends* (Stewart 1996).

  2. This, of course, depends on who "we" are. While Fukuyama's argument may be valid in the context of developed liberal democracies, its validity becomes more doubtful in other contexts. If, for example, as numerous commentators have pointed out, "we" happen to be Islamic fundamentalists or extreme nationalists, "we" are able to imagine quite different alternative worlds. In Fukuyama's terms, however, Islamic exceptionalism (along with resurgent nationalism) is either retrograde or provincial—or both. It has virtually none of the universalist claim that characterizes liberal democracy at the close of the twentieth century. It should also be noted that Fukuyama

Despite repeated attempts to do so, this extraordinary claim cannot be simply dismissed as the predictable fulminations of a sometime pupil of the Chicago-based conservative guru Allan Bloom, nor is it merely the result, as Paul Johnson suggests in a review of Fukuyama's book, of the unfounded speculations of a naive believer in the "the absurd declaration" of a nineteenth-century German philosopher that history had ended, a philosopher who had, what is more, subsequently gone on to write a quantity of "clever and influential nonsense" (1992, 51). Such counterclaims lose much of whatever force they may have possessed, when other, more dispassionate and better-informed voices are taken into account, particularly when those voices belong to prominent left-wing intellectuals like Russell Jacoby. In his recent book *The End of Utopia: Politics and Culture in an Age of Apathy* (1999), Jacoby argues that "Fukuyama stated a verity that many refuse to acknowledge. Today socialists and leftists do not dream of a future qualitatively different from the present. To put it differently, radicalism no longer believes in itself" (10).[3]

Before going further, however, with our discussion of Fukuyama, we need to address a point of possible misunderstanding, namely, that for Fukuyama the word "history" does not mean what it usually means to most of us. History, for Fukuyama, it is essential to bear in mind, is not just the continuing flow of time and the social, economic, and political events that take place within that flow. Fukuyama does not deny that such events will go on happening in the future or that, in this sense, history will never end. However, in the way that

does not take into account a theory such as is expressed in James Burnham's *Managerial Revolution* (1941), which maintains that the formal institutions of modern society, be they fascist, communist, or capitalist, are of little account. What really matters is that the managerial class (or Max Weber's bureaucrats) holds the strings of power. Fundamentally, therefore, these outwardly dissimilar societies are inwardly the same. History ends, in other words, not as Hegel predicted, but as Kafka depicted.

3. This is an insight that, as is apparent from Huxley's epigraph to *Brave New World,* had occurred to other observers long before. In that epigraph, taken from Nicolai Berdyaev's *The End of Our Time* (1927), the question is not how to achieve utopia but how to avoid it.

Fukuyama employs the word in *The End of History and the Last Man,* "history" has a very narrow Hegelian meaning that must not be confused with more general uses of the term. For Fukuyama, following Hegel, history begins with a primal struggle to the death between individuals striving for mutual recognition. In this conflict, one of the parties, fearing that his life may be lost, yields to the other and thereby forfeits his freedom. This conflict between masters (or winners) and slaves (or losers) represents the beginning of history. The relation of master and slave is not an unchanging one, however, for in performing his enforced labor for the master, the slave over time gains consciousness of a sort which the master, in his unchallenged—and unrelieved—leisure, cannot match. As a consequence and reflection of this increased consciousness, the master/slave relation assumes a series of different and increasingly noncontradictory social forms. Given this more or less inevitable progression of social forms, history must one day culminate or "end" in a society which manifests no systemic contradictions, in which, in other words, there will be no remnant of the original inequality between master and slave. That society, for Hegel, was the liberal democracy proclaimed by the French Revolution. And so it is too for Fukuyama, though his preferred manifestation of liberal democracy is the American consumerist variant of the late twentieth century, to which he, however, adds some important Nietzschean qualifications. More on these later.[4]

In short, in Fukuyama's view, liberal-democratic institutions plus consumer-capitalist economics spell the end of history. The master

4. The notion that such a state of social harmony is desirable in and of itself receives incisive criticism in J. L. Talmon's *The Rise of the Totalitarian Democracy* (1952). There Talmon describes the task of the "social analyst" as resembling that of the psychoanalyst, but on a collective rather than individual basis. His job is "to attack the human urge which calls totalitarian democracy into existence, namely the longing for a final resolution [the end of history?] of all contradictions and conflicts into a state of total harmony. It is a harsh, but nonetheless necessary task to drive home the truth that human society and human life can never reach a state of repose. That imagined repose is another name for the security offered by a prison, and the longing for it may in a sense be an expression of cowardice and laziness, of the inability to face the fact that life is a perpetual and never resolved crisis" (254–55).

and the slave have grown reconciled under the sign of the Big Yellow M. Reviewing in July 1999 his journalist friend Thomas Friedman's book, *The Lexus and the Olive Tree,* Fukuyama agrees with that book's consumerist conclusions, which he finds "particularly satisfying for me because it confirms, vividly and in rich detail, the truth that we have indeed reached the end of history: the ambassador from McDonald's is more highly regarded than the ambassador from the U.S." (Fukuyama 1999a, 54). Or, as he puts it less personally, and more soberly, in *The End of History and the Last Man,* "while not every country is capable of becoming a consumer society in the near future, there is hardly a society in the world that does not embrace the goal itself" (126). Despite appearances to the contrary, Fukuyama is, of course, not simply a follower and endorser of Hegel's quasi-mythological account of the origins of history. For him, Hegel—and along with Hegel, the elaborations of Hegelian doctrine by the Russo-French philosopher Alexandre Kojève—simply provides a convenient (and coherent) structure on which to hang his own analysis of social development at the end of the second millennium.

Two aspects of this analysis are particularly significant. The first concerns a fundamental redefinition of human nature. According to Fukuyama, both capitalist and Marxist historians are wrong in assuming that there is only one primary motive force in human psychology and therefore in history, namely, the economic impulse. For Fukuyama, *homo economicus* alone is inadequate as an explanation of how humans behave and history develops. To *homo economicus* he therefore adds *homo thymoticus,* the human being who (as in Hegel's parable) strives for recognition of his essential status as a free human being. The thymotic motive, for Fukuyama, explains human actions in history in a way that the simple pursuit of wealth or security (i.e., greed) cannot. Hegel's account of human and historical development is therefore superior to those of Hobbes and Locke, or even Marx. "Revolutionary situations cannot occur," Fukuyama argues persuasively, "unless at least some people are willing to risk their lives and their comfort for a cause. The courage to do so cannot arise out of the desiring part of the soul, but must come from the thymotic part. The man of desire, Economic Man, the true *bourgeois*, will perform an internal 'cost-benefit analysis' which will always give him a reason for working 'within the system.' It is only thymotic man, the man of anger who is jealous of his own dignity and the dignity of his fellow citizens"—and here Fukuyama alludes to another crucial event of the late 1980s—"who is willing to walk in front of a tank or confront a line of soldiers" (1992, 180).[5]

The other innovative element of Fukuyama's argument is his contention that the unilateral and irreversible progress of the accumulation of scientific (and technological) knowledge implies a concomitant and equally irreversible progression in the historical development of social organizations. Indeed, in his view, science is not merely a model for social development but an irresistible force that compels societies to reorganize themselves in order to maximize technological development. It is this unilateral, irreversible progression of scientific and technological development that ultimately confirms Hegel's thesis about the unilateral, irreversible, progressive movement of history. "Technology," according to Fukuyama, "provides a uniform horizon of production possibilities at any given level of scientific knowledge, and forces all societies employing technology to organize themselves in certain ways" (1989, 244). An important consequence flows from this insight, the full implications of which Fukuyama himself would, however, only realize several years later, namely, that "if our lives and our forms of social organization are governed by the inner logic of the development of science, we cannot know with finality what social arrangements will be dictated by a given level of scientific knowledge in the future" (1989, 247).

One important consequence of the end of history, however, Fu-

5. For Huxley, too, man is not to be simply equated with economic man. As he says in *Do What You Will*, "nothing could be more chimerical than the notion that man is the same thing as the Economic Man and that the problems of life, Man's life, can be solved by any merely economic arrangement" (224).

kuyama was fully aware of from near the beginning of his revival of Hegelian historiography, namely, that the end of history would also bring with it the end of humanity. The end of history, in other words, heralds the arrival of the Last Man as foretold by Friedrich Nietzsche's Zarathustra in the Prologue to Nietzsche's great prose poem *Also Sprach Zarathustra* (Thus Spake Zarathustra). "'Alas,'" Zarathustra says to the uncomprehending masses, "'the time of the most despicable man is coming, he that is no longer able to despise himself. Behold, I show you the *last man. . . .*' 'We have invented happiness,' say the last men, and they blink. They have left the regions where it was hard to live, for one needs warmth. One still loves one's neighbor and rubs against him, for one needs warmth. . . . No shepherd and one herd! Everybody wants the same, everybody is the same: whoever feels different goes voluntarily into a madhouse." And what do the masses reply to Zarathustra's warning about the impending end of humanity? "'Give us this last man, O Zarathustra,' they shouted. 'Turn us into these last men!'" (Nietzsche 1971, 129–30).

Fukuyama realizes full well that in announcing the end of history, he has, like Zarathustra, though a good deal less dithyrhambically, also announced the arrival of the last man. This last man is, in just about all respects, identical with the typical American consumer of the close of the twentieth century. "The end of history," he says in the final paragraph of his original essay, "will be a very sad time. The struggle for recognition, the willingness to risk one's own life for a purely abstract goal, the worldwide ideological struggle that called forth daring, courage, imagination, and idealism, will be replaced by economic calculation, the endless solving of technical problems, environmental concerns, and the satisfaction of sophisticated consumer demands. In the post-historical period there will be neither art nor philosophy, just the perpetual caretaking of the museum of human history." Viewing this melancholy and seemingly utterly monotonous prospect, Fukuyama himself draws back and, as it were, blinks. Perhaps, he thinks, history will not end after all;

perhaps "this very prospect of centuries of boredom at the end of history will serve to get history started again" (1989, 18).

Huxley's First and Last Men

In Aldous Huxley's dystopian New World State of AF 632, the last man has triumphed and happiness reigns supreme in a technologically sophisticated consumer society that, while clearly based on that of the United States in the twentieth century, allows no room for boredom and therefore precludes all possibility of a resumption of history. Huxley's future society, however, is anything but a liberal democracy. In fact, in Huxley's future world state liberal democracy is just as dead as history, for the simple reason that liberal democracy does not remove the deep sources of continuing conflict in the way that Hegel (and Fukuyama) had assumed. On the contrary, as we learn implicitly from Mustapha Mond, in the post–twentieth century era liberal democracies not only engaged in deadly international wars, they also fought devastating civil wars, a situation which in the long run became intolerable.[6] The true source of these conflicts lay, however, not so much in faulty social organization as in a fundamental misapprehension about what human beings were really like. The external social and collective conflict was in reality only a reflection of the internal, individual conflict. The final contradictions were in humanity itself, not in the way human beings organized themselves socially. The faults of the latter simply followed inevitably from the flaws in the former. To resolve that final inner contradiction, therefore, there had first to be a final inner revolution, one that would alter the human condition by altering humanity itself. That final revolution would bring with it the birth of the last man,

---

6. Here Huxley differs from Fukuyama, who cites "a substantial body of literature noting the fact that there have been few, if any, instances of one liberal democracy going to war with another" (1992, 262). As Fukuyama is aware, much of the force of this argument depends on how (and how narrowly) "liberal democracy" is defined.

but not as Nietzsche—or Fukuyama, for that matter—had foretold or envisioned it but in sterilized bottles moving silently along vast assembly lines in human embryo factories thirty-four stories high.

Still, though the political constitution of the New World State appears to have little to do with liberal democracy—if anything, it resembles an ecclesiastical model, governed by a self-selected and self-perpetuating council of bishops (the ten World Controllers)—it does, like Hegel's final state, quite consciously derive in important ways from the French Revolution. The motto of the New World State— COMMUNITY, IDENTITY, STABILITY—deliberately, and ironically, evokes the motto of the first French Republic ("Liberty, Equality, Fraternity").[7] Indeed the very notion of a World State is linked to the expansionist and universalist French Revolution, for which Hegel uses the term "universal homogeneous state."

For Huxley, however, as we have seen, the end of history does not really begin to happen, as it famously did for Hegel in 1806, when he saw Napoleon astride his horse after the great victory of the French armies at Jena. For Huxley, the French Revolution was merely the first and most superficial of a series of three revolutions that were to radically alter human history before conclusively ending it. The first revolution was a political revolution which Huxley explicitly identifies in his 1947 preface to *Brave New World* with Robespierre's role in establishing an egalitarian liberal democracy. More important in the long run than Robespierre, however, is François Babeuf, because Babeuf, despite his failures in the short term, adumbrated the next revolutionary stage, the economic revolution, which, though Huxley does not discuss it in any detail, radically altered social conditions in

7. In *Jesting Pilate* (1926) Huxley had already suggested that the motto of the French Revolution needed to be adjusted to contemporary circumstances: "Now that liberty is out of date, equality an exploded notion and fraternity a proven impossibility, republics should change their mottoes. Intelligence, Sterility, Insolvency: that would do for contemporary France. But not for America . . . what I should write under America's flapping eagle would be: Vitality, Prosperity, Modernity" (1957a, 280). Huxley goes on to define "Modernity" as "the freedom, in a word, from history" (281).

the nineteenth and twentieth centuries. The third or "final" or "really revolutionary" revolution, however, the revolution that brings history to a close and creates the New World State, only occurs several centuries later. Significantly, it is a revolution inspired much less by Rousseau and Robespierre than by Freud, William Sheldon, and Pavlov. It is only this third or final revolution—"achieved," as Huxley explicitly says, "not in the external world, but in the souls and flesh of human beings"—that has managed to resolve the last "contradictions" in the social order (xi–xii).

The continuity of the aims of the New World State with those of the French Revolution—but even more important, its differences—are signaled by the triple motto of Huxley's World State. Instead of liberty, there is community—that is, the sense of being part of a social collective rather than an independent, free-standing individual. This reflects a policy on the part of the New World State that has far more in common with the anti-individualist outlook of communism and fascism than it does with liberal democracy. Instead of equality, there is identity, but identity not in the liberal humanist sense of developing a notion of who one really is as an individual but rather in the sense of being as much like other members of the society as possible. This kind of identity is established in the New World State in two ways: primarily through bioengineering (especially cloning) for the three "slave" castes (gamma, delta, and epsilon), and secondarily for the most part through behaviorist conditioning for the two remaining "master" castes, alpha and beta. Finally and most important, the New World State insists on stability rather than fraternity, for only if the social organism is stable can it guarantee any kind of well-being for its citizens. "Stability," as Mustapha Mond insists, "stability. The primal and the ultimate need" (42). It is to ensure stability that the third revolution has been carried out. It is to ensure stability that there are innumerable entertaining but trivial ways of spending one's money—such as Obstacle Golf and the Feelies—but virtually no serious ones. It is to ensure stability that there is enjoined an unrestricted sexual promiscuity. It is to ensure stability that there is

bioengineering and hypnopedia and conditioning. It is to ensure stability that the World State has divided its citizenry into castes rather
than classes, so that there will be no class conflict—as well as, perhaps, to satisfy the thymotic urges of all but the lowest of the low,
the epsilon semi-morons. It is to ensure stability, finally, that there is
soma, a drug with few side effects which transports its users into a
happy neverland whenever reality threatens to impinge on them.[8]

But then, in the New World State, reality rarely does. For here
even the uncloned alphas and betas are conditioned to avoid any
kind of strong feeling or independent thought. They can hardly help
but conform to Our Freud's injunction never to delay a possible grat-
ification, but have to live their adult lives in the mental equivalent of
the bottle in which they were conceived and nurtured. Any sign of
potentially adult behavior is strongly censured. As the CEO of the
baby-producing factory angrily tells one of his nonconforming man-
agers, "My workers must be above suspicion, particularly those of
the highest castes. Alphas are conditioned that they do not *have* to be
infantile in their emotional behavior. But it is all the more reason for
their making a special effort to conform. It is their duty to be infantile, even against their inclination" (98).

Into this future world of posthistory irrupts John Savage, a devoted reader of Shakespeare and the sometime inhabitant of a world
of prehistory. He is a Zarathustra-like figure, come down from the
lofty isolation of his New Mexico reservation to a live a brief and
violently unhappy existence among those last men of the future
whom he had tragically mistaken at first sight for real men like himself. It is in the great dialogue between John and Mustapha Mond
near the end of the book—a dialogue reminiscent of the encounter between the Grand Inquisitor and Christ in *The Brothers Karam-
azov*—that the contrast between the values of the world within his-

---

8. Huxley's choice of name for this drug is profoundly ironic. As he points out
in *Brave New World Revisited,* "the original soma . . . was an unknown plant (possibly
Asclepias acida) used by the ancient Aryan invaders of India in one of the most solemn
of their religious rites" (68).

tory are most dramatically, and truthfully, contrasted with those of the world that has passed out of history. Like the masterful, thymotic man he is, John asks Mond if he does not agree that living dangerously is something that humans need. Surprisingly, Mond hastens to agree. Indeed humans need danger, he says—or at any rate, they need the biochemical equivalent of danger, they need to have "their adrenals stimulated from time to time." This is the reason why the New World State provides for regular V.P.S. treatments, the abbreviation standing for "Violent Passion Surrogate." Regularly, once every month, Mond tells John, "[w]e flood the whole system with adrenalin. It's the complete psychological equivalent of fear and rage. All the tonic effects of murdering Desdemona and being murdered by Othello, without any of the inconveniences."

To John's reply that he wants those inconveniences, that he wants God, poetry, real danger, and freedom, that he wants goodness and even sin, Mond says, ironically echoing the great founding document of our American liberal democracy, "in fact . . . you're claiming the right to be unhappy." That right, the right of the man still within history, also entails, however, as Mond goes on to point out in graphic detail, "the right to grow old and ugly and impotent; the right to have syphilis and cancer; the right to have too little to eat; the right to be lousy; the right to live in constant apprehension of what may happen tomorrow; the right to catch typhoid; the right to be tortured by unspeakable pains of every kind.'"

To which, after a long silence, John replies: "I claim them all" (247).

Marcuse's Happy Consciousness

Fukuyama does not mention Huxley or *Brave New World* in either the initial essay or in the later book-length version of his argument. Just why he should omit him is unclear. (He does, however, mention Huxley and *Brave New World,* though only in passing, in subsequent remarks about the then current state of the debate about the end of history.) It may be that Huxley's dystopia was not sufficiently "social scientific" for him to be given serious consideration in venues and for audiences that were primarily concerned with profound political and economic issues, rather than with what might be thought of as marginally cultural or even frivolous literary matters. But, if so, why then the prominence given Nietzsche, who may hardly be said to enjoy great respect, or even acquaintance, among social and political scientists? Or is it merely because Nietzsche is currently more fashionable among intellectuals of the right (and even the left) than Huxley?[9] Or could it be that a philosopher, even one who went mad, is nevertheless preferable to a novelist who notoriously took drugs? Perhaps. The answer may "simply" and quite unconsciously be that the dividing line between the two cultures runs not merely between the hard sciences and the humanities, as C. P. Snow once postulated, but also and almost as deeply (with occasional exceptions like Nietzsche) between the soft sciences and the humanities. It is certainly true, as I can vouch from personal experience, of the sharp dividing lines drawn at my own university, where humanists who wish to be taken seriously by their softly scientific colleagues had better learn to speak their language.[10] If, as Max Weber suggests, the "last men" are those who locate their identities in their specialized professional functions, then the American university, as currently constituted, is arguably in the vanguard of such ultimate humanity (Hennies 1988, 153).

9. It may be significant that Nietzsche is not mentioned by name in the original *National Interest* essay, whereas he is featured (or alluded to, at least) in the title of the later book version. The difference may be due to Nietzsche's having been specifically brought into the discussion by Allan Bloom in his response to Fukuyama's original essay, published in the same issue of the *National Interest*. There, after pointing out that Kojève's analysis of the human situation at the end of history was closer to Nietzsche's pessimism than to Hegel's optimism, Bloom goes on to argue that "if, as Nietzsche believed, the 'last man' is the ultimate product of reason, then reason is bad and we must look more closely to unreason for hope of salvation. God is dead and we need new gods. The consequences of this analysis are earth-shaking, and this is the thought of the most modern modernity" (Bloom 1989, 21).

10. See my article "Comparative Literature and Cultural Illiterates" (Firchow 1987).

What *is* surprising, however, about *The End of History* (that is, both the essay and the book) is the omission of Herbert Marcuse, whose *One-Dimensional Man* was a classic of the 1960s and anticipates, in many ways, the specific concerns as well as some of the conclusions of Fukuyama's work. (And, of course, it also echoes, though again without explicitly acknowledging it, Huxley's *Brave New World.*) Like Fukuyama too, Marcuse is profoundly influenced by Hegel (as well as, of course, by Marx), whose thought is recurrently invoked in *One-Dimensional Man*. Indeed, Marcuse had devoted the whole of an earlier book, *Reason and Revolution: Hegel and the Rise of Social Theory* (1941) to the impact of Hegel's philosophy on the modern state.[11] In that book, addressing specifically the Hegelian idea of the end of history, he both agrees and strongly disagrees with Hegel's conclusions. "There is a stark truth," he writes, "in Hegel's strangely certain announcement that history has reached its end. But it announces the funeral of a class, not of history. At the close of the book [*Philosophy of Right*], Hegel writes, after a description of the Restoration, 'This is the point which consciousness has attained.' This hardly sounds like an end. Consciousness is historical consciousness" (227). In other words, Hegel's chief error, according to Marcuse, was that he identified absolute consciousness with bourgeois consciousness. It took Marx to set him straight about the true nature of historical consciousness and to set forth the necessary conditions under which history would finally end.

While still profoundly influenced by Hegel and Marx, *One-Dimensional Man* is not a work of philosophical or intellectual history but consists rather of a critical analysis, as the title implies, of the sorry condition of contemporary humanity, especially in the United States. It seeks to determine the degree to which postmodern Americans have become dehumanized by the establishment of a consumer society and hoodwinked by the proliferation of its con-

---

11. This work is also not mentioned by Fukuyama.

comitant false needs. "The products indoctrinate and manipulate," Marcuse argues, "they promote a false consciousness which is immune against its falsehood. And as these beneficial products become available to more individuals in more social classes, the indoctrination they carry ceases to be publicity; it becomes a way of life. It is a good way of life—much better than before—and as a good way of life it militates against qualitative change. Thus emerges a pattern of *one-dimensional thought and behavior* in which ideas, aspirations, and objectives that, by their content, transcend the established universe of discourse and action are either repelled or reduced to terms of this universe" (1972, 24).

Like Fukuyama, Marcuse views the modern fusion of democratic institutions, consumer capitalism, and technological innovation as so potent as to be virtually irresistible. In combination these elements produce a stable society in which any kind of meaningful social change or development is improbable and perhaps even impossible. It is this fact of the "containment of social change" that Marcuse sees as "perhaps the most singular achievement of advanced industrial society" (11). But what is "singular" is, of course, not necessarily good. On the contrary, the absence of social change (or, better, of social development) in the postmodern world is, in Marcuse's view, utterly deplorable. Just because a gullible citizenry has been seduced or hoodwinked into accepting and even endorsing consumerist ideals and institutions does not make them any "less irrational and less reprehensible." Such apparently willing acceptance on the part of a brainwashed population does not—and here Marcuse is very adamant—invalidate the distinction between "true and false consciousness" (12). Nor does such acceptance mean that the innate contradictions of a faulty social organization have disappeared. They have merely been covered up so artfully and successfully that they are no longer perceived as contradictions. Just because the masters are now elected to office rather than imposed by force as formerly, does not mean, Marcuse concludes ironically, that the distinction between masters and slaves has been abolished (21).[12]

The real problem with postmodern society for Marcuse, as for Huxley, is that its foundations are ultimately more psychological than social. It is the individual and collective consciousness of this society that needs to be changed if meaningful social progress is to be achieved, but, even though that consciousness is demonstrably *false,* it is so deeply entrenched that there appears to be no discernible way to alter it. Thus, in a profoundly ironic and even paradoxical manner, Hegel's famous contention that history is the progressive realization of consciousness is here both endorsed and denied. For, if, as Marcuse observes, "[a]ll liberation depends on the consciousness of servitude," then in a society where such consciousness of servitude is permanently stifled, there can be no liberation (20). The end of history has thus been reached, but in a way not anticipated by either Hegel or his Marxist followers, including the younger Marcuse.

Though Marcuse never mentions him by name, it is clear that Nietzsche's condemnation of the last man in *Also Sprach Zarathustra* plays an important role in his conception of postmodern society. (And, as we shall see, behind Nietzsche, Huxley as well, who is also not mentioned by name.) This Nietzschean influence is particularly apparent in Marcuse's description of what he calls the "Happy Consciousness." Because of the postmodern society's proven ability to absorb and co-opt all opposition—in politics, culture, and even in the "instinctual sphere" (i.e., sexual behavior)—"the mental organs for grasping the contradictions and the alternatives" have become atrophied and, as a result, the Happy Consciousness has triumphed (74). This Happy Consciousness is defined (in Marcuse's curious mixture of Hegelian terminology and hip-speak) as "the belief that the real is rational and the system delivers the goods" (78). It is a consciousness which knows no limits, arranging as it does "games

12. Elsewhere in the book, however, Marcuse claims that postmodern society *has* abolished the distinction between master and slave by the simple expedient of making both slaves (40). Consistency is not a notable feature of Marcuse's argument.

with death and disfiguration in which fun, team work, and strate-
gic importance mix in rewarding social harmony" (75). Life is lived
as a means rather than as an end, and people exist as instruments
or things rather than as fully aware human beings. "This is the pure
form of servitude," Marcuse observes: "to exist as an instrument, as
a thing" (40). History—the past—has been abolished, as it will also
be in Huxley's New World State, or is at any rate much discouraged,
for "[r]emembrance of the past may give rise to dangerous insights,
and the established society seems to be apprehensive of the subver-
sive contents of memory" (88). In a passage that might almost be
lifted from the concluding debate between John Savage and Mustapha Mond in *Brave New World,* Marcuse contends that, although the
"romantic pre-technical world was permeated with misery, toil, and
filth, and these in turn were the background of all pleasure and joy,"
nevertheless "there was a 'landscape,' a medium of libidinal experience which no longer exists" (69). Now, at the end of history, there
is instead only a profoundly false Happy Consciousness enjoyed by a
profoundly despicable herd of one-dimensional Last Men.

Fukuyama and Marcuse: Hegel or Nietzsche?

Neither Fukuyama nor Marcuse, as we have seen, cites the precedent of Huxley's *Brave New World* in developing their arguments
about the present state of capitalist, consumerist, technologically advanced liberal-democratic society, especially in its American manifestation. Though their political origins and convictions are, on the surface at least, very different, with Fukuyama an avowed conservative
and Marcuse a celebrated radical Marxist of the Frankfurt School,
both arrive at surprisingly similar conclusions when it comes to pre-
dicting the immediate—and even the long-term—prospects for mankind. Though they employ somewhat different means to get there,
both manage to arrive at what looks like the same end of history, a
destination which dismays and even horrifies them. History, for both
(and especially for Marcuse), comes to an end not with a bang or

even a whimper, but with a squeal of porcine bliss uttered by a mass
of consumers metamorphosed by the Circe of modern capitalist
technology and wholly unconscious of their lost humanity.

Despite their divergent starting points, then, for both Fukuyama
and Marcuse history ends in much the same way. Is this because
both are Hegelians, albeit Hegelians of the Right and of the Left?
Or is it because both, faced with having to explain the indisputable
and unrivaled success, as well as the apparent stability, of American
society in the latter half of the twentieth century, concluded that
the facts of American consumerism do not confirm Hegel's analysis of historical development but rather Nietzsche's prophecy of the
last man, who prefers the Happy Consciousness to real intellectual
and spiritual awareness? The surprising answer would seem to be
the latter. Nietzsche, so far as both Fukuyama and Marcuse are concerned, sees further—and deeper—than Hegel. Indeed, for Marcuse
there is no real prospect of humanity's ever being able to find an
exit from the present dead end of history, with its ingrained false or
"happy" consciousness, in order to re-enter the real march of history and thereby reach its true (Marxist) climax. All Marcuse holds
out for us is the vague and rather uncertain hope that a kind of neo-
Marxist *Lumpenproletariat* (Marcuse does not use the word) or what
he calls "the substratum of the outcasts and outsiders, the exploit-
ed and persecuted of other races and other colors, the unemployed
and the unemployable," will rise up and protest (peacefully!) "for the
most primitive civil rights" while heroically facing "dogs, stones, and
bombs, jail, concentration camps, even death." In this way, Marcuse
concludes, the people of the substratum—here the sometime Cali-
fornian Marcuse was probably identifying the "substratum" with the
San Francisco Beats, hippies, and hobos of the late fifties and early
sixties—may be the harbingers of a new world: "The fact that they
start refusing to play the game may be the fact which marks the beginning of the end of a period" (256–57). In the subsequent anti–
Vietnam War protests and especially in the great student uprising
of 1968, Marcuse must have briefly seen his hopes for the potential

overthrow of the existing system confirmed. But it was not to be, as
he seems to have known all along. For Marcuse, the hope of an actual resumption of history was really just a matter of whistling in
the dark.

Not so, however, for Fukuyama—or at least not in the long run.
In the first version of his argument, the end of history is—or rather
"will be," for despite having asserted that we have already reached
the end of history, the "real" end is apparently yet to come—the end
of history will be a "very sad time," a time which will be not only
posthistorical but also posthuman. Though the end of history will
bring with it stable happiness and universal contentment, it will also
entail the end of artistic endeavor and philosophical speculation.[13]
That is why, though he acknowledges the "inevitability of such a future," he also feels in himself (and perceives in others) "a powerful
nostalgia for the time when history existed." Therefore, rather than
face "centuries of boredom at the end of history," he hopes that the
very idea of such a soporific fate will impel (if not compel) people
and nations to make a very un-Hegelian return to history. Like Tennyson before him, but less certainly and much less heroically, a suddenly adventurous Fukuyama does not wish

> to herd with narrow foreheads, vacant of our glorious gains,
> Like a beast with lower pleasures, like a beast with lower pains!
> . . .
> Not in vain the distance beacons. Forward, forward let us range,
> Let the great world spin forever down the ringing grooves of
> change.

13. This gloomy prospect is, as Bloom points out, belied by Kojève's belief that
the end of history would bring with it "the possibility of unconstrained philosophiz-
ing" as well as "the moral recognition of all human beings as ends in themselves." At
the same time, however, Bloom acknowledges that Fukuyama's pessimism is grounded in Kojève's later writings, where "there is much to suggest that he began to believe
that we are witnessing the ultimate trivialization of man and his re-entry into the
merely animal order" (Bloom 1989, 20–21). Fukuyama specifically addresses Kojève's
thoughts about humanity at the end of history in the book-length version of his argument (1992, 310–11).

Through the shadow of the globe we sweep into the younger day;
Better fifty years of Europe than a cycle of Cathay.[14]

(Tennyson 1955, 49)

Seeing Further: Huxley's Dystopian Prophecies

In the conclusion to the 1992 version of *The End of History and the Last Man,* Fukuyama provides a fuller account of how and why humanity may return to history after having left it. As in his earlier speculations, however, the primary motive force will still be a kind of boredom, a refusal on the part of a relatively few individuals to live in a world of animal contentment.[15] Impelled by their powerful need for real, rather than merely surrogate or metaphoric, recognition, they will insist on "proving themselves by that very act that constituted their humanness at the very beginning of history: they will want to risk their lives in a violent battle, and thereby prove beyond any shadow of a doubt to themselves and their fellows that they are free. They will deliberately seek discomfort and sacrifice because the pain will be the only way they have of proving definitively that they can *think well of themselves,* that they remain *human beings*" (329). What Fukuyama says here about the likely end of the end of history is, of course (as all readers of Huxley's *Brave New World* will immediately recognize), precisely what happens when John Savage and his friend Helmholtz Watson confront an enraged mass of drug-deprived Deltas in order to free them from what John is convinced is their slavery:

14. The "younger day" has overtones both of historically "younger" nations, such as England, and what in German is referred to as "der jüngste Tag" (i.e., the Last Judgment), signifying the end of history in Christian eschatology. Cathay refers to China, which was once mistakenly thought to have enjoyed more than two millennia of social stability and peace.

15. For Arnold Toynbee, too, the real problem at the end of history is how to keep people from being bored to death. In the conclusion to *A Study of History,* he writes that if "we could imagine a World Society in which Mankind had first rid itself of war and class-conflict and had gone on to solve the population problem, we might surmise that mankind's next problem would be the role of leisure in this life of a mechanized society" (1957, 345).

"Free, free!" the Savage shouted, and with one hand continued to throw the *soma* into the area while, with the other, he punched the indistinguishable faces of his assailants. "Free!" And suddenly there was Helmholtz at his side—"Good old Helmholtz!"—also punching—"Men at last!"—and in the interval also throwing the poison out by handfuls through the open window. "Yes, men, men!" and there was no more poison left. He picked up the cash-box and showed them its black emptiness. "You're free!" (219)

John is, of course, quite wrong about freeing the Deltas or about having restored them to humanity. Their bioengineering and deep-seated conditioning have made such a restoration impossible. But he is right—more right perhaps than he knows himself at this stage—that he has freed himself by his act of thymotic violence, by his willingness to risk his life in the cause of freedom, and that, in doing so, both he and Helmholtz have themselves become free, and have turned not into Last Men but into "Men at last!"[16] "To live human-

16. Whether Huxley is consciously alluding to Nietzsche's Last Man here, or elsewhere in *Brave New World*, is unclear. That he was aware of Nietzsche and had read some of his work at least by 1927 is apparent from a letter, written in January of that year, to his friend Robert Nichols. There he tells of reading a number of biographies, including one about Nietzsche by M. A. Mügge (1969, 282). One of the sections of Mügge's book contains excerpts from Nietzsche's writings, including the relevant "Last Man" passage from *Also Sprach Zarathustra* (192–93). Huxley's conception of Nietzsche may also have been influenced by his friendship with D. H. Lawrence, which was particularly close at this time. Lawrence was instrumental in helping to soften the largely negative attitudes toward Nietzsche in Britain, attitudes which had been primarily shaped by the massive propaganda onslaught during World War I, in which Nietzsche (along with Hegel and other German philosophers, particularly Fichte) was blamed for the war. A passage like the following about the baleful effects of democracy, taken from Huxley's most Lawrentian book, *Do What You Will* (1929), suggests at least an indirect influence of Nietzsche: "the complete practical realization of the democratic ideal . . . would mean, almost inevitably, the apotheosis of the lowest human values and the rule, spiritual and material, of the worst men" (224). Nietzsche's thinking may also be behind John Savage's (and the Zuñi Reservation's) preference for pain over pleasure. In the essay on Swift in *Do What You Will*, Huxley notes that "Nietzsche advised men to be cruel to themselves, not because asceticism was pleasing to some hypothetical god, but because it was a good spiritual exercise, because it wound up the will and enhanced the sense of power and of conscious, voluntary life" (97). Finally, of course, at the very close of the novel when John encounters Lenina for the last time, he literally heeds Zarathustra's notorious advice: "Gehst du zum Weibe, vergiss die Peitsche nicht."

ly" means, as Joseph Wood Krutch maintains, "to live dangerously" (1956, 31).

In the end, then, it is Huxley who sees furthest—further than Marcuse, further than Fukuyama, and further even than Nietzsche—and deeper too. He sees that by putting his faith in the marginalized people of the "substratum," Marcuse is really harking back to Orwell's "Last Man in Europe," Winston Smith, who had pinned his futile and pathetic hopes on the "proles" in *Nineteen Eighty-Four.* There is, as Huxley realizes, no salvation to be expected from that quarter. He also sees what Fukuyama sees, namely, that the real danger to the established society of Last Men is a society (even a very small society) of determined and courageous First Men. The real danger to that society lies in risk-taking primitive man, thymotic man, the man whom Huxley fittingly names "the Savage." It is only when the wild confronts the tame—or when, as in the case of Helmholtz Watson (and to a lesser degree, Bernard Marx) the tame reverts to a state approximating wildness—that the New World State is endangered. But Huxley also sees further than Fukuyama because he sees that, even when challenged by wild thymotic men, the New World State will always succeed in overcoming that threat by means of either exiling nonconformists or consigning them to the lethal chamber. Huxley knows what Fukuyama is afraid to admit, namely, that once you have left history, there is no going back to it—or at least not for long, and not for more than a few heroic individuals.

Huxley also sees what Fukuyama only saw several years after he had first proposed his seemingly controversial thesis that history was drawing to an end in the America of the late twentieth century. For Huxley sees that it is ultimately innovations in modern science or technology (that is, in applied science, especially in the fields of biology, psychology, and pharmacology) that will both force changes in social organization and, paradoxically, also keep such changes from being made. Huxley actually anticipates Fukuyama's reasons for repudiating his own thesis about the end of history. Specifically, he anticipates (and refutes) Fukuyama's 1999 revisionary conclusion that the argument which he had earlier used "to demonstrate that History is directional, progressive and that it culminates in the modern liberal state, is fundamentally flawed. . . . History cannot come to an end as long as modern natural science has no end; and we are on the brink of new developments in science that will, in essence, abolish what Alexandre Kojève called 'mankind as such'" (1999b, 17).[17]

Fukuyama's argument assumes an even more specifically Huxleyan dimension when he goes on to state that the "most radical outcome of ongoing research in biotechnology is its potential for changing human nature itself," and that by this means science will in future be able to "accomplish what the radical ideologies of the past, with their unbelievably crude techniques, were unable to accomplish: to bring about a new type of human being" (1999b, 28). In Huxley's New World State this transformation has already taken place, in primarily biological terms for the three lower castes, psychopharmacologically for the two higher ones. In Huxley's New World,

17. What Fukuyama does not acknowledge at this point in his essay, however, is that this argument is in itself fundamentally flawed. For one thing, it is self-contradictory. That is, if it is indeed true that history cannot end so long as science progresses, then it must also be true that, if the progress of science entails, as Kojève maintains, the end of humanity, history itself will logically come to an end. Or is history perhaps not human history, but something else? Fukuyama, however, does acknowledge this fundamental contradiction at the end of his essay, when he concludes that the "open-ended character of modern natural science suggests that within the next couple of generations we will have knowledge and technologies that will allow us to accomplish what social engineers of the past failed to do. At that point we will have definitively finished human History because we will have abolished human beings as such. And then, a new, Posthuman history will begin" (1999b, 33). Just what "posthuman history" is supposed to signify, in Hegelian or even Nietzschean, terms, Fukuyama leaves unsaid. But even granting his assumption (also Huxley's) that science will be able to create a new species of humanity, Fukuyama still fails to perceive that posthumans will then also have the power, as they do already in *Brave New World,* to make history—even posthuman history—stop. In his original essay, Fukuyama had, to be sure, already asserted that posthistory would bring with it posthumanity, but there posthumanity meant subhuman (animal) rather than, as here, superhuman humanity. Fukuyama's idea of a super-posthumanity, then, as shaped by science, may in fact owe less to Huxley's bottled embryos than to Nietzsche's notion of the Overman. This nonhuman superhuman will one day transcend ordinary humanity but, by virtue of his heroic characteristics, will nevertheless remain within the realm of history—or of posthuman history, anyway.

history has come to an end, not only, however, because humanity as we know it has (with a few isolated exceptions) ceased to exist but because, once this radical transformation has taken place, science is no longer permitted to "progress." As Mustapha Mond points out, if the final goal of good government is permanent social stability (i.e., the end of history, as defined by Hegel), then it "isn't only art that's incompatible with happiness; it's also science. Science is dangerous; we have to keep it most carefully chained and muzzled" (231). Lest there be any misunderstanding, Mond goes on to stress his conviction that "truth's a menace, science is a public danger. As dangerous as it's been beneficent. It has given us the stablest equilibrium in history. . . . But we can't allow science to undo its own good work. That's why we so carefully limit the scope of its researches" (234). To remake humanity, in other words, you first need to remake the world, or at any rate you need to remake (and radically limit) the human perception/conception of the world. Here again, Huxley sees further than Fukuyama. If a future humanity has the ability to control its social and biological destiny, then it also has—and will make use of—the ability to control scientific investigation and its applications to humanity itself.[18]

Huxley also sees further than Fukuyama—or even than Hegel and Nietzsche, for that matter—when he takes into account the distinct possibility that history may indeed end, but with a loud bang and many cries of pain, rather than with the blissful squealing of Last Men. The world Huxley describes in *Ape and Essence* (1948) re-

---

18. As Gertrude Himmelfarb remarks, without referring to Huxley, this is a "far more radical vision than Hegel's 'end of history' or Nietzsche's Last Man" (38). Fukuyama does mention *Brave New World* in connection with recent developments in pharmacology, particularly the drug Ritalin, which, in his view, resembles Huxley's *soma*. Fukuyama even goes so far as to suggest that Ritalin may be thought of as "Nietzsche's Last Man in a bottle," and then speculates, somewhat whimsically, "what the careers of tormented geniuses like Blaise Pascal or Nietzsche himself would have looked like if they had been born to American parents and had Ritalin and Prozac available to them at an early age" (1999b, 30–31).

sembles the real world of 1945 in being a wasteland produced by the ravages of the recent world war, especially in terms of its "saturation" bombing and nuclear weapons; but the destruction of the twenty-first century is/will be on so much vaster a scale than that of the twentieth that only a few, isolated remnants of the old world survive in remote areas, such as New Zealand and central Africa. For the rest, wherever actual bombing has not caused complete devastation, the effects of radiation have brought about radical biological and psychological changes in humanity. This is especially true of Los Angeles and surroundings, where just about all of the action of the "novel" is set. (*Ape and Essence* is actually, or at least pretends to be, more of a screenplay than a novel.) These seemingly random changes are quite different from the planned genetic manipulation and psychological conditioning described in *Brave New World*. With relatively few exceptions, human females have reverted to oestrus, so that sexual activity is limited to only a very brief period each year (two weeks). Babies born with more than what is considered an acceptable degree of mutation are sacrificially killed. Technical culture has regressed to a level approximating the stone—or, at most, the bronze—age. Worship of the Christian god has been wholly replaced by devil worship, since human history is more credibly explained as the result of diabolic rather than divine agency. "The longer you study modern history," so the Arch-Vicar (a character who bears some resemblance to Mustapha Mond) tells the protagonist, Dr. Alfred Poole, "the more evidence you find of Belial's Guiding Hand" (126).

Though there are once again masters and slaves in this post-Christian, postatomic world, history has nevertheless essentially come to a stop. That is no doubt the primary reason why, among the books used as fuel to bake bread (the primary function of books in this grim dystopia), Huxley singles out Hegel's *Phenomenology of the Spirit* for dishonorable mention, that is, the very book in which the progressive theory of history is enunciated and in which the triumphant march of the rational Idea is proclaimed.[19] It is an irony that Huxley will not allow to go unnoticed or unsavored, for, as the Arch-Vicar of Belial points out, it was precisely those motive forces in history that Hegel identified as the carriers of the rational that have brought humanity to its present lamentable and quite irrational pass: "Progress and Nationalism—those were the two ideas He [Belial] put in their heads" (125).

The Arch-Vicar is, however, fully aware that history might have proceeded (and eventually ended) otherwise, that the triumph of Belial was not inevitable. The elements for a better world, even for the achievement of utopia, were there all along. Humanity only needed the will to choose the existing means to achieve a nobler and more meaningful end.[20] The wisdom of the East and the technology of the West could in combination have prevented the bombs from falling. In this sense, Belial is merely the symbolic expression of the inadequacy of the collective human will. "'Just think if they'd

19. Unlike Nietzsche, for whom he usually expressed tolerance if not admiration, Huxley had no sympathy whatever for Hegel. Elsewhere in *Ape and Essence,* he refers to Hegel as having composed his "Patent History" while performing as a "pimp for Prussia" (15). And in *Proper Studies* (1927) he writes that *"The Nature's Philosophy* [presumably *Philosophy of Nature*] reads for me like the ravings of a lunatic. And yet there were, and I believe still are, Hegelians for whom the book is full of the profoundest significance" (46). In *The Hegel Myths,* Huxley is included among the perpetrators of falsehoods about Hegel's work (Stewart 1996).

20. In the 1947 foreword to *Brave New World,* Huxley writes that, though he knows that "sanity" has in the past been an unusual state for humanity, he is "convinced that it can be achieved and would like to see more of it." The response he has received for having said so, however, was not encouraging, especially not the response from the universities. "I have been told by an eminent academic critic," Huxley goes on to say, "that I am a sad symptom of the failure of the intellectual class in a time of crisis. The implication being, I suppose, that the professor and his colleagues are hilarious symptoms of success. The benefactors of humanity deserve due honor and commemoration. Let us build a Pantheon for professors. It should be located among the ruins of one of the gutted cities of Europe and Japan, and over the entrance of the ossuary I would inscribe, in letters six or seven feet high, the simple words: SACRED TO THE MEMORY OF THE WORLD'S EDUCATORS. SI MONUMENTUM REQUIRIS CIRCUMSPICE" (ix). In *Ape and Essence* the professors are represented by two Einsteins, kept on leashes by military madmen and forced to detonate the bombs that will destroy civilization.

made the best!' squeaks the Arch-Vicar. [He squeaks because in the Belialistic future all priests are castrati.] 'Eastern mysticism making sure that Western science should be properly used, the Eastern art of living refining Western energy; Western individualism tempering Eastern totalitarianism.'" But it was not to be. "Happily the grace of Belial," so the Arch-Vicar concludes, "was stronger than the Other One's grace" (184–85).

But not always and not everywhere. In Huxley's last completed novel, *Island,* published only a year before his death in 1963, the Other One's grace turns out to be a great deal stronger, at any rate until his creation is overrun by a nearby disciple of Belial whose primary concern is to foster not greater human sanity but greater profits for the multinational petroleum interests. Still, the disaster does not occur until we have had ample opportunity to witness just how successful a society can be that is founded on a fusion of the best parts of the Eastern and the Western worlds. As Dr. Robert MacPhail (the Mustapha Mond, as it were, of this novel) tells a sophisticated, skeptical, but receptive equivalent of John Savage:

> To make the best of both worlds—what am I saying? To make the best of *all* the worlds—the worlds already realized within the various cultures and, beyond them, the worlds of still unrealized potentialities. . . . They never succeeded, of course, in making the best of all the worlds; but by dint of boldly trying, they made the best of many more worlds than any merely prudent or sensible person would have dreamed of being able to reconcile and combine. (129)

Huxley's End to the End of History

In *Island* Huxley created a society that was stable, free of internal contradictions, and not populated by Last Men. In this sense it is the only society, among all the ones that have been proposed by the various thinkers discussed in this chapter, which fully—and in a positive sense—corresponds to Hegel's idea of a society at the end

of history. That is, it meets Hegel's (and even Fukuyama's) criteria
in all but one important respect: it is not a universal homogeneous
state. It could become one, perhaps, for there is nothing inherently
exclusive about it. But its loosely democratic constitution, its ecolog-
ically sensitive, cooperatively functioning economy is (deliberately)
not designed to deal with the challenges of worldwide consumerism
and territorial aggression. As a result it fails. At the end of the novel, the island utopia is invaded by an armed force assisted by a quis-
ling who has converted to consumerism. The future looks gloomy:
there is little cause for supposing that the quasi-ideal conditions existing prior to the invasion can or will be ever reestablished. Nevertheless, it is a failure that, by its example alone, is more successful
than all other apparent successes. So long as the memory persists
that human beings can be organized in a social framework that pre-
serves and even fosters their humanity, history will not end in the
petty pursuits of Last Men.

CHAPTER 4

GEORGE ORWELL'S DYSTOPIAS

From Animal Farm *to* Nineteen Eighty-Four

*Happiness is notoriously difficult to describe, and pictures of a just
and well-ordered society are seldom either attractive or convincing.*
George Orwell

Authentic Orwell

More than any other British writer of the first half of the twentieth century, with the possible exception of the otherwise very different E. M. Forster, George Orwell had an uncanny gift for quickly establishing a relationship of trust with his readers. Encountering him, one has the feeling almost at once that he is an intelligent, basically decent person who is being "straight" with us, who is trying as honestly as he can to avoid mouthing the party line, whether it's the party line of the Right, Left, or middle. At the same time, he doesn't ostentatiously bare his chest or seek to occupy the limelight as the greatest sinner or truth teller of all or even just his own time. Not only does he not metaphorically raise his own voice in his writing; he despises others who raise theirs. Witness the contempt with which he treats the fanatical Marxist sloganeer at the Left Book Club meeting in *Coming Up for Air* (175ff.). Orwell's self-image of the quiet, diffident, fiercely independent commentator on politics and life in general is especially evident in his essays—like Huxley and Forster, Orwell is one of the great essayists of the period—as well as in his documentary books, *Down and Out in Paris and London, The Road to Wigan Pier,* and, most of all, *Homage to Catalonia,* which is about his participation in the Spanish Civil War.[1]

While his personality—his "persona," if you prefer—is a good part of the reason why we trust him, we also trust him because he is authentic. When one reads Orwell on the Spanish War, one knows that he's been there. One feels very differently too, I think, about reading a novel like *Animal Farm* or *Nineteen Eighty-Four* when one knows that the author has actually *experienced* what he is writing about. Not that George Orwell ever was an "animal"—though there undoubtedly is something very Orwellian about the skeptical donkey Benjamin in *Animal Farm*—or lived in the year 1984 (for him of course still thirty-five years into a future he never lived to see), but he had actually raised animals (as Alex Zwerdling says, the book "could only have been written by someone who had observed life on a farm and how animals behave very closely") and experienced life at the very bottom of the social ladder, as, among other things, a dishwasher in a Paris hotel and a hobo drifting through London and surroundings; and he had lived in some of the worst industrial slums of the black country during the most depressing years, as he did in Wigan. In very different circumstances, he had also experienced at first hand how brutally the Stalinist Communist Party operated in Spain, where he saw and felt how they fanatically tried to suppress and even "liquidate" him and his fellow anti-Franco fighters in the Trotskyist POUM (Partido Obrero de Unificación Marxista or "Workers' Party of Marxist Unification").[2]

1. For more on Orwell's success in establishing his "persona," see Firchow (1992).

2. Orwell may have partly modeled the Thought Police in *Nineteen Eighty-Four* on memories of being observed by Stalinist police in Barcelona at the end of his stay there. What he probably did not know, however, is that the British Secret Service (MI5) had been keeping tabs on him as far back as 1936, primarily because they (somewhat obtusely) suspected him of being a Communist. The Wigan police report to MI5 opined that "[i]t would appear from his mode of living that he is an author, or has some connection with literary work, as he devotes most of his time to writing" (Travis 2005).

In other words, George Orwell's books always rest on a solid foundation of lived experience. Though he is not afraid to generalize or criticize others from the perspective of that experience, he is never a mere windbag or "theoretician." When he notoriously censured W. H. Auden for justifying "necessary murders" during the Spanish War though Auden had never witnessed an actual murder himself, Orwell could point out that he, on the other hand, *had* experienced murder and not just killing (in Spain and probably in Burma too). By doing so he was claiming the authority of experience over mere theory. "So much of left-wing thought," he went on to generalize about what he took at the time to be martini-Marxists like Auden, "is a kind of playing with fire by people who don't even know that fire is hot" (1954, 243).

Interestingly, Orwell's experience exists on *both* sides. That is, not only was Orwell down and out in Paris and London, but he was also, as it were, up and inside in Rangoon and on the Irrawaddy. His first job—and the only one that he was ever fully trained to do, including his subsequent jobs as a journalist and novelist—was that of an officer in the Indian Colonial Constabulary in Burma, so that when he writes about O'Brien in *Nineteen Eighty-Four* or about Napoleon's specially trained dogs in *Animal Farm*, he is also writing in part from actual police experience. This is even true to some extent of Winston Smith's work at the Ministry of Truth. After all, it is probably not coincidental that Winston Smith's participation in the manufacture and re-manufacture of truth bears a resemblance to Orwell's wartime work in the propaganda section of the BBC. The two activities are not the same, of course, but they are close enough in a general way to count as real experience.

Orwell, in short, is an *authentic* writer whether he is describing the social depths or the social heights. (As a graduate of Eton College he also had personal experience of the uppermost segment of the upper classes in Britain.) That is why we trust him. And we trust him too because he is willing to admit to what might be thought of as flaws in his own character, as when in 1940, after expressing his

readiness to kill Hitler if given the chance, he admits that he nevertheless can't help feeling a sneaking sympathy for him as an underdog. Then there is Orwell's notoriously sensitive nose, one that was
able to ferret out stenches which he would go on to describe in lov-
ingly nauseating detail, e.g., the odiferous chamber pot placed under the breakfast table in the disgusting lodgings he occupied while
gathering the material that would eventually congeal into *The Road
to Wigan Pier*. While we may not share Orwell's sympathy for the
"underdog" Hitler or his olfactory obsessions and may even be put
off a little by them, they definitely do serve to make him more "human."

Animal Farm as History and Dystopia

Among other things, *Animal Farm* is based on authentic farm-
ing experience. During the 1930s Orwell had tried his hand, admittedly not very successfully, at raising vegetables and even a select variety of small animals. Later, when he could afford to—ironically,
partly as a result of the very good sales of *Animal Farm*—he lived for
a time on a remote farm on the Scottish island of Jura, a farm that
had no electricity and was accessible only on foot. It was something
he had dreamed about doing for years. That dream is emblematic
of the deep rift in Orwell's personality between downright, practical hands-on experience—his ingrained realism, if you like—and an
idyllic, quite impractical nostalgia for a Romantic "golden" countryside such as never existed outside his imagination. His real nose may
testify to the vile smells of his Wigan boarding house, but his visionary eye is always longing for the pristine bliss of an ideal Golden
Country.

Though it would become hugely successful, *Animal Farm* was
probably Orwell's most difficult book to get published. This despite
the fact that Orwell was by then fairly well known as a sort of mav-
erick left-wing writer of essays and reviews. Written in 1943–44, at
a time when just about everybody else in England was enthusiastic

about the Red Army's costly and unexpected success against Hitler's initially seemingly invincible army (and had already more or less forgotten about the Soviet Union's erstwhile alliance with Hitler and their joint invasion of Poland), *Animal Farm* was felt by the publishers to whom Orwell submitted the book to be the work of a traitor to the cause of social progress, rather like his friend Arthur Koestler's *Darkness at Noon*. Orwell, however, refused to be intimidated and continued to insist that he was a *socialist*, indeed far more of a socialist than those who were mouthing the Communist Party line and who were taking, as he put it in a telling phrase, "their cookery from Paris and their opinions from Moscow" (1954, 279). As he was also to remark later, in the Preface that he wrote for the Ukrainian translation of *Animal Farm:* "Indeed, in my opinion, nothing has contributed so much to the corruption of the original idea of Socialism as the belief that Russia is a Socialist country and that every act of its rulers must be excused, if not imitated" (1968b, 405).

Animal Farm was eventually accepted by a small, new publisher, Secker & Warburg, who brought it out in August 1945. In the United States it was rejected by eight publishers and did not actually appear until 1946 under the Harcourt, Brace & Company imprint. As all of this more or less concerted opposition suggests, *Animal Farm,* and of course Orwell too, were widely known to be potentially disruptive commodities, even though a few observers, such as the fellow-traveling Kingsley Martin, tried to dismiss them as merely trivial and ridiculous.[3] It was only after the collapse of the Soviet Union in 1989 that Orwell's status as a realistic commentator on the "socialism" of the Soviet Empire was fully vindicated.

3. Shortly before his death Orwell provided the Foreign Office's Information Research Department (a semi-secret propaganda agency) with a list of people he suspected of being "crypto-communists." He intended the list to be used in preventing the IRD from hiring the wrong people for its work. Among the names is that of Kingsley Martin, described by Orwell as "too dishonest to be outright 'crypto', or fellow traveller, but reliably pro-Russian on all major issues" (Ash 2003). Such lists seem to have been a kind of habit with Orwell. According to Stephen Spender, Orwell had expressed his willingness to "draw up a list of intellectuals who would be willing to collaborate with the Nazis if they succeeded in invading England" (Steinhoff 1975, 221).

Animal Farm, as virtually everyone realized who read the book at the time, either before or after it was published, and who reacted either positively or negatively to it, is intended to be read as a very close allegory of Soviet history from the time of the Revolution until about 1945 or at least until the Teheran Conference. In case, however, anyone still needs the allegory to be translated, here are the animal/historical equivalents:

Jones is the pre-1917 Russian ruling class. Manor Farm is tsarist Russia. Animal Farm is the Soviet Union. Old Major is a combination of Marx and Lenin.[4] Animalism is Marxism-Leninism. Snowball is Leon Trotsky. Napoleon is Josef Stalin. Squealer is Andrei Zdanov. Whymper is the generic capitalist intermediary, also representative of the so-called New Economic Policy of the 1920s. The pigs are the Communist Party membership. The domestic animals are the working class, especially the hard-working horses Boxer and Clover, with the sheep being the naive believers of all aspects of party doctrine. The wild animals are the rural peasantry, especially perhaps the kulaks, but possibly also the "Lumpenproletariat." (Even Old Major is unsure what to make of them.) The dogs trained by Napoleon are the NKVD (later the KGB). The humans are the bourgeoisie. Pilkington and Foxwood are Great Britain, and perhaps France too. Frederick and Pinchwood are Germany. Building the windmill is the electrification and industrialization of the Soviet Union. (According to a famous slogan attributed to Stalin, socialism plus electricity equals communism.) The Battle of the Cowshed is the defeat of the White Russians. The Battle of the Windmill is World War II.

---

4. More Marx than Lenin probably, given Orwell's view, expressed in 1945, that "one ought, I believe, to admit that all the seeds of evil were there from the start and that things would not have been substantially different if Lenin or Trotsky had remained in control" (1968a, 18). Since Old Major dies before the uprising of the animals, it would seem more likely that he is to be identified with Marx than Lenin. Otto Friedrich, however, claims that Old Major *is* Lenin, whereas Bernard Crick states with equal certainty that Old Major is Marx and that Lenin "does not figure in the story" (Friedrich 1984, 92; Crick 1989, 172).

Moses the Raven is the Russian Orthodox Church, and his Sugar-candy Mountain is heaven. Mollie the vain horse represents those members of the working class who left the Soviet Union for opportunistic reasons. The hypocritical cat seems to have no specifically allegorical function. Benjamin the donkey is the novel's *raisonneur,* who expresses the outlook that comes closest to Orwell's own.[5]

Into the framework of this allegory Orwell places many, if not most, of the important historical and political events of the Soviet period, such as: (1) the expulsion of Trotsky by Stalin, along with the gradual "rectification" of the former's role in the Revolution—Trotsky, like both Snowball and, later, Emmanuel Goldstein in *Nineteen Eighty-Four,* is transformed into a traitor and universal scapegoat;[6] (2) the creation of a secret police loyal only to Stalin and his totalitarian regime; (3) the cunning but ultimately stupid and self-defeating "diplomacy" of Stalin in the 1930s, who thought he would be able to play off Great Britain and France against Germany; (4) the infamous show trials of the late thirties, with their trumped-up charges and confessions along with their summary executions; and (5) the gradual metamorphosis of the Communist Party from the "voice" of the people to the protective mask of a privileged caste, or, in Orwell's terms, the ultimate interchangeability of pigs and humans.[7]

More difficult to grasp than the political and historical allegory of *Animal Farm* is what the point of it all might be. That is, why

5. According to Robert Lee, Benjamin "is essentially selfish, representing a view of human nature that is apolitical, and thus can hardly be, as some readers hold, the spokesman for Orwell within the book" (1986, 50).

6. Orwell's use of a Trotsky figure as the scapegoat in both *Animal Farm* and *Nineteen Eighty-Four* has its obvious historical origin in the treatment of Trotsky and Trotskyists after the expulsion (and "expunging") of Trotsky by Stalin, but there are also personal reasons for Orwell's intense, almost obsessive concern with the fate of Trotsky and his followers. This obsession is probably traceable to Orwell's being hounded out of Barcelona (and nearly killed there) for supposedly being a "Trotskyist" (Shelden 1991, 270).

7. An overly literal reading of *Animal Farm,* however, as in the case of Northrop Frye, can lead to absurd conclusions, such as that the end of the story affirms the reinstitution of the tsar (1986, 10).

didn't Orwell just tell us the "story" of how socialism was pervert-
ed in Stalin's Russia in straightforward and readily comprehensible
terms? Why was it necessary for him to disguise that story in animal
dress? And what are we to make of Orwell's rather odd claim in the
subtitle that *Animal Farm* is a "fairy story"?

To these questions there are several possible answers.[8] To begin
with, we need to remember that Orwell is writing fiction in *Animal
Farm,* not history. Though the historical element is very strong in
the novel—and indeed is essential to understanding what's going on
in it—history has been coherently transposed into the very different and quite nonhistorical context of a fable, a context so far re-
moved from the usual way history is written that, initially at least,
readers are not aware that what they are reading is a peculiar retelling of Soviet history. It is precisely this unfamiliarity of context, and
the gradual realization on the part of readers of what the book is
really about, that causes them to see the historical events in a new
light. Ironically, Orwell has succeeded in *Animal Farm* by using what
has since come to be seen as a characteristically Soviet literary technique—"defamiliarization"—first described by the so-called Russian
Formalists in the 1920s, to expose the crafty, underhanded maneu-
verings behind the Communist Party's accession to power.

This technique of defamiliarizing already familiar historical material and thereby making it "new" also has, literarily speaking, other interesting and positive side effects. For example, it helps to make
the actions of the Party seem at times absurd and ridiculous, if not
actually pathetic, as, for example, when, not long after the overthrow of Jones, under the leadership of the pigs the animals tour the
farmhouse and find some hams hanging in the kitchen which they
then proceed to take out for formal burial. So too with the account
of Napoleon's supposedly imminent death after having, for the first

8. According to C. M. Woodhouse's somewhat murky analysis, Orwell uses the
fairy story to further his purpose of writing a story set "in a world beyond good and
evil," one which when transcribed "into terms of highly simplified symbols . . . leaves
us with a deep indefinable feeling of truth" (Orwell 1996, xviii–xix).

time, sampled rather too much of old Jones's whisky. Furthermore, it allows Orwell to expose satirically the absurdity of the Stalinist cult of personality by having one hen remark to another: "Under the guidance of our Leader, Comrade Napoleon, I have laid five eggs in six days" (67). Also the "fairy" tale designation of the story serves to defamiliarize our response, since it implies that the historical allegory is really part of some incredible "fairy" tale that no adult person would ever accept as real or even realistic.[9] The strong implication is that most histories of the Soviet Union up to this point have been "fairy tales."

Even more interesting and probably significant, however, are the implications of transposing a story that is fundamentally social (i.e., the story of the development of the Soviet Union) into a primarily biological or essentialist framework. The story then becomes one of nature rather than nurture, of the essential "animal condition," as seen especially from the donkey Benjamin's point of view. If such a reading of the book holds up, then it would seem that Orwell is presenting here a critique of the Soviet Union from what looks like a conservative point of view. That is, he is apparently arguing that basic human (or, rather, "animal") nature is such that, no matter what the political system might be, the "pigs" will inevitably rise to the top. The lesson then would be that those creatures who are the greediest, least scrupulous, and most power-hungry, regardless of whether they are human or animal, are the ones who will rule, no matter what the current official political doctrine or theory is. What takes place at the Animal Farm, then, or in the Soviet Union, for that matter, is less an example of Marxist dialectical materialism and more a version of Vilfredo Pareto's notorious "circulation of the elites." Instead of elite humans, we are here confronted with elite pigs—not a big difference, as it turns out. *Plus ça change,* as it were, *plus ça reste la même chose.*[10]

9. In his essay on fairy tales J. R. R. Tolkien does not mention *Animal Farm* and specifically excludes "beast-fables" from the category (1984, 117).

10. William Empson pointed out this aspect of *Animal Farm* to Orwell in a letter

Is Orwell implying something like this? Yes, I think he is. Toward the end of his life he did, after all, become a kind of Tory anarchist—as he once described himself (Crick 1980, 174)—or even Tory
socialist, someone, that is, who, though without exercising doublethink, managed to fuse conservative ideas (about patriotism, for example) with radical ones (about the equitable distribution of wealth,
for example).[11] Not that reading *Animal Farm* in essentialist terms really represents a radical deviation from the socialist perspective. In
orthodox Marxist doctrine there is, after all, a fundamental assumption about human "economic" nature that resembles the one that
Orwell appears to be making in *Animal Farm,* namely, that those
who own the means of production are also those who exercise the
power in any society. And hidden behind this assumption is yet another assumption that it takes a certain kind of creature to secure
the ownership of those means of production in the first place. (This
second, more or less invisible assumption goes back to Hegel's theory about the origin and development of the master/slave dichot-
omy. Marx, as the usual cliché has it, notoriously turned Hegel on
his head.) In *Animal Farm,* though Napoleon and the pigs may not
"own" the means of production in the technical sense of possess-
ing a legal piece of paper that says they do—though at the end of
the story there is in fact such a piece of paper—the pigs behave as
if they own the farm and have a canine police force to back up their
claim. Furthermore, there is the fact that, from the reader's point of
view, it is Benjamin (and not, as Boxer maintains, Napoleon) who is
proved "always right." This too would seem to support the essentialist position. Finally, there is a connection here to James Burnham's
argument in *The Managerial Revolution*—a book from which Orwell

written not long after the book's publication: "the effect of the farmyard, with its unescapable racial differences, is to suggest that the Russian scene had unescapable social differences too—so the metaphor suggests that the Russian revolution was always
a pathetically impossible attempt" (quoted in Crick 1989, 190).

   11. In the essay on "Politics and Literature" (1946), however, Orwell refers to Jonathan Swift disparagingly as a "Tory anarchist," that is, someone who despises "authority while disbelieving in liberty" (1968a, 216).

borrowed several important ideas and which he admired, though with many reservations—that the real power in all contemporary societies (whether socialist, fascist, or capitalist) is vested in the managerial class. The pigs, therefore, will always behave like pigs, which in effect means that a pig will always be Pig Brother.

Choosing the genre of the fable for his retelling of the Soviet experiment had the additional advantage that it allowed Orwell more readily to present his material in the form of a satire than would have been the case if he had written it up as straightforward history. The continuing juxtaposition of the initially ideal seven commandments (and their continuing downward revision) with the reality of the pigs' behavior constitutes one of the most effective means of showing what sort of dystopia the farm of the animals is turning into. It provides an easily comprehensible—for most readers if not for most animals—frame of reference by which to gauge the moral deterioration of the revolution and its eventual collapse into a moral pigsty. The initial hopes for the establishment of a utopia, as promised both in Old Major's "I have a dream" speech and in the singing of "Beasts of England," are dashed as the pigs progressively pervert or subvert the "principles of Animalism" on which the Animal Farm had been based.[12] The utopian "golden future time" which the song foretells grows increasingly gray and drab—not to say "leaden"—despite the claims made by Squealer when, at the behest of "Comrade" Napoleon, he announces that "Beasts of England" is no longer to be sung. The reason? Because in the song the animals had "expressed our longing for a better society in the days to come. But that society has now been established. Clearly this song has no longer any purpose" (62).[13]

12. That there is also some humor (and skepticism) here is indicated by the narrator's remark that the "stirring tune" to which "Beasts of England" was sung was "something between *Clementine* and *La Cucaracha*" (9).

13. Orwell is here satirizing the abolition of the "International" as the anthem of the Soviet Union in March 1944, when it was replaced by the "Song of Stalin." In the novel, the new anthem, composed by the pig Minimus, is called "Comrade Napoleon."

Are we therefore to read *Animal Farm* primarily as a satire on the
folly of trying to establish a fair and equitable society in which workers would be treated justly? Is the dream of a "golden future time" a
pipe dream pure and simple? Are the conclusions to be drawn from
the attempt to establish an animal farm entirely pessimistic? Is the
sardonic Benjamin the only animal who is, in the final analysis, always right?

There is certainly a large body of evidence to support this sort
of negative view of the story. The pessimism is especially evident in
the recurrent preoccupation of the animals (and the narrator) with
determining whether the farm is better off under animal (or, rather, porcine) management than it was under Jones's. More and more,
as Napoleon's policies take effect, the implication seems to be that
the farm is worse off. Initially, despite a variety of hardships and set-
backs, the animals had at least managed to get as much food (though
no more) as they did in Jones's day. This is because, while they may
be working longer hours, their work has become more efficient; and
since "no animal now stole," certain kinds of jobs, such as maintaining fences and hedges, were now unnecessary (46).[14] And, of course,
the farm now "belongs" to the animals, and, what is even more important, no animals are being slaughtered.

This difficult but still tolerable and even hopeful situation on
the farm changes radically for the worse when, at Napoleon's com-
mand, a number of animals are killed by his dogs after confessing
to a secret collaboration with Snowball. At the end of these "show
trials" and summary executions, the air becomes "heavy with the
smell of blood, which had been unknown there since the expulsion
of Jones." Though these killings are no more numerous than they
had been under Jones, they are perceived to be "far worse" because
they are carried out by the animals themselves on the orders of other animals (61). Whatever else may or may not be true about these

14. Either Orwell is forgetting here about the pigs' stealing the milk and the
windfall apples or else the pigs are already undergoing their transformation from animals to humans and hence are no longer to be counted as fellow "animals."

killings, there can be no question that a moral deterioration has set in.

This is confirmed when it becomes apparent that, although the farm itself eventually becomes richer and more prosperous, the animals themselves are no better off "except of course for the pigs and dogs" (92). The remaining animals seem to work harder and get less food than before, though even the older ones are increasingly unable to remember if even "in the early days of the rebellion . . . things had been better or worse than now." They can't tell because there is no reliable measure by which they can compare their present condition with their former one; there are only "Squealer's lists, which invariably demonstrated that everything was getting better and better" (93).[15] Only Benjamin, whose memory seems to work more reliably, claims that in his experience there is not much difference between conditions prevailing now and then—"hunger, hardship, and disappointment being, so he said, the unalterable law of life" (93). But even Benjamin may occasionally be wrong. When, at the very end of the novel, Mr. Pilkington and some other farmers visit the farm, they conclude with some satisfaction that "the lower animals on Animal Farm did more work and received less food than any animals in the county" (98).

So the experiment of the animals taking over and running their own farm is to be judged a failure? Yes, apparently so, though neither Orwell nor his narrator takes much joy in arriving at such a conclusion. If the evidence clearly shows that in practice the farm is no better off, as far as most of the animals are concerned, than it was before the expulsion of Jones, still in theory that expulsion retains a great part of its justification. In other words, the final mes-

15. In this connection it is worth remembering Orwell's remark in "In Front of Your Nose" (1946) that "the Russian people were taught for years that they were better off than anybody else, and propaganda posters showed Russian families sitting down to abundant meals while the proletariat of other countries starved in the gutter. Meanwhile the workers in the Western countries were so much better off than those of the USSR that non-contact between Soviet citizens and outsiders had to be a guiding principle of policy" (1968a, 125).

sage seems to be that however much the reality may disappoint us, we should nevertheless adhere to the ideal. For this reason *Animal Farm* should not be read merely as a satire. Or, put another way, its satirical parts are so bitter precisely because the ideal is still believed in. The lies and cruelty of Napoleon, and the boundless chutzpah of his apologist Squealer in justifying every violation of the original seven commandments, are a gross perversion of Old Major's dream of universal animal equality and happiness. Orwell's task, as he saw it, was to expose that chutzpah, that perversion, not to question the original dream. After all, if those original commandments were not the potential basis for a good society, why bother to expose their violation? In the end, then, *Animal Farm* affirms the dream of a "golden future time," while at the same time denying that such a golden future time has yet arrived. It also shows that, no matter how disappointing the outcome, there once had been at least a glimpse of what such a time might be like during the days immediately following the rebellion and the takeover of Manor Farm by the animals.

In 1943, at more or less the same moment when he was starting work on *Animal Farm*, Orwell put down some reflections on how the working class could never accommodate itself to fascism. These reflections are also relevant to how we should respond to the failure of the socialist experiment in *Animal Farm*. "The struggle of the working class," Orwell tells us in his essay on "Looking Back on the Spanish War," "is like the growth of a plant. The plant is blind and stupid, but it knows enough to keep pushing upwards towards the light, and it will do this in the face of endless discouragements. What are the workers struggling for? Simply for the decent life which they are more and more aware is now technically possible." Not that the working-class "plant" always succeeds in getting what it wants, any more than the working-class "animals" do. But there are occasions when it does happen, even if only briefly. One such occasion, according to Orwell, was the period just at the beginning of the war in Spain, when "for a while, people were acting consciously, moving towards a goal which they wanted to reach and believed they could reach. It accounted for the curiously buoyant feeling that life in Government Spain had during the early months of the war. The common people knew in their bones that the Republic was their friend and Franco was their enemy" (1954, 208). What are we to conclude from these reflections? I think we are meant to conclude that there is and always will be hope; and that this hope resides principally, as Winston Smith will put it in Orwell's next novel, in the "proles," that is, in the human and animal embodiments of what is best in the working class, such as the Italian antifascist soldier whom Orwell met at the beginning of his stay in Barcelona (and about whom he later wrote one of his rare poems), or, for that matter, in such animals as the rather stupid but nonetheless noble and admirable Boxer in *Animal Farm*.

The End of Oceania

Nineteen Eighty-Four has a distinguished and variegated literary ancestry.[16] To begin with, there is Evgenij Zamiatin's *We*, which Orwell had read with admiration in 1944 on the recommendation of Gleb Struve.[17] Then there is his friend Arthur Koestler's *Darkness at Noon*, and behind Koestler, Dostoevsky's *The Possessed*, both of which helped to shape the debate between O'Brien and Winston Smith in the last part of Orwell's novel. Also, and rather more obviously, there is Aldous Huxley's *Brave New World*, which Orwell may

16. Since it is often claimed that *Nineteen Eighty-Four* has little literary value, it is relevant to note here that the novelist Anthony Burgess admired *Nineteen Eighty-Four* so much that he not only wrote a kind of continuation-commentary, *1985*, but claimed to have read the novel thirty times (Aldiss 1984, 10).

17. Orwell reviewed the book for the *Tribune* in January 1946. In the review he argues, mistakenly I believe, that Aldous Huxley had read *We* and borrowed from it. Indisputable, however, is the debt that *Nineteen Eighty-Four* owes to Zamiatin's dsytopian novel. The betrayal by the narrator D-503 of his lover I-330 (prefiguring the betrayal of Julia by Winston) is among the most obvious similarities, if only because Orwell discusses it himself in his review (1968a, 74). According to George Steiner, "Without 'We,' 'Nineteen Eighty-Four,' in the guise in which we have it, simply would not exist" (1983, 174). For additional possible sources of the novel, see Rose (1992).

be said to stand on its head, replacing Our Freud's sex drive with Big Brother's lust for power.

There is at least one scene in Orwell's novel which directly recalls Huxley's, namely, when Julia and Winston are just about to make love for the first time: "She stood looking at him for an instant, then felt at the zipper of her overalls. And yes! It was almost as in his dream. Almost as swiftly as he had imagined it, she had torn her clothes off, and when she flung them aside it was with that same magnificent gesture by which a whole civilization seemed to be annihilated" (110). In *Brave New World,* it is Lenina who disrobes before John Savage: "Zip! Zip! . . . She stepped out of her bell-bottomed trousers. Her zippicamicknicks were a pale shell pink . . . Zip! The rounded pinkness fell apart like a neatly divided apple. . . . Still wearing her shoes and socks, and her rakishly tilted round white cap she advanced towards him" (193). Unlike John, however, who interprets Lenina's behavior (quite rightly) as evidence of her promiscuity and proceeds to revile her, Winston delights in the evidence of Julia's sexual experience. "The more men you've had," he tells her, "the more I love you. . . . I hate purity, I hate goodness. I don't want any virtue to exist anywhere. I want everyone to be corrupt to the bones" (111).

Here the influence of *Brave New World* is at one and the same time acknowledged and rejected. For Orwell, at this point in the novel at any rate, it is the sex drive that is the most dangerous enemy of the power drive.[18] That, no doubt, is also why, as O'Brien tells Winston later, Oceania's neurologists are busily at work on ways to abolish the orgasm. (This is an idea that would be utterly abhorrent to O'Brien's counterpart in *Brave New World,* the gentle World Controller, Mustapha Mond.) It may also be why for Winston the em-

---

18. For Irving Howe the sex drive is the primary source of danger to the stability of the Oceanic state, though he implies that this is something that Orwell himself may not have been aware of. Howe reasons that if Winston and Julia's "needs as human beings force these two quite ordinary people to rebellion, may not the same thing happen to others?" (1971, 50).

bodiment of his persistent hope in the "proles" is the massive figure of the woman whom he hears singing and whom he also sees from the window of his love nest above Charrington's junk shop. She has hips at least a meter across, as Julia disparagingly points out, and possesses practically no mind, but Winston finds her beautiful nevertheless. She has "strong arms, a warm heart, and a fertile belly," so fertile indeed that Winston speculates she may have given birth to as many as fifteen children. Where O'Brien destroys, in other and somewhat hopeful words, she creates. In Winston's mind, she represents the "hundreds or thousands of millions of people just like this, people ignorant of one another's existence, held apart by walls of hatred and lies, and yet almost exactly the same—people who had never learned to think but were storing up in their hearts and bellies and muscles the power that would one day overturn the world. . . . The future belonged to the proles. . . . The proles were immortal. You could not doubt it when you looked at that valiant figure in the yard. In the end their awakening would come" (195–96). Significantly, in *Brave New World* John Savage shares, for a time at least, a similar hope that the lower-caste workers will rise up and destroy the New World State—a hope that turns out to be just as deluded as Winston's.

Small wonder, then, that Orwell should have sent Huxley a copy of his new book immediately after its publication, and was anxious to know what Huxley's verdict would be.[19]

And, of course, there is also the influence of *Animal Farm*. Both novels share a preoccupation with the Soviet Union's betrayal of the ideals (as Orwell saw them) of socialism. Both feature prominently the transformation of Trotsky into a scapegoat for all the inadequacies of the Soviet system, though in *Nineteen Eighty-Four* the Trotsky figure, Emmanuel Goldstein, is provided with some (apparently fictitious) opportunity to justify himself by means of "The Book,"

19. See Chapter 5 of Firchow (1984) for a more extended discussion of the relation between *Nineteen Eighty-Four* and *Brave New World*.

something Snowball was not able to do in *Animal Farm*. Both novels make much of the massive personality cult devoted to Stalin, with the glaring, larger-than-life depictions of the heavily moustachioed face of Big Brother being virtually omnipresent in Oceania.[20] Both books devote a good deal of attention to the ways in which the Party brainwashes its adherents (e.g., notably the sheep in *Animal Farm* and the bumbling, brainwashed Parsons in *Nineteen Eighty-Four*), as well as to the disproportionate and utterly irrational punishments meted out to alleged traitors and saboteurs. Both books are also centrally concerned with the inability of the working class—though in *Nineteen Eighty-Four*, it's primarily the Outer Party—to gauge whether the postrevolutionary society is better off than the prerevolutionary one. This preoccupation also extends beyond practical concerns to a larger, metaphysical worry about how totalitarian states are able to reshape the past for their own purposes, thereby controlling the identity not only of their societies but also of their individual citizens.

There are also important differences between the two books. Most obviously, there is in *Animal Farm* no protagonist like Winston Smith, no love affair with someone like Julia, and no talkative torturer like O'Brien. There is also no distinction between the Inner and Outer Parties, no vast population of working-class people (representing 85 percent of the total population) who are left more or less undisturbed by the Party, which subjects them only to occasional outbursts of propaganda and designates for liquidation only the most obvious potential proletarian rebels. There is also the im-

---

20. Though some Western critics of *Nineteen Eighty-Four* (notably Raymond Williams, A. L. Rowse, and Scott Lucas) have attacked Orwell for betraying socialism, there was nothing like the vicious attack launched by the Soviet government, which denounced Orwell as "a former 'police agent and yellow correspondent' [journalist?] . . . who passes in England for a writer 'because there is a great demand for garbage there'" (quoted in Rodden 1988, 132). In this connection, it seems odd that even a relatively objective critic like Krishan Kumar claims that only "careless readers" of *Nineteen Eighty-Four* are given to identifying the world depicted in the novel with that of Stalin's Russia (Kumar 1993, 65).

portant difference that Oceania is characterized by continuous war, with enemy prisoners being reviled and sometimes executed, and with (enemy?) rockets regularly exploding and killing people. In *Animal Farm*, while war may be a continual danger—at least until the pigs become fully "human"—there are only two actual interludes of warfare: the Battle of the Cowshed and the Battle of the Windmill.

The most important difference may actually be that *Animal Farm* is about the past (as well as a little about the present), whereas *Nineteen Eighty-Four* is entirely about the future. *Animal Farm* ends more or less with the consolidation of power by the pigs following the Battle of the Windmill, that is, translated into historical terms, with the end of World War II in 1945—also the year when the novel was published. *Nineteen Eighty-Four*, on the other hand, differs radically in that it imagines a future based on the tendencies of the present. Completed in 1948, *Nineteen Eighty-Four* simply reverses the last two digits of that year, unmistakably indicating thereby that it is a book about what the present will likely turn into in the not too distant future. *Animal Farm* ends with pigs and humans becoming indistinguishable, an idea which, though bitterly ironic, can still raise a smile; not so, however, *Nineteen Eighty-Four*, which leaves the reader with little to laugh or even smile about. Pig Brother, swinish though he may be, still isn't Big Brother. Paradoxically, Pig Brother is still "human"; he is selfish, egotistical, vain, full of foibles like getting drunk or hogging the milk and apples. He is even cruel and conniving, like Jones, but he is not a monster.

That is not the case, however, with Big Brother or with his principal representative in *Nineteen Eighty-Four*, O'Brien. The most remarkable thing about O'Brien is that, in the ordinary way, he seems to have no vices at all. Though he is not an "animal," he definitely isn't "human." So far as we can tell, he devotes just about all of his time to discovering, manipulating, "curing," and eliminating social deviants like Winston Smith. Judging from the minute detail that he seems to have accumulated over the previous seven years about Winston's life and mind, along with the elaborate premeditated malice with which he responds to Winston's allegedly errant ways, he must be putting in nearly twenty-four-hour days at the Ministry of Love (with additional, briefer interludes at the Ministry of Truth). No wonder Winston Smith thinks O'Brien looks tired.[21]

If O'Brien is typical of the elite of the Inner Party—and it's clear we are meant to think so, just as we are meant to think of Winston Smith as typical of the Outer Party—then it's hard to escape the conclusion that already by 1984 human/porcine nature has changed dramatically, at least so far as the Inner Party is concerned. Most obviously, it has become monomaniacally focused on one thing only: POWER. Unlike, say, *Brave New World,* it is a power deliberately based on hatred rather than on love. Nothing else matters, as O'Brien explains to Winston, and in the future beyond 1984, nothing else will matter, if possible, even less:

> The old civilizations claimed that they were founded on love and justice. Ours is founded upon hatred. In our world there will be no emotions except fear, rage, triumph, and self-abasement. Everything else we shall destroy—everything. Already we are breaking down the habits of thought which have survived from before the Revolution. . . . Children will be taken from their mothers as one takes eggs from a hen. The sex instinct will be eradicated. Procreation will be an annual formality like the renewal of a ration card. We shall abolish the orgasm. . . . All competing pleasures will be destroyed. But always—do not forget this, Winston—there will be the intoxication of power, constantly increasing and constantly growing subtler. Always, at every moment, there will be the thrill of victory, the sensation of trampling on an enemy who is helpless. If you want a picture of the future, imagine a boot stamping on a human face—forever. (238–39)

21. It is true, however, as Brian Aldiss reminds us, that in his apartment O'Brien does enjoy some compensating comforts, which Winston can only marvel at: "There is wallpaper on the walls, the floors are carpeted, the telescreen can be switched off, the butler pours wine from a decanter, and there are good cigarettes in a silver box. Not sybaritic, exactly; more the sort of thing to which typical Old Etonians (Orwell was an untypical example) could be said to be accustomed" (1984, 9). Or, perhaps more to the point, these are the sorts of comforts and privileges which higher-ups in

Though admittedly one should be careful about reaching definitive conclusions before all the evidence is in, still, after the momentous events of 1989, it definitely looks like O'Brien's insane predictions have not proved particularly accurate.[22] No doubt, the boot on the human face is still stamping away busily in various parts of the world, including places that are fairly close to home—and such sadistic stamping may even continue "forever" into the future—but it unquestionably is not the exclusive "intoxication" in the post-1984 world that O'Brien thought it would become. On the contrary, as Francis Fukuyama has famously observed, the currently triumphant consumerist society, with its videos, burgers, drugs, and sexually "pneumatic" delights, looks far more likely to be the final form of the future for most of us living in the West (i.e., in "Oceania"), if, that is, it has not already turned into our present.[23] These days, no matter what one may think of our devotion to consumerism, one can still say that, comparatively speaking, it is fortunate that O'Brien—or whatever other name an equivalent contemporary sa-

---

the Party came to expect as their due, as anyone who ever visited the former Soviet Union or its satellite states can testify.

22. Aldous Huxley pointed this out to Orwell in a letter thanking him for the gift of *Nineteen Eighty-Four,* saying: "Whether in actual fact the policy of the boot-on-the-face can go on indefinitely seems doubtful" (Huxley 1971, 102).

23. As is perhaps to be expected from someone with an almost professional interest in Marxism, Orwell may have been aware of Hegel's concept of the "end of history," though for him history appeared to be ending in a very un-Hegelian sense. In his 1943 essay on the war in Spain, Orwell remembered "saying once to Arthur Koestler, 'History stopped in 1936,' at which he nodded in immediate understanding." What the two friends were thinking about, Orwell claims, was not the triumph of bourgeois, representative democracy but the systematic distortion of historical fact to the point where it was impossible to verify what had really happened—i.e., Winston's job at the ironically named Ministry of Truth. According to Bernard Crick, however, Orwell's knowledge of Marxist doctrine was less than complete, though he apparently was able to impress even orthodox Marxists with that knowledge (Crick 1980, 305). Though, like Crick, Werner von Koppenfels finds little evidence in Orwell of a profound knowledge of Marx's writings, he does cite a disguised allusion to the *Communist Manifesto* (in *The Road to Wigan Pier*) and points out that Orwell had a dog named Marx (1984, 660). William Steinhoff, on the other hand, claims that Orwell "knew a great deal about Marxism and he regarded Marx's theory as a 'useful instrument for testing other theories of thought'" (Steinhoff 1975, 73).

dist might be operating under—is more likely to be found playing some virtual-reality chainsaw video game than conducting electric shock sessions in Room 101. The idea that eliminating all pleasures, except the unique "pleasure" of stamping with one's boot on some hapless face, would satisfy an intelligent person "forever" is, in retrospect (but not only in retrospect), absurd. On the surface, at least, such single-minded focus on just one "pleasure" seems self-defeating even in O'Brien's own terms, since the elimination of other ways of enjoying power, such as, say, depriving people of sexual pleasure, is unlikely to make the "intoxication of power" grow "subtler." Cruder is what it would make it grow, even boring, like reading the Marquis de Sade's *120 Days of Sodom*. For most people, it seems fair to conclude, even the vicarious experience of a couple of days in Sodom is more than enough. And de Sade, though no doubt quite as mad as O'Brien, at least had enough sense to retain the orgasm.

O'Brien is actually a far better and more realistic metaphysician than he is a prophet or moralist.[24] His insistence that the nature of reality is internal rather than external, that it can be solely determined by the Party, represents an interesting revision of the famous verdict of heresy by the Church regarding Galileo's contention that the earth revolved around the sun.[25] Though, like Galileo, Winston

24. Orwell, in retrospect, was not particularly good at prophecy either. In "England Your England" (1941) he predicts that unless Britain loses the war against Germany, the conclusion of hostilities "will wipe out most of the existing class privileges" (1954, 283). As William Steinhoff points out, Orwell also readily admitted that he had been wrong to predict Churchill's resignation after the disaster of the loss of Singapore to the Japanese in 1942 or, for that matter, the continued, long-term collaboration of Germany and the Soviet Union (1975, 102). In his two essays on James Burnham, Orwell faults Burnham for his inaccurate and frequently revised prophecies, though he does not mention his own flawed predictions in those contexts.

25. O'Brien's obviously Irish name is probably also intended to evoke associations with Catholicism and the Inquisition. According to Carl Freedman, Orwell's aversion for the Catholic Church was almost as intense as his hostility to the Soviet Union (1986, 98). As Crick also points out, "O'Brien's reference to the regime holding a Ptolemaic rather than Copernican cosmology must be intended to make us think of Galileo facing the papal inquisition and reveals a religiosity in O'Brien" (1989, 157). And according to William Steinhoff, Orwell had read Boris Souvarine's *Cauchemar en U.R.S.S.*, which uses as its epigraph a quotation linking Galileo's submission

initially reacts with the equivalent of the former's whispered "ep-pur se muove" ("nevertheless it [the earth] moves"), he is finally per-suaded that 2 + 2 actually make 5, and that, if he so wished, O'Brien could levitate. In the end Winston is even persuaded to love Big Brother, something the Church was never able to make Galileo do with the pope.

Party reality, in other words, is a kind of "bottled" reality, very much as in *Brave New World,* though the "reality" contained in the bottles is, in each case, very different. And, as in Huxley's novel, where the Alphas enjoy a certain freedom not to be infantile (that is, they are able, when absolutely necessary, to emerge from the "bot-tles" of their conditioning), members of the Inner Party also have access, at least to the extent permitted by "doublethink," to an "un-bottled" reality.[26] This is notably proved by O'Brien's possession of the supposedly destroyed photograph of the discredited former In-ner Party members, Rutherford, Aronson, and Jones. Somewhere, then, in the Ministry of Truth, there must be a separate set of files preserving an unrevised record of actual historical events. Big Brother, so it would appear, endorses not only doublethink but also double-entry bookkeeping.[27]

---

to Church doctrine with the phony Moscow trial confessions (1975, 33). Orwell may also be thinking of the fanatic Irish Catholic villain of Joseph Conrad's *Romance.* His name is O'Brien. (At about the time Orwell was writing *Nineteen Eighty-Four* he was planning a long essay on Conrad which he did not live to complete.) O'Brien's link with Catholicism—and with Communism as well, of course—is especially evident in his compulsive need to have Winston make a full and genuinely contrite confession. Only then can Winston be absolved of his "sins," that is, when he sincerely express-es his love for Big Brother (i.e., God). It's worth noting in this connection, however, that O'Brien, the supposed devotee of "hatred," contradicts himself when he wants Winston's "treatment" to culminate in love. Or is this simply another manifestation of "doublethink"?

26. In "Writers and Leviathan" (1948) Orwell implicitly defines doublethink with reference to the alleged habit of the English Left to think of the word "socialism" as having the same meaning both in Russia and in England: "Hence there has arisen a sort of schizophrenic manner of thinking, in which words like 'democracy' can bear two irreconcilable meanings, and such things as concentration camps and mass de-portations can be right and wrong simultaneously" (1968a, 410).

27. It's worth noting here that the vast effort expended at the Ministry of Truth

In this connection, it is probably significant that Newspeak, at least on the evidence of Orwell's novel, is never spoken—not by the proles, not by members of the Outer Party, and not even by members of the Inner Party. While the Appendix on Newspeak does explicitly address the issue of how the language is to be spoken in the future (in a "gabbling style . . . at once staccato and monotonous" [275]), it provides no convincing examples of such speech, and, in any event, the Appendix is not really relevant for reasons that will become apparent a little later in this chapter. The reality that Newspeak is designed to "bottle" is, so far as Winston and his contemporaries are concerned, strictly a written reality. All spoken language continues to be entirely in "Oldspeak," which means that forbidden thoughts can still be expressed so long as they are expressed orally. In that sense, "Newspeak" is a misnomer; it should really be called "Newwrite."[28]

Given O'Brien's stated predilection for the supposedly ever subtler "intoxications of power," it seems, initially at least, rather puzzling why O'Brien should be devoting so much time and effort in the reformation of Winston Smith's character by means of a variety of rather crude methods of torture. Though Winston is not stupid, his life so far has not been in any way unusual or distinguished. While

---

to keep altering the past to conform with the currently expedient political facts makes very little sense in the context of the kind of police state Oceania is described as being. What citizen of this state, in his or her right mind, would dare to examine the files of past newspapers in order to verify what had "actually" happened? Doing so would be an obvious invitation to the Thought Police to "examine" such a person more carefully in Room 101. In *Animal Farm,* however, the revision of the seven commandments by Squealer makes sense, since the animals are not hindered when they check the back of the barn to see what "new truth" the latest revision has brought them.

28. The assertion that forbidden thoughts cannot be expressed in Newspeak is not entirely accurate. For example, the Newspeak names of the various ministries—of love, peace, truth, and plenty—respectively, Miniluv, Minipax, Minitrue, and Miniplenty—strongly and ironically imply that they possess a "minimum" amount of love, peace, truth, and plenty. According to William Steinhoff, Orwell may have modeled Newspeak on the "cablese" that journalists used to write formerly when transmitting their copy to their editors via telegraph from overseas (1975, 169).

he evidently possesses a certain gift for rewriting snippets of history, especially as contained in old newspapers, and even produces occasional quasi-Newspeak articles for the *Times,* he is otherwise quite as nondescript as his surname suggests he must be. What's more, as he tells Julia at the first opportunity, he is thirty-nine years old, has a wife he can't get rid of, suffers from varicose veins, and has false teeth. Small wonder that he can't quite grasp what she sees in him. For that matter, it's hard to grasp what O'Brien sees in him either.

One explanation for O'Brien's concentrated interest in Winston might be that he thinks of Winston as a kind of "Everyman," which would at least account for Winston's ordinariness. An everyman, after all, has to be ordinary if he is to qualify as an everyman. Still, Winston's ordinariness does not help explain why Julia should be attracted to him. Her reason—that she "saw something" potentially rebellious in his face (108)—seems rather lame and even unlikely, since, if Winston is good at anything, he's good at maintaining the "ordinary" orthodox poker face required to escape the attentions of the omnipresent telescreens.[29] Perhaps the real reason for Julia's otherwise inexplicable attraction to Winston is to be found in Orwell's own private preconceptions about women, whom in actual life he usually considered undersexed and even frigid. Julia, in other words, is a kind of wish fulfillment, for Orwell as well as for Winston. As for Winston's ordinariness, the primary reason for that, other than camouflage, may be to allow the reader to identify with someone who is "ordinary" in much the same way most readers are. In this way readers can be made to feel (even "bellyfeel," as the Newspeak word has it) what it's like to live in the Oceania of 1984. Otherwise the novel

29. By now the telescreens have become synonymous with the idea of continuous surveillance, a feature of Orwell's state that contemporary Americans, especially, fear may be adopted by their own government. For Orwell the origins of this sort of universal surveillance are probably to be found in the universal spy mania prevalent in World War II but also relevant, if we are to believe Vita Fortunati (along with Michel Foucault), may be the so-called "panopticon," which permitted guards to keep a continual eye on prisoners in Jeremy Bentham's hypothetical prison (Fortunati 1987, 115).

might easily have degenerated into a mere treatise along the lines of Emmanuel Goldstein's "Book," only longer. As it is, *Nineteen Eighty-Four* already bears a heavy burden of discursiveness, not only in the assigned readings in "The Book" but also in the discussions between O'Brien and Winston that take up much of the last part of the novel. For this reason we should perhaps be grateful that Julia is only a revolutionary from the waist down, someone who barely manages to keep awake when Winston starts reading out loud from "The Book."

The most compelling explanation for O'Brien's curiously intense interest in Winston, however, is to be found in O'Brien's own explicit assertion and prediction that "[t]his drama that I have played out with you during seven years will be played out over and over again, generation after generation. Always in subtler forms" (239). Here O'Brien acknowledges that he has been systematically manipulating Winston's physical and mental life since 1977. In ways that ironically resemble Winston's revising and even inventing historical and biographical facts, O'Brien has apparently spent much of his time during the last seven years totally reinventing Winston's life and mind. This persistent and massive interference with and involvement in Winston's behavior and thinking (even dreaming) is apparent only when one goes back and looks more closely at earlier scenes in the book that now assume additional significance. Then one suddenly realizes that *Nineteen Eighty-Four* is really a book with two plots: an overt and a covert one. So, for example, the fact that Winston's room possesses a nook where he can hide from the telescreen seems fortuitous until we recognize that this too was part of O'Brien's plan to lull Winston into a false sense of security. Months later, languishing in the cellars of the Ministry of Truth, Winston himself realizes that "for seven years the Thought Police had watched him like a beetle under a magnifying glass. There was no physical act, no word spoken aloud, that they had not noticed, no train of thought that they had not been able to infer. Even the speck of whitish dust on the cover of his diary they had carefully replaced" (247). There seems to be no length to which O'Brien is not prepared to go, no expense that he is not willing to incur, in order to entrap Winston. The "junk shop" with its "owner," the elaborately disguised Thought Police official Charrington, has been set up and kept in readiness for years—Potemkin Village–style—apparently just in order to deceive Winston. The effort and the planning that must have gone into these stage props stagger the imagination.

Winston's dream seven years earlier—and the association of that dream with the as yet unfamiliar face of O'Brien—that they will meet "in the room where there is no darkness," seems at first promising (the absence of darkness suggests hope) and only in retrospect becomes ominous (22, 91). His detailed envisioning of the "Golden Country" even before he goes there to meet Julia for the first time may strike the reader as odd, but it only becomes suspicious on rereading. Then it becomes clear that somehow either Julia herself must have been complicit with O'Brien from the beginning or else she too has been manipulated by him in much the same way as Winston has been. How else to explain the proleptic vision Winston has of a "girl with dark hair coming toward him across the field" who overwhelms him with "admiration for the gesture with which she had thrown her clothes aside. With its grace and carelessness it seemed to annihilate a whole culture, a whole system of thought . . ." (27). At this point Winston has not even met Julia. Later, when they do meet in the Golden Country and Winston sees Julia act out in reality what he had earlier dreamed she would do, he says to himself, ". . . yes! It was almost as in his dream. Almost as swiftly . . . she flung [her clothes] aside . . . with that same magnificent gesture by which a whole civilization seemed to be annihilated" (110).[30]

30. It is suspicious that Julia disappears from the novel after the couple's apprehension by the Thought Police, only to reappear briefly when the two meet "by chance" and engage in a pointless conversation that makes Winston want to break off contact permanently. By this time Winston, to be sure, has found a new love interest in Big Brother. While it may be that Julia has indeed been subjected to torture in much the same way that Winston has been, there is no specific evidence for it; and, given the skill with which O'Brien and his cohorts contrive to disguise people (e.g.,

Once we as readers become aware of the extent of the covert plot of the novel, we are inevitably led to wonder what the point of it might be. The most obvious answer to this question is, once again, provided by O'Brien, at least implicitly. His extraordinary manipulation of Winston is both proof of his immense, almost godlike power and also proof of its "subtlety." The more obvious and therefore cruder expressions of his power only follow later, in the beatings and in the electroshock treatments carried out in Room 101. The boot in the face, in other words, is only the culmination, as it were, of the stab in the back, or, more accurately, of the twist of the mind.

So O'Brien's "intoxication of power" is subtle after all? On the evidence of Winston's experience, yes, it would seem to be. But what about O'Brien's claim that Winston's experience is a mere preliminary to the drama that "will be played out over and over again, generation after generation, always in subtler forms?" This claim seems to border on madness and may be intended to be read as an example of O'Brien's hubris. After all, if the sex impulse and even the orgasm are to be abolished in the future, the possible areas for "subtle" expressions of power will be drastically diminished rather than increased. If there's no interest in sex, there obviously can be no future equivalent of the Winston/Julia relationship; and if, as O'Brien claims, the parent/child bond will also be destroyed, there can be no guilt feelings of the sort that Winston repeatedly feels about being responsible for the death of his mother and younger sister. There is the further complication that the future refinements in Newspeak will increasingly prohibit the expression—and ultimately even the conception—of subtlety. The point of Newspeak, after all, is to eliminate complexity and subtlety, not to foster them. What then will be the future sources of the supposedly ever more subtle

---

Charrington), it's perhaps justifiable to speculate that Julia's new appearance may simply be another development in O'Brien's "subtle" drama. Another small piece of evidence suggesting that Julia may be O'Brien's stooge is her failure to react when Winston tells her that he recognizes the details of the landscape of the Golden Country because he has seen it before "sometimes in a dream" (109).

playing out of the drama of power? Is it to be always the boot in the face? Forever? Unless he is utterly mad, this must seem an unattractive prospect even for O'Brien. That it apparently does not strike him as unattractive inevitably raises suspicions that he *is* utterly mad and that his madness will have "subtle" and rather drastic consequences.[31] Readers of *Nineteen Eighty-Four* should be careful, as William Steinhoff points out, not to confuse O'Brien's views on these matters with Orwell's. He "did not believe that Machiavelli, Burnham, and O'Brien were right. He did not believe that 'sadistic power-hunger' is the ultimate motive for human conduct" (1975, 203–4).

These suspicions are confirmed in the Appendix on "The Principles of Newspeak." Unlike Goldstein's "Book," there is no indication that this Appendix has been fabricated by O'Brien and/or other members of the Inner Party in order to mislead people like Winston. We can therefore accept it as a "genuine" description of the status of Newspeak and, by implication at least, of the status of the

---

31. I, for one, strongly sympathize with the long tradition of Orwell criticism, including such distinguished figures as George Kateb and Irving Howe, that shares Morris Dickstein's view about O'Brien, namely, that "he may embody the system but he cannot plausibly speak for it. O'Brien is no Grand Inquisitor, whose arguments he tries to match." The earlier critics differ, however, from Dickstein by taking O'Brien's mania seriously, or, rather, by not supporting Dickstein's claims that Orwell means us to think of O'Brien as relatively normal, since in his view "the book offers little support for seeing this thuggish creature as a madman who plays mind games with his victims" (2004, 65). Dickstein also shows no awareness of the existence of the double plot in *Nineteen Eighty-Four,* though Thomas Pynchon apparently does in his introduction to a recent edition of *Nineteen Eighty-Four* (Deery 2005, 123). (I pointed out its existence as long ago as 1984 in the concluding chapter of my *End of Utopia.*) That O'Brien's lust for power is psychologically unmotivated was noted as early as 1949 by Philip Rahv in his review of *Nineteen Eighty-Four,* when he said that even Dostoyevsky's Grand Inquisitor felt the need to justify his exercise of arbitrary power, whereas O'Brien does not. Irving Howe, after quoting Rahv, argues that Orwell is depicting a totalitarian society that has reached a stage "when belief in the total state is crumbling while its power survives" (Howe 1983, 12–13). The absence of any justifying ideology is also problematic for George Kateb, who, in what is probably the best discussion of this important aspect of the novel, faults Orwell for failing to explain why men like O'Brien want power. In his view Orwell, like Winston, seems to know a great deal about the "how" but not much about the "why" of the power motive (Kateb 1971, 82–87).

society that has developed it. We can infer that the Appendix seems
to have been written sometime after 1984, "when Oldspeak was still
the normal means of communication" (277), and 2050, the date for
which "the final adoption of Newspeak had been fixed" (279). The
opening sentence of the Appendix reads as follows: "Newspeak was
the official language of Oceania and had been devised to meet the
ideological needs of Ingsoc, or English Socialism."

There are several odd things about this sentence. To begin with,
it's odd that any likely Oceanic reader of the Appendix would need
to be told that Ingsoc means "English Socialism." Indeed, it's unlikely that such a reader would even understand what the reference to
"English" means, since, according to the novel, England no longer
exists but has long ago been replaced by an "Airstrip One" that is
part of a larger international conglomerate named Oceania. Even
odder is the statement that "Newspeak was the language of Oceania." If it *was* the language of Oceania, what *is* the language of Oceania now? Apparently, it's English, for that is the language in which
the Appendix is written. But if English still is the language of Oceania, even long after 1984, and if the meaning of Ingsoc still needs
to be explained at a time when the development of Newspeak was
scheduled to be completed, then the kind of society described in
Nineteen Eighty-Four either no longer exists or has changed beyond
recognition. From all these peculiarities it appears that the Appendix, very much like the novel that precedes it, has both an overt and
a covert meaning.

It could of course be argued that the fact that the Appendix is
written in the past tense constitutes no proof that Oceania is no longer functioning as described in the novel. The novel itself, after all, is
written in the past tense. To this objection, one can raise the coun-
terobjection that the Appendix is not part of the novel but is clearly
designated as an "appendix"; in other words it is something that follows the principal part of the book and presumably helps to clarify it
or some part of it. Significantly, its form is not narrative but discursive. The Appendix therefore could and probably should have been

written in the present tense, the tense in which most descriptive essays (e.g., like this one) are written. That it wasn't suggests Orwell had an ulterior motive in not doing so. This hypothesis may become more convincing when it is apparent that there is nothing grammatically or idiomatically wrong with changing the opening sentence into the present tense: "Newspeak is the language of Oceania and has been devised to meet the ideological needs of Ingsoc."

Even so, there is an additional problem even after the sentence has been transposed into the present, because it is still written in English, not in Newspeak. However, that objection can be discounted by noting that no contemporary reader of *Nineteen Eighty-Four,* either now or in 1949, would be able, or would have been able, to make out the meaning of so complex a document as the Appendix if it had been written in Newspeak, even supposing that Orwell had had the ability or desire to write it in that "language." (He could, of course, have used "cablese," which would have been comprehensible to most journalists at least.) Besides, there is the further objection that Newspeak was designed to eliminate the possibility of writing complex documents like this one.[32]

All in all, then, there seems to be a good deal of evidence to support the conclusion that we are meant to read the Appendix as conveying a double meaning, much as the novel itself does. Assuming, however, that this conclusion is indeed valid, there then follows another, perhaps even more momentous problem that needs

32. The most thorough discussion of the relation of the Appendix to the story of Winston Smith is Richard Sanderson's 1988 essay, which argues that there is no way of telling if the Appendix is told by a different narrative voice from the one in *Nineteen Eighty-Four.* In his view, one should therefore not take into account "the essay's clues" as reliable indications of "the future downfall of Big Brother." Sanderson also professes to be puzzled as to why Orwell would have signaled the demise of Oceania in so indirect and ambiguous a fashion if he really meant to leave his readers with the sense of a happy ending (589–90). By way of an answer, one might point out that Orwell after all was a literary artist and not a mere propagandist, and that, as such, he had a right to expect his readers to extrapolate from the evidence he provided, including the evidence of the covert plot in the novel proper—something that Sanderson seems to be unaware of.

to be addressed, namely, what was it that brought Ingsoc and the Party down? Was it, as Winston hoped and even predicted, the pro-les?[33] Are we to conclude that the "beautiful" working-class wom-an with her fertile meter-wide hips was too formidable an adversary for O'Brien after all? Or was it Goldstein's Brotherhood that, despite O'Brien's boastful claims, was not mythical after all, but in fact final-ly managed to infiltrate the Inner Party and destroy it?

There is and can be no definitive answer to these questions, or at least no direct answer. Indirectly, however, one can surmise that it was O'Brien himself (and his fellow Inner Party members) who brought down the prevailing system. The evidence for this conclu-sion is contained in O'Brien's own words and behavior. His peculiar predictions about the abolition of the orgasm and even of the sex drive as such, his ravings about the "ever subtler" intoxications of power when it is obvious that those "intoxications" could only be-come ever cruder and more boring, suggest that O'Brien, intelligent and hard-working though he is, is also utterly mad. But if this is so, there is no escaping the conclusion that no stable state can be built on the speculations of a madman. If nothing else, in 1948 the drastic and horrifying results wrought by the power-intoxicated and utterly mad Adolf Hitler were as yet staring everyone in Europe in the face. Hitler's thousand-year *Reich* lasted exactly twelve years. O'Brien's "forever" may last a little longer. But in the end, while O'Brien is able to convince Winston that $2 + 2 = 5$, and while he is even able to abolish history when he wants to, he nevertheless cannot con-trol the future or abolish it.[34] Instead, the future will abolish him.

33. William Casement is one of the few critics of the novel who shares, though with qualifications, some of Winston's hope in the possibility of the proles bringing about the destruction of Oceania (1989, 219).

34. As William Steinhoff points out, Orwell's use of the "$2 + 2 = 5$" formula is derived from the first Soviet five-year plan, which was supposed to be completed in four rather than five years (1975, 172). While the placement of such an apparently ab-surd notion in a historical context makes it appear rational—and therefore may make O'Brien seem rational too—few readers of *Nineteen Eighty-Four* would have caught the allusion, and even if they had, they might have missed the irony in Orwell's reference to a propagandistic plan which had not succeeded either in four or even in five years.

Despite his grandiose and overweening claims, there are limits to O'Brien's power, as well as to the power of an institutionalized Ingsoc. The last and greatest of the many ironies of *Nineteen Eighty-Four*, then, is that the hope for the overthrow of Oceania resides neither in the proles nor in Emmanuel Goldstein's Trotskyists. The hope is in O'Brien.[35]

35. Additional evidence that Orwell must have meant his readers to treat O'Brien's claims skeptically is to be found in his essay "James Burnham and the Managerial Revolution" (1946), which he wrote after he had already begun work on *Nineteen Eighty-Four*. In that essay Orwell wonders why Burnham, who, like O'Brien, is obsessed with power, "never stops to ask *why* people want power. He seems to assume that power hunger, although only dominant in comparatively few people, is a natural instinct that does not have to be explained, like the desire for food" (1968a, 177). Later in the essay, Orwell goes on to question Burnham's claim that "literally anything can become right or wrong if the dominant class wills it." Not so, says Orwell, because Burnham "ignores the fact that certain rules of conduct have to be observed if human society is to hold together at all." Orwell then goes on to speculate that Russian policy will probably lead to atomic war, but even if it doesn't, "the Russian regime will either democratise itself or it will perish. The huge, invincible, everlasting ["Forever!"] empire of which Burnham appears to dream will not be established, or, if established, will not endure, because slavery is no longer a stable basis for human society" (180). Are we to suppose from this evidence that Orwell made one prediction about the future of totalitarianism in the essay on Burnham and another, utterly different one, in the approximately contemporaneous *Nineteen Eighty-Four*? It's possible, of course, but I'm inclined to doubt it.

CHAPTER 5

WILLIAM GOLDING'S
LORD OF THE FLIES

An Island Utopia?

It is a thankless task to be a fabulist.

William Golding

Fabulous Fun

Until 1961, when he decided that he could make a living from his writing, William Golding was a teacher of English and philosophy at Bishop Wordsworth's School, a relatively obscure private school in Salisbury in the west of England. Teaching had provided him with a good deal of firsthand experience with the kinds of boys he describes in *Lord of the Flies*. As he points out in his essay on fable (originally a talk given during his year as writer-in-residence at Hollins College in Virginia), he was "well situated" for this task, having served for many years not only as a schoolmaster but also, as he pointed out in his lecture, as "a son, brother, and father. I have lived for many years with small boys and understand and know them with awful precision" (1965, 88).

These last words are, I must confess, a little (actually more than a little) chilling. Despite Golding's obvious literary gifts, gifts that must have informed his teaching as well as his writing, these words suggest that one ought not to envy the boys at Bishop Wordsworth's the experience of having had him as their teacher. No doubt he was a formidable taskmaster, definitely not someone to be easily deceived into believing in the potential of immature noble savages to transform themselves someday, under appropriate tutelage, into educated and civilized human beings.

Given this background, it's clear that *Lord of the Flies* is absolutely authentic, even, in its own way, as authentic as Orwell's two dystopian fictions. It's also clear that the novel is at least as dark and pessimistic as Orwell's books, perhaps even darker. As one should be able to deduce from its title, it also has a religious dimension that is largely absent in Orwell. Lest anyone fail to see it when reading the novel, Golding, who apparently was as skeptical of his readers as he was of his pupils, takes pains to make it explicit in his essay on fable: "Man is a fallen being. He is gripped by original sin. His nature is sinful and his state perilous. . . . I decided to take the literary convention of boys on an island [notably in Ballantyne's *Coral Island*], only make them real boys instead of paper cutouts with no life in them; and try to show how the shape of the society they evolved would be conditioned by their diseased, their fallen nature" (88). There is not much doubt here about the outlook for the boys on the island. The guiding hand of their author, rather like the controlling hand of the wrathful God of the Old Testament, will soon make them feel, with "awful precision," what it's like to be "gripped" by the disease of original sin.

Though Golding went on to write several more novels, culminating in the award of the Nobel Prize in 1983, *Lord of the Flies,* his first published novel, is still the book by which he is remembered today. Ironically, the novel would not have been published at all if Golding had not been so extraordinarily (awfully?) persistent in sending it around, clearly an indication of his confidence in the quality of the book. After twenty-one refusals, Faber & Faber finally accepted it and brought it out in 1954. For a first novel it sold very well, though by no means spectacularly. It wasn't until it was reissued as a paperback in 1959 that it turned into a best-seller and became one of the four or

so key books of the American sixties generation, along with J. D. Salinger's *Catcher in the Rye* (with which it is often compared), Tolkien's
Lord of the Rings, and Hermann Hesse's *Steppenwolf* (published in the
1920s in Germany but virtually unknown in the United States until
the 1950s). Like these other books, *Lord of the Flies* succeeded in tran-
scending the usual fairly limited audience for serious fiction and soon
reached an immensely large public. Hence the claims made on the
cover of paperback editions of the novel that more than ten million
copies have been sold, claims more reminiscent of the hamburger industry than of the publishing business.

By the time Golding came to the United States in 1961 to teach
for a year at Hollins College, the book was already a must-read on
just about all American campuses. For example, on the obverse side
of the title page of my copy, published in 1959, is listed the information that it's part of the "fifty-third impression," and the front cover
is headed by the boastful announcement that more than three and a
half million copies were then in print. Inevitably one wonders why.
What made the book so popular? Was it because the sixties generation was possessed by so powerful a sense of their fallen nature that
they saw themselves mirrored in the various and variously dreary or
at best tragic fates of the stranded boys? Or was it the implication
that an impending World War III—still very much a source of anxiety in the sixties—was less due to impersonal historical forces than to
innate human folly (or worse)? Was it perhaps the gradually deterio-
rating political and social atmosphere caused by the war in Vietnam
that brought with it a loss of faith in American innocence paralleling
the loss of innocence of the boys in the story? Or was it something
else? Was it perhaps the very violence of the story that made it attractive to a generation that, unlike any other before it, was witness
to the violence of war every evening on the television news?

Perhaps all of these were factors in contributing to the book's
vast popularity. Oddly, however, according to the book's author, its
popularity was not attributable to the fact that it is a fable, since for
him (even after the book had been impressed more than fifty-three

times and had sold more than three and half million copies), "fabulists are never popular" (1965, 85). Perhaps Golding could say this with a straight face because he had not bothered to define in clear terms what a "fable" was, other than that it is a tale told by a "moralist" (85). (That's also why he says it's unpopular.) But is this really so? *Gulliver's Travels,* for example, is both a fable and very moral, but it is also a very popular story, in both its children's and its adult versions. To be sure, it's also very funny, which *Lord of the Flies* definitely is not. For that matter, just about all utopias and dystopias are to some significant degree fables, though by no means are all of them funny, and many of them—including all of the ones discussed in this book—are still at least moderately popular.

But then perhaps when Golding uttered these words about the supposed unpopularity of fabulists, he was thinking more of his subsequent novels than of *Lord of the Flies.* For, fable or no, *Lord of the Flies* is undoubtedly a good read, despite its sometimes (and ultimately) depressing overtones. It's a good read because it is, on one level at least, a rousing adventure story, with lots of fantasy (about "beasties," for example) and suspense (e.g., will Jack and his gang of savages catch up with and kill Ralph?). In this respect it definitely resembles Tolkien's *Lord of the Rings,* whose great popularity is also due in part to its ability to tell an engrossing story. Both narratives have a great deal of the "and then" quality that E. M. Forster defined as the essential characteristic of a good story, a characteristic that in his view was necessary if one wanted to engage "a gaping audience of cave men" or "their modern descendant the movie-public" ([1966], 86).

This hypothesis would be more persuasive if only the other two great campus successes of the sixties were also "good reads" of the adventurous sort. But of course they aren't. Both Salinger's *Catcher in the Rye* and Hesse's *Steppenwolf* are quite different kinds of novels whose popularity is almost certainly not attributable to their rousing narrative line but rather to their intense concern with describing how their protagonists find their "identities" (or fail to) in the usually hostile context of their respective societies. Things happen in the two books, of course, but there's nothing like the absorbing series of episodic and often violent adventures that make up Golding's and, especially, Tolkien's books.

How to account for this difference? Did Golding and Tolkien appeal to a different segment of the campus audience than Salinger and Hesse? To the dimmer "caveman" segment, to put it bluntly if somewhat unkindly? Perhaps so, though I suspect that if there was a distinct separation between these two groups of readers, there was also a considerable overlap. Why? Not only because most bright young people need (then as well as now) and are looking both for fun and for answers as to "who" they are, but also because neither Golding's nor Tolkien's books are "merely" adventure stories. They also address important issues of a moral nature—e.g., what makes us behave as we do? Is it possible to avoid the corrupting influence of power? Why do kids who seem to start out with similar gifts and outlooks develop in radically different ways? Golding's and Tolkien's novels address these crucial issues in the unpretentious context of adventure fiction. They are also, it is important to remember, "novels"; that is, they are very different from the textbooks students might be (or might have been) reading in introductory classes in philosophy or psychology, and they are also very different from old-fashioned adventure stories like those of H. Rider Haggard or, for that matter, new-fashioned ones like Ian Fleming's. They are "serious" adventure stories. *Pace* Forster, their audience does not just consist of gaping cavemen. That's why no serious student need be ashamed at being caught reading a novel by Golding or Tolkien. They may be good reads, but they are not escapist fiction.

Golding and Tolkien also share another quality that, paradoxically, may help to account for their vast popularity, namely, their sexual "innocence." Though there have been attempts to read sexuality into *Lord of the Rings,* these attempts have not been particularly persuasive. It's hard, for example, to believe that the popularity of Golding's novel is attributable to its multitudinous readers savoring

the Oedipal aspects of Roger's killing the sow by ramming a stick up
her anus. That's an idea that might even have shocked Freud. Not,
of course, that Freud would have been shocked by the bit about the
stick in the anus, but rather by the claim that this scene parodies the
Oedipus complex. After all, Freud thought he knew quite well that
it was the father whom the male child wished to kill and the mother
with whom he wished to sleep. Just how killing the mother, rather
than sleeping with her, is parodic of the Oedipal complex is left unclear, even if we assume that Edmund Epstein, in his afterword to
the Capricorn edition (he was an editor there at the time), means
us to think that it's funny for the boys to think of their mothers as a
sow. As for the Beastie being the Id, another one of Epstein's claims,
while that's undoubtedly more acceptable from a Freudian point of
view, to my mind the allegory works better if applied to the boys
themselves, so that Jack would represent the Id, Ralph the Ego, and
Piggy the Superego. But even such a Freudian allegorical reading
still leaves out the important figure of Simon, and besides, as Golding was at pains to point out, he had not read Freud when he wrote
Lord of the Flies.[1]

Surely, putting aside this Freudian red herring (or fat sow), it
seems obvious that much of the proven appeal of Golding's story
is due to its being set in an earthly paradise—a boy's utopia. When
at the beginning of the novel, not long after having lived through a
harrowing plane crash, Ralph, Jack, and Simon set out to explore the
island, they are filled not with terror at what they might discover,
but with tremendous joy at the adventure they find themselves in:

"Wacco."
"Wizard."
"Smashing." (23)

1. Not having read Freud might, however, actually reinforce the argument that
Freud is relevant to an interpretation of the story. Relevant too is the likelihood of
Golding's having gained at least a superficial knowledge of Freudian theory without
having read any actual work by Freud. It's hard to believe that a forty-three-year-old
Oxford graduate and teacher (among other things, admittedly) of philosophy would
not have known at least the basics of Freudian psychology.

In Golding's words, "[t]he boys find an earthly paradise, a world, in fact like our world, of boundless wealth, beauty, and resource" (1965, 89). Actually, the island is not quite "boundless" in its wealth, though there does seem to be an inexhaustible supply of fruit growing just about all of the time that the boys are on the island (evidently less than a year, or from the end of one rainy season to the beginning of the next). And, of course, there are the pigs, if one also wishes to classify these under the rubric of "boundless wealth." Or perhaps they should belong to the category of what Golding calls "resource"? Whatever the case, "boundless fun" describes much better how the boys initially respond to their environment. As Ralph later tells the assembled boys, "[t]his is our island. It's a good island. Until the grownups come to fetch us we'll have fun" (30). The three boys don't pause on their way up to exploring the mountain that first morning to savor the beauty of the landscape, but rather look forward to the excitement of getting to know a mysterious island. They are less juvenile Wordsworths than twentieth-century reincarnations of the Ralph, Jack, and Peterkin of Ballantyne's *Coral Island*. For them the worlds of fantasy and reality have suddenly fused, something that just about all adolescent boys (and perhaps girls too) dream about happening. It's only gradually that some of the boys (and presumably all of the readers) become aware of the grave dangers of (con)fusing fantasy and reality. It's only gradually that the good island becomes a bad island, that utopia turns into dystopia.

What is the appeal of the uninhabited island? It's partly the appeal of being free, of returning to a state of innocent or seemingly innocent nature. Hence the explicit absence of sexuality. But it is also the tremendous appeal for many adolescent boys of being freed from adult responsibility, as is the case, for example, in another celebrated and influential fantasy, James Barrie's *Peter Pan*. (Not coincidentally, I suspect, the cover of recent editions of the Putnam "Capricorn" paperback edition depicts a Ralph [Jack?] who looks very much like Peter Pan.) "Neverland," like Golding's island, is a place where the main aim is to have "fun"—a fun which is more threatened by the semi-adult responsibility of Wendy than it is by Captain Hook or the Indians. As in Barrie's fantasy world, so too in Golding's, the breakup of what initially seems like a juvenile utopia is caused by the insistence of would-be adults like Piggy (and to a lesser extent, Ralph) that "fun" is not enough, or even that "fun" poses a danger that needs to be eliminated. Toward the end of *Lord of the Flies,* Piggy and Ralph, as is also the case with Barrie's Wendy, represent a boring adult and even specifically female world (paradoxically in Golding too) of having to take care of the "littluns," of watching and feeding the fire, and of keeping a lookout for possible rescue.

It's likely, then, that some of the popularity of the book is attributable to the absence of sexuality on the island. That there is no overt sexual dimension to the novel is also clearly the result of a deliberate choice on Golding's part. "The boys were below the age of overt sex," he says in his essay on fable, "for I did not want to complicate the issue with that relative triviality" (89). Let me say here that I, for one, am left a little puzzled by this assertion. If sexuality is indeed "a relative triviality"—a conclusion reached, presumably, by means of the "awful precision" of Golding's understanding of small boys— then how could/would it possibly "complicate the issue," except (relatively) trivially? My sense is that Golding really means to say something different. What he means, I think, when he says that there's no overt sexuality in the novel is that he hasn't allowed any girls to come along. (The "littluns," however, may be viewed as possible substitutes for girls.) There certainly seems to be no suggestion of homosexuality among the boys, though traditionally this was a widespread "problem" among British public schoolboys—as Golding must have known, given his "awful understanding"—up to the time that he published his novel and even beyond. (Jack and his "choir" boys would have been another link to homosexuality, if Golding had wished to exploit it. They are clearly identified as public school boys, with Jack acting as prefect, though he is not explicitly referred to as such.)[2]

2. Jack, however, does complain that Ralph gives orders even though he is not a prefect. As "chapter chorister and head boy," Jack is in a position that in the English

Leaving girls out of the story therefore may not "simplify" matters, but it certainly emphasizes the story's maleness. I suspect this exclusively male focus contributes considerably to its appeal to young men; and I suspect therefore that most of its readers are male. Not that males don't like reading about sex, but there is a sense in which strictly male adventure stories do help provide male role models for adolescents. Like just about all fiction, adventure stories, and *Lord of the Flies* in particular, have a "bovaristic" dimension; that is, they allow (encourage?) readers to try out various fictional guises or masks to see which one fits best. If, as it turns out, one reader happens to think of himself as a possible Ralph, he had better watch out for problematic encounters with Jacks. If one sees oneself as a potential Jack, one had better avoid situations where there is no check on one's innate inclination toward violence. And so on. (It's possible, given Golding's known admiration for Aldous Huxley, that he may have been consciously using Sheldonian psychosomatic categories in establishing his characters.) In addition, *Lord of the Flies* exercises an appeal to most readers who are probably older than the boys in the story that is perhaps best described as "nostalgia." It's a longing— one that is also present in the Tolkien stories—for a presexual Edenic world before one had eaten of the sexual Tree of Knowledge. In Eden, after all, it was the very nontrivial knowledge of sexuality that brought about the loss of innocence and the subsequent expulsion of Adam and Eve. In Golding's retelling of this archetypal narrative, there is no Eve and, instead of sexuality, it is the boys' eating of the "tree of power" that brings about their loss of innocence and expulsion from the island of Eden.

---

system is usually occupied by a prefect, that is, of a public school student in his last year. It is therefore peculiar that Jack is no older than the other boys, though, to be sure, it is also peculiar that the choir is made up of boys who are all about the same age.

Getting to Utopia

Though few critics have remarked on it or even noted it, there is something very odd about how the novel begins.[3] As far as we can tell, the boys have arrived on the island after their plane has been shot down at night by enemy aircraft during what seems to be part of a nuclear World War III. They were apparently being evacuated—much as English children had been in the early stages of World War II—from England and were being flown to safety in Australia (?) or New Zealand (?).[4] (Why all of this is never made explicit is a question that was left unanswered until Charles Monteith, Golding's editor at Faber, addressed it in 1986.) The novel begins on the morning after the plane has crashed, with one of the boys (it turns out to be Ralph) making his way out of the jungle by way of the "long scar" that the plane had smashed into the jungle as it crashed. He is followed a little later by another boy (Piggy), who emerges from more or less the same place and who has evidently been gorging himself on fruit. The two then engage in a contrived conversation about what occurred the previous night. Piggy first wonders what happened to "the man with the megaphone" and then about what happened to the pilot. Ralph asserts that there probably aren't any grownups on the island, something that seems to delight rather than distress him. He also claims that the pilot "must have flown away after he dropped us. He couldn't land here. Not in a plane with wheels."[5] He also thinks that the pilot will be back to pick them up. Piggy, however, is evidently more realis-

---

3. According to Stephen Medcalf, however, high school teachers in Britain who use this novel to introduce their students to "high literature" for the first time "still rather irritably explain in answer to their complaints that we do not know how the boys of the story arrived" on the island. On the whole, it seems that the critics have shown rather less curiosity—or irritability, for that matter—in this respect than many high school students (2005, 12).

4. That the island is somewhere in the Indian Ocean is suggested by the intertextual reference to Ballantyne's *Coral Island*. However, it is also made clear in the novel itself that the plane must have been flying in this direction, since it is said to have made two prior stops in Gibraltar and Addis Ababa (17).

5. Readers of the published book could not have known that in the version Gold-

tic and does not agree. He points out that the plane was under attack and went down in flames, with the cabin of the plane producing the aforementioned scar in the jungle as it crashed. To Ralph's question, as to where the remains of the plane might be, Piggy speculates that the plane was swept out to sea by the storm that was then raging, probably with some of the children (and of course the two adults) still on board (5–6).

Does all of this make any sense?

Not really. To begin with, it's very peculiar that neither boy—or, for that matter, any of the other boys who later join them, some of them from places quite distant from the site of the crash—has been injured in any way, not even slightly, nor has their clothing been torn or even singed or soiled. (Jack's choir, for example, is fully dressed in caps and gowns.) What's more, there is no trace whatever of the plane that came down, except for the deep scar that it left behind as it smashed through the jungle. There is no detritus of metal, glass, propellers, food, tools, or weapons. There is simply nothing, not even corpses or body parts. Even if we accept Piggy's hypothesis that the plane was swept out to sea by the force of the storm, the fact that it has left nothing behind is *very* peculiar. Peculiar too is the circumstance that the plane evidently disappeared into the relatively shallow lagoon protecting the beach side of the island from the sea. The reef blocking the surf and the open sea is said to be "perhaps a mile away," which means that, no matter how great the force of the storm might have been, the plane could not have been swept beyond the reef (8). (In fact, the storm was evidently not particularly powerful, since none of the trees on either side of the scar appears

___

ing originally submitted to his eventual publisher there were several planes rather than just one, and that these planes were equipped with detachable "passenger tubes" which could be released by the pilots to float down to earth on giant parachutes. These futuristic details were eliminated on revision, at the suggestion of Charles Monteith (Monteith 1986, 58). That Golding retained aspects of the original version (the distribution of the boys over various parts of the island, for example) while adding new ones (notably the "scar") makes the beginning of the novel confusing, apparently deliberately so.

to have been blown down.) But if the remains of the plane are resting at the bottom of the shallow lagoon, then they should at least be visible from more elevated parts of the island and might possibly even be accessible. Such is, however, evidently not the case, for none of the boys ever mentions seeing the plane or, Robinson Crusoe–like, attempts to retrieve useful items from it.[6]

All of this is very curious. Curious too is what the point of all this mystery surrounding the boys' arrival on the island might be. It is clearly not due to carelessness on Golding's part, since, in speaking with Frank Kermode about *Lord of the Flies* in 1959, he said that "it was worked out very carefully in every possible way, this novel" (Kermode 1983, 201). Several years later, in conversation with Jack Biles, he reaffirmed his conviction that the novelist is a fully conscious craftsman: "I'm against the picture of the artist as the starry-eyed visionary not really in control or knowing what he does. I think I'd almost prefer the word 'craftsman.' He's like one of the old-fashioned shipbuilders, who conceived the boat in their mind and then, after that, touched every single piece that went into the boat. They were in complete control; they knew it inch by inch, and I think the novelist is very much like that" (Biles 1971, 177). These remarks obviously negate any supposition that Golding was simply unaware of what he was doing when he placed his boys on the island in so peculiar a manner. But if it was not an oversight or a blunder, then what? Certainly, all prior island fantasies, from *Robinson Crusoe* to *Peter Pan,* including Golding's explicit model, *Coral Island,* are at pains to show how their characters got there. Not Golding, however.

One possible answer might be to approach this apparently deliberate mystery from the perspective of the kind of philosophy that was current and most fashionable at the time *Lord of the Flies* was

6. None of these details seems to bother Mark Kinkead-Weekes and Ian Gregor, who simply assert that all the boys landed in a "detachable tube" which was then swept out to sea by a "great storm," together with some of the children on board. There is no discussion of why there are no injuries to the surviving children, or why some of them appear scattered over the island, or why there is a "scar" that has been caused by a plane crash (Kinkead-Weekes and Gregor 2002, 7–8).

first published, namely, existentialism. Existentialism would account for the otherwise inexplicable way the boys "drop in" on the island by analogy to the way we have all "dropped in" on life—also an inexplicable and even "absurd" event. It's a given, in other words, which we simply have to accept without any further explanation, as with Martin Heidegger's idea of human beings being "thrown" into life. This existentialist answer to the problems raised by the strange beginning of the novel is admittedly an attractive solution to a difficult problem. It is especially attractive also because one of Golding's subjects of instruction at Bishop Wordsworth's School happens to have been philosophy, which presumably means that he would have been aware of existentialism even at this relatively early stage of its introduction into the English-speaking world. Still, I don't think it's the main reason why Golding arranged for the novel to begin as it did.

The main reason, I believe, is the utopian reason. Golding's intention is to establish, even at the cost of a drastic lack of realism, something like a laboratory situation.[7] Or, if lack of realism is too strong a phrase, then at least a "nonrealistic" laboratory situation, one, in other words, that is outside of, or more accurately, beside, reality. As he remarks in his essay on fables, "[t]he point of the fable under imaginative consideration does not become more real than the real world; it shoves the real world to one side" (1965, 97). Golding's aim in *Lord of the Flies* seems to be to set up the right conditions for an "experiment." Here, in other words, representative humanity (or at least representative male humanity between the ages of six and about twelve) is to be subjected to a "test," something rather like what the Hungarian critic Georg Lukacs in his study of the historical novel calls an "extreme situation." Such a situation, though on the surface utterly atypical, is actually the most effective way of presenting a truly typical situation, since a more obviously "typical" situation would actually be "average" and therefore unconvincing.

7. Although, as we have seen, the original typescript version of the novel did provide more details about how and why the boys got to the island, Golding's revisions in the published version obscured those details, presumably deliberately.

The very lack of realism, the very extremity of the situation, calls attention to the "experiment" that is being conducted in the novel. This kind of test or "gimmick," as both Frederick Karl and James Gindin call it (taking their cue from Golding himself), is also apparent in the ending of the novel, not only in its beginning. There a *deus ex machina* in the guise of a British naval officer, along with several members of his crew, steps ashore to "rescue" the boys. The way the book ends, in short, is quite as "absurd" and unpredictable as the way it begins.

An Island Laboratory

This situation raises the further question presented by another odd aspect of the novel, namely, the clear division of the boys into two distinct age groups, the "littluns," who are all about six years old, and the "biguns," who are all about twelve. In this respect, *Lord of the Flies* differs radically from its principal intertext, Ballantyne's *Coral Island,* and actually resembles more the island section of *Peter Pan.* In Ballantyne's novel, Jack Martin (Jack Merridew in *Lord of the Flies*) is eighteen, Ralph Rover is fifteen, and Peterkin Gay (Simon in *Lord of the Flies*) is thirteen. In other words, though the age differences among them are not insignificant, the boys are all past the age of puberty; they are, in other words, already young adults. However, because of his greater age and experience, as well as because of his much greater physical strength, Ballantyne's Jack automatically assumes and is willingly granted leadership of the small group. There is none of the rivalry so evident in *Lord of the Flies.*

Why does Golding divide his boys into two distinct groups of littluns and biguns? Is it to suggest that littluns are just waiting to become biguns, just as the biguns are merely biding time to become adults like the naval officer (or the dead pilots)? There is some evidence that we are to interpret the division in these terms. In the only scene in the novel where the littluns are provided with something more than a background role, the behavior of three of them, Henry, Perceval, and Johnny, is shown to mirror the behavior of Jack, Ralph, and Piggy, as is evident from the following description of the three small children playing on the beach:

> Henry [Jack] was a bit of a leader this afternoon, because the other two were Perceval and Johnny, the smallest boys on the island. Perceval [Piggy] was mouse-colored and had not been very attractive even to his mother; Johnny [Ralph] was well built, with fair hair and a natural belligerence. Just now he was being obedient because he was interested; and the three children, kneeling in the sand, were at peace. (55)

There is, however, at least one other persuasive reason for the division, namely, to provide an opportunity for the older boys to show whether or not they are willing to assume a (boring?) responsibility for those who are less able, or even unable, to care for themselves. In the passage cited above, for example, it turns out that the three littluns are being watched by two biguns, Roger and Maurice, who proceed to destroy a number of the littluns' sand castles, and Maurice also kicks sand into Perceval's eyes. Still, both of the older boys are somewhat inhibited in their behavior toward the littluns, especially Maurice, who goes off to swim by himself. Roger, however, remains behind, apparently waiting for an opportunity to satisfy his sadistic impulses, of which he seems to possess more than any of the other older boys on the island. A little later, when Henry leaves the two other littluns to play alone at the edge of the water, Roger proceeds to throw stones in his direction, more to frighten him, however, than to hurt him.[8] He, like Maurice, is as yet inhibited by the conditioning of the "outside" world: "Here, invisible yet strong, was the taboo of the old life. Round the squatting child was the protection of parents and school and policemen and the law. Roger's arm was conditioned by a civilization that knew nothing of him and was in ruins" (57).

Roger's overtly sadistic behavior toward the littluns is atypical,

---

8. Roger's throwing stones in Henry's direction is clearly intended as a foreshadowing of Roger's releasing the rock that will kill Piggy toward the close of the novel.

but it's clear that just about all of the biguns, including Ralph and perhaps even Piggy, have difficulty in shouldering responsibility for them. This difficulty is revealed not only in their persistent failure to establish a list of the names of the littluns or a clear count of their number, but in their more ominous failure to prevent the death by fire of the little boy with the mulberry mark on his face.[9] Only one of the older boys shows any real concern for the welfare of the littluns, namely, Simon, who on his way into the interior of the island stops to help some of the little boys get at ripe fruit that is beyond their reach. Lest we miss the point here, Golding specifically draws our attention to it in his 1964 interview with James Keating, where he also observes that he deliberately intended Simon to be perceived as a "Christ figure" (Baker 2000, 192).

Here again it's worth recalling the absence of overt sexuality in the novel. There is no sense that Simon's assistance to the littluns— or, for that matter, Roger's and Maurice's earlier hostility to them— is prompted by secret or sublimated sexual impulses. Simon's behavior is undoubtedly altruistic. (Perhaps this incident is what Golding is thinking of when he describes himself as an optimist.) Judging from the example of Simon, it is at least possible in his world to act altruistically. The absence of sexuality, as we have seen, also fits the idea of a fictional laboratory where the basic human drive(s) can be identified and examined in isolation. Here it is the drive for power that is the center of attention, but, as is evident from Simon's behavior, it also becomes clear that not all of the boys are affected by this drive, and, further, that some of them are less affected by it than others (Ralph and Piggy).

Golding's intention here appears to be to evoke "the state of nature," that hypothetical utopian/dystopian condition postulated by seventeenth- and eighteenth-century philosophers from Hobbes to Rousseau. Golding wants us to return to the place where it all be-

---

9. Another one of the odd and even incredible aspects of this narrative is that none of these boys—all of them schoolchildren—is in possession of pencil and paper with which to make such a list.

gan, which is perhaps also why he confines his novel to young and youngish children. Not that the "state of nature" is identical for all of these foundational philosophers, as Golding the sometime philosophy teacher must have known full well. In both Rousseau's and Locke's views, primitive humanity was essentially good, a world of "noble savages," whereas for Hobbes it was essentially bad, with his primitive men inhabiting a world where life was, as Hobbes famously put it, "solitary, poore, nasty, brutish and short." Which of these two views of humanity Golding preferred as being closest to reality should not be a question readers of *Lord of the Flies* need to ask.

Aside from evoking/invoking this Enlightenment debate about the origins of human society, Golding also appears to want his readers to think of the specifically Judeo-Christian tradition of the origin of the human species. Thus the rationally inexplicable presence of the boys on the island—i.e., how they got there—reflects, I think, the biblical story of the creation, the story of Genesis. This is perhaps why all of the boys first step out of the dark background of chaos (the jungle) before they enter the world of light on the beach. This is also why they need to know the names of the littluns and why the "word," as embodied in the conch, is so important. It may also be why the smoke becomes for the older boys the primary means for rescue as well as a matter of contention, though neither Ralph nor Jack may actually be aware of the echoes of the Abel/Cain story. (Jack's later adoption of facial markings to provide camouflage and to foster group solidarity seems to identify him even more with the Cain story.) There is also something of an allusion to the fallen angels in the transformation, during the course of the novel, of Jack's choir into a gang of diabolic hunters.

What is not quite so clear in all of this socioreligious intertextuality, is why Golding should have chosen children exclusively to conduct his "experiment" with. This is certainly not what Hobbes, Locke, Rousseau, or even the Bible do when they depict the state of nature. Why then Golding?

Part of the reason, I think, is that children between the ages of six and thirteen are old enough to be able to survive under favorable conditions, at least for a while, independent of adult care, while at the same time not yet being fully socialized. It is therefore possible and even believable that they would begin to forget what little socialization they once possessed and start to revert to a "state of nature." Another part of the reason perhaps is that children are much less adept at suppressing or disguising their true feelings and motives than adults are, with the result that they inevitably reveal their "true" natures more fully and clearly. Furthermore, there is a long and very influential tradition in the West that attaches value to childhood, a tradition that views children as innocent and unspoiled by adult society. In this connection, it is worth noting that Christianity is a religion—the only major religion—that places a child at its center. Also, for the Romantics, that is, for the immediate successors of Rousseau, the child is, as Wordsworth famously put it, the "father of the man." The child is, as he is also in Blake's songs, an innocent who is corrupted by experience. In Rousseau's words, man is born free—and born of course as a child—yet everywhere he is in chains, both in the sense of the real chains made by an authoritarian adult society as well as in the sense of Blake's mind-forged manacles.

In *Lord of the Flies*, who or what is to blame for the corruption of the initially innocent children?

The answer to this question is easy, on the surface at least. It is the "Lord of the Flies," who is prominently referred to in the title of the novel.[10] Most readers undoubtedly realize who is to blame long before the interview between Simon and the severed head of the pig (in the chapter entitled "Gift for the Darkness"). The "fly-lord" or Beelzebub is only the externalized form of an evil that dwells within the boys themselves. That evil is present even in Simon, who is un-

10. According to James Baker, the original title of the book was *Strangers from Within*, and Golding only adopted *Lord of the Flies* as his title at the urging of the publisher (Baker 2000, 122). According to Charles Monteith, the final title was suggested by Alan Pringle, another editor at Faber & Faber (Monteith 1986, 62). It may be that by referring to "inner" strangers Golding wished to suggest a link with Camus's novel, *L'étranger*, thereby emphasizing the existential aspects of his novel.

doubtedly, morally speaking, the best of the whole lot. Not that this indwelling evil (which Golding would later identify as "original sin") is here easily defined or understood, for adult readers or, much less, for the boys themselves. Unlike, say, the world depicted in Tolkien's novels, where creation is on the whole neatly divided into good and bad, Golding's is a mixed or gray-scale world, not a sharply dualistic black-and-white one. It is a world, as E. M. Forster once said, not of good and evil but of good-and-evil. It should not be surprising, therefore, that some boys have a greater share of original sin—of evil—than others.

Simon is the boy with the least inherent evil. That is no doubt why, paradoxically, evil manifests itself to him most clearly, as in the temptation of Christ. There is also some ambiguity as to whether the scene in which the Lord of the Flies speaks to Simon is meant to be seen as a purely symbolic event or as an actual, real one. The answer to this question depends in part on how we view Simon himself. Though in some superficial ways he is only a boy much like the other boys—he likes to explore, for example—Simon differs from the others in that he seems to possess a genuine visionary gift. He exercises this gift when he accurately foretells Ralph's escape from the island (103). Significantly, Simon is also an epileptic, a condition that is sometimes associated with extrasensory perception. Among so-called primitive peoples, the shaman is often an epileptic (hence shaman / Simon?).

Whether the scene—and with it the Lord of the Flies—is real or unreal (or merely symbolic) is ultimately impossible to determine. What is clear, however, is that Simon is unmistakably associated with the head of the pig. When he faints he envisions himself inside that head. His own head also bleeds and, like the pig's, attracts the flies. On some level and to some extent, therefore, we are apparently intended to think of Simon's head as identical with the pig's head, which, if true, means that, since the pig's head is one manifestation of the essential "beastie," Simon too must be another such manifestation (127–28). This identification is literally (and ironically) proved when Simon is "mistaken" for the "beastie" and bludgeoned to death a short time later, when he joins the hysterical group on the beach.[11] (The irony of course is that Jack and his hunter-killers are much more bestial than Simon.) The other chief manifestation of the "beastie," namely, the dead parachutist on top of the mountain, is also associated with Simon. It is Simon alone who dares to confront him and so comes to realize what he is, a dead human being.[12] Simon then takes pity on him—he is, after all, a Christ figure—and releases him. He can do so perhaps because, as with the pig's head, he recognizes his kinship with the fallen figure. Both are subject, though in different ways, to the "falling disease." Fittingly, both in the end are swept out into the sea (of eternity?), where they disappear, mysteriously leaving no trace of their bodies behind. Only the spirit survives, as it were.

Simon is obviously the most interesting because the most complex character in the book. For the rest, despite Golding's hope that he could avoid depicting boys who were mere "cut-outs," the other characters are so predictable that one almost always knows what they are going to say or do beforehand: Piggy will always whine; Ralph will always try to do the right thing; Jack will always try to do the wrong one; and Roger will always try to do someone or something in. Given Golding's preoccupation with setting up a laboratory on

11. Piggy's name also inevitably associates him with the pig's head. Like Simon (and of course the pig itself), Piggy is killed by the other boys; he too is apparently another manifestation of the "beastie." Golding's identification of the "beastie" with the morally superior characters like Simon and Piggy (and later with Ralph), rather than with Jack et al., is quite deliberate. He wants his readers to be aware that "original sin" is present even among those who seem least affected/infected by it. That the other boys, along with their leader Jack, are bestial hardly needs pointing out.

12. In Golding's complex private allegory, the parachutist represents so-called "off-campus history," which is Golding's name for the mass of national prejudices that pass popularly for history. (Real or objective history, on the other hand, is academic or "campus" history.) As Golding writes in "Fable," the League of Nations (symbolized in the book by fire) was a "great effort at international sanity [that] fell before the pressures of nationalism which were founded in ignorance, jealousy, greed—before the pressures of off-campus history which was dead but would not lie down"—like the parachutist, in other words (1965, 96).

the island in which to study human nature, he is almost forced into having at least one representative example from each of the important human categories, though, given his shortage of characters (a brief novel like this one can only accommodate relatively few characters and still remain a novel), he has to make a single character fulfill slightly different roles at different times. Simon, as we have already seen, is the shaman, the religious mystic, but he is also the individualist, the solitary. Piggy is the rationalist and intellectual, but he is also the inevitable outsider. (Piggy, so far as we can tell, is also the only boy who comes from a working-class background.) He has all the faults of the intellectual—he's physically lazy; he's near-sighted; and he's a chronic complainer and nag—but he also has the compensating virtues. He knows how to organize people and things; he has a more lucid and objective overview of the situation; and he is able to foresee if not forestall potential dangers.

Jack is also a familiar type, but at the other end of the scale. Red-haired, courageous, somatotonic, competitive, he is a "natural leader" who has charisma but no ability to think much beyond the immediate situation. Lacking a sense of the future, Jack reverts entirely to the past, literally becoming the "chief" of a tribe (the word is actually used) of primitive hunters. When he puts on his "mask" of colored markings and insists that his followers do the same, he thereby eliminates not only all semblance of civilization but also all individual identity. It is in these respects that Jack can reasonably be called a "fascist"; that is, he promotes a cult of uncritical worship of, and obedience to, the "leader" while at the same time placing group solidarity above individual rights. Ralph, on the other hand, shares qualities possessed by both Piggy and Jack, with the Piggy-like characteristics mostly dominating. His problem is that, being a divided personality, he looks both ways. Ralph's inner ambiguity is evidently too much for his frail psyche, with the result that Ralph increasingly "forgets" the civilized rationale for his actions (e.g., why the fire needs to be kept lit) and comes to resemble Jack's instinctual "savages" more and more without being able (or perhaps really wanting) to join their group.

Each of these boys is, it's clear, representative of a fairly large and typical category of humans. But why so? What is it that has produced these different categories? Who or what is it that has created not one type of human being, but various types? Why is Jack different from Ralph, and why are both different from Piggy? Or, put in more general terms, what is the principal shaping force here, nature or nurture?

The unambiguous answer to this question seems to be: nature. So, for example, Piggy can't help being fat. His inability to change is symbolized by the fact that he never loses any weight. He remains the same Piggy from his absurd beginning to his lamentable end, despite being forced to abstain entirely from the fattening candy that his "auntie" used to feed him. So too Jack apparently can't help being aggressive or Roger sadistic; and even among the littluns the same types are visible in embryonic state. Simon's epileptic condition is relevant here too. One is born an epileptic, not made one.

Given these basic, genetically determined human "facts," it seems inevitable that, in the laboratory conditions of the island, the fundamental, innate human drive for power should triumph over all other, relatively speaking "trivial," competing drives, such as benevolence and altruism. (Altruism, too, however, as we can see from Simon's example, is just as innate as the lust for power; it's just weaker.) In other words, might will always triumph over right, power will always crush morality, "fun" will always take precedence over responsibility, death over life, primitive emotion over civilized thought, the group over the individual. The shift of power from the democratically elected Ralph to the self-appointed "führer" Jack reverberates with ominous echoes through the corridors of contemporary history. World War II, we seem meant to learn, was not the last word on what human beings are really like. We need another World War, one that is even more devastating—one that will finally leave the whole world in ruins—to prove to us that the fly-lord is the real master of the world.[13]

Is this the depressing conclusion that we should take away from this novel?

Yes and no, I think. Certainly civilization is shown to be very fragile. The conch, the symbol of civil society, can and does break. And Piggy's glasses break too, or are stolen and misused. The glasses are a particularly interesting symbol, rather like the crystal ball that Winston Smith buys in Charrington's junk shop in *Nineteen Eighty-Four*, and which is also smashed in the end (but totally smashed, unlike Piggy's glasses). The glasses that are meant to help Piggy see (and "see") also produce the fire that may (and will!) rescue the boys, though not Piggy himself.[14] However, they also light the fire that kills the boy with the mulberry mark and that will eventually destroy most of the nonhuman life on the island. Civilization, in the form of fire, is not only fragile, it is also profoundly dangerous, both on the island and off it. Golding, so it would appear, has once again proved that, as Gilbert Murray once put it in a famous epigram, when you scratch a European, you will find a savage. Or, if not a savage—for neither Piggy nor Ralph ever turns savage—then at least a human being "gripped" by original sin.

But, if this is true, if Golding's scientific "experiment" has inexorably led to this conclusion, then it also follows logically that civilization could never have arisen in the first place, at least not to the

13. It is the destruction of the civilized world by atomic bombs, as well as Beelzebub's ultimate responsibility for that destruction, that makes James Baker believe that Golding is here in some way reworking Aldous Huxley's dystopian "novel," *Ape and Essence* (1948). In that dystopia Huxley posits a post–World War III Los Angeles devastated by atomic warfare and given over entirely to a satanic cult. To my mind the parallel is interesting but not persuasive, though it is undoubtedly significant that Golding did acknowledge being influenced by Huxley's pessimism to the extent of liberating him from "a certain starry-eyed optimism which stemmed from the optimistic rationalism of the nineteenth century" (quoted in Baker 2000, 116).

14. According to Julian Barnes, it is actually impossible to light a fire using the eyeglasses that would have been prescribed for the kind of nearsightedness that Piggy suffers from. The error is presumably not deliberate (Barnes 1990, 77).

point where Ralphs and Piggies could ever have exercised power over Jacks and Rogers. Of course, perhaps they never really did, perhaps so-called civilization consists only of brief intervals when the "Jack" boot (as it were) is not forever, as O'Brien puts it so vividly and memorably in *Nineteen Eighty-Four,* smashing the face of the innocent victim. Perhaps even Jacks and O'Briens need to take a rest once in a while. As Napoleon reputedly said, you can do everything with bayonets except sit on them. If this is actually the case, then there can be no rescue—not for the boys, not for us.

But if there is no rescue for the boys on the island, if there is only a continuation on a much vaster and technologically more sophisticated scale of the "hunt" of an arbitrarily designated "enemy," then what is or was the point of keeping the fire going in the first place? If the final rescue is no real rescue but merely another way of having "fun" in a different and even more destructive guise—that is, in naval uniforms and with submachine guns rather than with facial markings and sharpened sticks—then Jack was right after all in not worrying about being rescued. Then Jack, and not Ralph or even Piggy, is the truly radical thinker. Then it is Ralph and Piggy and not Jack who remain trapped in the illusion that there is such a thing as conventional safety or civilization in the adult world. If adult decency and altruism are only illusions, then there can be little consolation in the fact that the world will end not with a whimper, but with a bang—a very big bang.

CHAPTER 6

SUBJECTIVITY AND UTOPIA IN IRIS MURDOCH'S *THE BELL*

For me philosophical problems are the problems of my own life.
                                                        Iris Murdoch

Despite repeated tendencies towards worldliness and corruption, the medieval monastery has appeared to many thinkers to come closest in conception and even achievement to the general form of the ideal society.
                                                        Krishan Kumar

Iris Murdoch's first published book was a book of mixed philosophical analysis and aesthetic criticism, *Sartre: Romantic Rationalist* (1953). Why start off a career in philosophy with Sartre? Partly, no doubt, because Sartre was still a relatively unknown writer in early fifties Britain, and Murdoch's little book was among the very first to introduce him to her more provincial contemporaries; but partly too, I think, because for Murdoch Sartre was already something she was destined to become herself, namely, a philosopher who was also a novelist, though in her case the proportions would turn out to be rather different, with Murdoch being more of a novelist and less of a philosopher.

The choice of Sartre was also significant in other ways, for Murdoch did not (and never would) practice "philosophy" as conceived of in contemporaneous Britain, a philosophy that was primarily theoretical, abstract, and academic. Though, as a professional philosopher, she was of course knowledgeable about the general tradition of British moral philosophy, for her, as for Sartre, philosophy was something intimately linked to experience and commitment, a connection that helps to explain her decision to devote her life, during the latter part of the war as well as in the period immediately following, to working in Belgium and Austria for the United Nations Relief and Rehabilitation Administration. Though it was in fact only through going abroad to pursue this work that she came to know of Sartre's philosophy, her choice had already prepared her for its favorable reception. Her enthusiasm for existentialism (and its influence) even before meeting the great man himself in November 1945 is unmistakable. "[W]hat excites me more than the philosophy itself," she remarked, "is the extraordinary bunch of good novelists it is inspiring." After actually meeting him, she confessed somewhat breathlessly to a friend that "[h]is talk is ruthlessly gorgeously lucid—& I begin to like his ideas more & more . . . his writing and talking on morals—will, liberty, choice—is hard & lucid & invigorating. It's the real thing—so exciting & so sobering, to meet at last—after running away in despair from the shallow stupid milk & water 'ethics' of English 'moralists' like Ross & Pritchard" (quoted in Conradi 2001a, 215–16). Not that she was ever "converted" to existentialism—indeed she was critical of it from the very beginning—but the Sartrean impact on her was and would continue to be great and undeniable (and undenied). One does not publish one's first book on someone whose life and thought one considers unimportant.

Still, the book on Sartre is very much an English book, not a French one. The book on Sartre is really a book about Sartre as seen from the point of view of someone who has been reading and thinking not only about Sartre but also about Wittgenstein. That is also why her first published novel, although partly set in France, has as its title a phrase taken from Wittgenstein and has also as one of its principal characters a figure strongly reminiscent of Wittgenstein. Like Sartre, the impact of Wittgenstein would be great and enduring.

Though she only overlapped with him at Cambridge just after his retirement, and only met him briefly in person, she was extremely close to several of his students, who were in the habit of discussing him "incessantly." According to Peter Conradi, Murdoch "dreamt of him [Wittgenstein] all her life (never of Sartre)," and as late as 1978 she wondered out loud about the way in which "the fact that I have known *very well* certain people . . . who were *imprinted* by Wittgenstein [has] affected my work as a writer" (quoted in Conradi 2001a, 262–63). Wittgenstein is indirectly referred to in *The Bell* by the name of the maker of one of the bells, Hugh Bellfounder (43)—also the name of the Wittgenstein character in *Under the Net*.[1]

Aside from numerous essays and reviews dealing with philosophical issues, Murdoch also published books of philosophy other than the one on Sartre. It is perhaps significant, however, that the book on Sartre is the only book on philosophy she published while she was still engaged as a full-time teacher of philosophy. Though, like it, the various essays that make up *The Sovereignty of Good* (1970) and even *Metaphysics as a Guide to Morals* (1992)—originally a series of lectures—are both more or less given to empirical (or *experiential*) rather than to abstract philosophy, still these two books are primarily concerned with ethics, with the nature of the "good." Her remaining books of philosophy, *The Fire and the Sun: Why Plato Banished the Artists* (1977) and *Acastos: Two Platonic Dialogues* (1986), are both, as the subtitles indicate, concerned with Plato, even to the point, in the latter case, of overt imitation.

The moral, experiential focus is also true, not surprisingly, of her novels. And it is perhaps true as well, as Murdoch suggests in her book on Sartre, of all novels, at least when the term "novel" is variously but narrowly defined. There she distinguishes between four kinds of novel: "the novel proper," as written, among others,

1. The Wittgensteinian presence is especially noticeable in the third chapter, "The Sickness of Language," in which, among other references, Murdoch quotes approvingly from the *Tractatus* to the effect that "'[i]n the world everything is as it is and happens as it does happen. *In* it there is no value'" (1974, 47).

by Jane Austen, Dostoyevsky, and Proust (and, prospectively, by herself, though she does not say so); the novel of ideas, for which she
gives as the only example Voltaire's *Candide;* the "plain tale," e.g.,
Defoe's *Moll Flanders;* and, finally, the "modern metaphysical tale,"
for which she provides, again, only one example, Kafka's *The Castle.*
"The novelist proper," she goes on to argue, "is, in his way, a sort
of phenomenologist. He has always implicitly understood what the
philosopher has grasped less clearly, that human reason is not a single unitary gadget the nature of which could be discovered once for
all. The novelist has had his eye fixed on what we do and not on
what we ought to do or must be presumed to do . . . [the novel] is
also a type of writing which is more important than" the admittedly
quite important writings of Nietzsche, Freud, and even "the philosophy of Sartre" (1974, 9–10).[2]

   While not as intimidating as her philosophical writings, Murdoch's novels can be and usually are formidable experiences. (This
is less true, however, of her historical fiction.) They are also, as of
course they should be, given the specialized background of their author, philosophical novels, that is, complex, intricate, and profound.
In addition, they are ironic, witty, and sometimes even farcical—as,
for example, when in *The Bell* Toby and Dora stumble into the hollow
of the eponymous bell in a sudden moment of awkward sexual embrace immediately after having raised the bell from its muddy bed.

   But difficult and challenging though the novels sometimes are,
it is not necessary to possess a whole philosophical/mythological
reference library to understand (at some significant level, at least)
and enjoy them—unlike the work, say, of another eminent literary
figure who started out to be a professional philosopher, T. S. Eliot.[3]

   2. And more important too than the novels of Jean-Paul Sartre, since these, along
with his plays, have, as she points out in a 1950 BBC broadcast, "a strictly didactic purpose" (1997, 103). For an explanation as to why didacticism in fiction is "of the essence of Romanticism," see "The Sublime and the Beautiful Revisited" (1997, 281).
   3. See Michael Levenson's essay, "Iris Murdoch: The Philosophic Fifties and *The
Bell,*" for the most thorough reading of the novel from the perspective of Murdoch's
philosophical writings, especially the early essays. One of Levenson's main conten-

One does not even need to read her own philosophical work in order to understand and enjoy her novels. Iris Murdoch is not a modernist novelist in this narrow sense, full of learned allusions and intertexts, clouded by obscurity. Which, to be sure, is not to say that there aren't intertexts, allusions, or myths (sometimes in plenty) in her fiction, but the difference with Murdoch is that these do not seem to get in the way of one's readerly enjoyment as they undoubtedly do, at least initially, with Eliot. The difference may be due to Murdoch's not taking all these, by now almost inevitable, accoutrements of modernist fiction at face value, as seems to be the case when she filters them through several consciousnesses of varying maturity and sensitivity, as she does in *The Bell* with Dora, Toby, and Michael. And even in those instances when she does not do so, as, for example, in the first-person narration of *A Severed Head,* the reader is allowed to follow a process whereby consciousness is increased in gradual stages. That is, the reader's consciousness is enlarged in the same ways and at the same rate as the characters'.

So, to repeat, it is not necessary to delve first into Murdoch's philosophical work before one reads her fiction. In fact, a good argument can be made that it is better to start with the fiction even if one's ultimate aim is to understand the philosophy, since the fiction is, almost explicitly at times, presented as a testing ground for the philosophy—hers or, for that matter, anyone else's.[4] Instead of in-

---

tions is that in *The Bell* Murdoch exposes "the hollowness . . . in the [existentialist] theory of freedom-as-choice. A choice is a momentary act of mind. But we often act against our conscious choices, just as Dora chooses not to surrender her seat and then immediately rises. Something else takes over: perhaps an instinct or a disposition. For Murdoch there is something far larger than the local movement of mind that we call free choice; there is the entire framework of our lives—our beliefs, our emotions, our memories—which can be more determining than any conscious act of freedom" (2001, 566). Sharon Kaehele and Howard German anticipate some of Levenson's argument when they note that "[i]n stressing the role of emotions and other irrational motives for behavior, Miss Murdoch is countering the contemporary emphasis upon reason which is found in empiricism and existentialism with their stress upon making choices and performing actions" (1967, 560).

4. As Jack Stewart argues, "[f]iction provides an existential dimension lacking in

quiring abstractly about the nature of the good and whether and under what circumstances it might be possible to be good—or to seek abstractly to examine the bases of what might make a good society, as, say, Thomas More or even Plato do—Murdoch presents us with individuals who are trying to live good lives or trying to establish a society in which it may be possible to live a good life. That indeed is what the plot and characters of *The Bell* are all about, but here the plot and the characters are not figments of an abstract, hypothetical situation but rather mimic in abundant detail situations and people as they might be encountered in actual life, which means that Murdoch never strives to provide her readers (as most philosophers generally do) with unambiguous answers. There is always a dialectic between various ethical positions of which no single one is obviously privileged. Murdoch's real success lies in making us believe that her characters are real people plagued by real problems—or not plagued by them, as the case may be. It is this success that makes her a genuine novelist, the best writing in English in the latter half of the twentieth century.

Murdoch's novels, then, one should never forget, are novels. They are not simply narrative frameworks on which to hang dummies (or even smarties) who spout her ideas. Her characters are never mere mouthpieces. That this should be so is quite extraordinary in the context of most utopian or even dystopian fiction. Her focus is never on describing in detail what the principles are on which a genuinely or, as the case may be, ironically good society has been established, but rather on the people who inhabit that only vaguely defined society. Although *The Bell* is unquestionably a novel with ideas, it is first and foremost a modern novel plain and simple, that is, a work in which the emphasis is on the exploration of the consciousness of the characters, not on the exploration of the validity or nonvalidity of the ideas themselves. Of course, this way of conceiving

---

philosophy, whereby the validity of opposing views may be tested within the context of the proponents' lives and motives" (1980, 215–16).

and practicing the art of the novel is not "plain and simple" at all, but actually very complex and, relatively speaking, quite recent.

Subjectivity and the Novel

If we are to believe Erich Auerbach, serious attempts to depict consciousness (or subjectivity) in fiction only began in early nineteenth-century France with Stendhal, a tradition that was subsequently picked up and developed in Britain during the later nineteenth and early twentieth centuries by Henry James, James Joyce, and Virginia Woolf.[5] That Murdoch wants her readers to be aware that she too is writing in this tradition is evident from her playful allusion near the beginning of *The Bell* to Woolf's classic essay on the "new" way to depict character in fiction, "Mr. Bennett and Mrs. Brown." In that essay Woolf memorably describes how she (or at any rate her "persona") overhears a conversation between two strangers while riding in a train compartment with them, and then, on the basis of this fragmentary exchange as well as their dress and appearance, draws conclusions about them. For Woolf this is the way we "really" understand (and, of course, also misunderstand) people, that is fragmentarily and inconclusively, not in the totalized, materialistic manner of realistic novelists like Arnold Bennett.[6]

This "Woolfian" experience of others is also what happens with Dora, who near the beginning of the novel shares a railway compartment with "some nondescript grey ladies, an elderly man" and, most notably, sitting opposite her, a boy whom she estimates to be about eighteen and a man of about forty (18). It is their appearance that she focuses on and their conversation that she overhears and

5. "We may ask ourselves," Auerbach writes, "how it came about that modern consciousness of reality began to find literary form for the first time precisely in Henri Beyle of Grenoble" (1971, 459).

6. According to Woolf, none of the so-called Edwardian novelists so much as even looks at Mrs. Brown. Instead, they look out the window of the railway carriage at "factories, at Utopias, even at the decoration and the upholstery of the carriage; but never at her, never at life, never at human nature" (1961, 223).

draws conclusions about, such as the (correct) conclusion that the older man was unlikely to be the boy's father since there was "something pedagogic" about him, a characteristic that, given her husband Paul's propensities, she is no doubt particularly sensitive about (19). Dora, feeling herself entirely mistress of the situation, is also amused by what she interprets as the rather awkward responses of the attractive young boy to what she believes are her charms.

Unlike Woolf, however, Dora's role is not merely spectatorial. Suddenly, hearing the older man refer to Imber,[7] the name of the place to which she herself is going, she realizes that these two people represent not merely a mildly amusing chance encounter on a train about which she can speculate imaginatively and with impunity (as in the case of Woolf), but two people whom she is almost certain to have personal dealings with in the immediate future. Now, instead of strangers, the man and the boy threaten to impinge upon on her own, as it turns out, very inadequate sense of self. Now, hearing their voices emanating from the compartment which she has

7. The real Imber is a small village in Wiltshire, now in the center of an artillery range and generally closed to the public since 1943. Of the original buildings only Imber Court (the Manor House) and the church, St. Giles, are still standing, protected from military intervention. However, Murdoch's fictional Imber Court and Imber Abbey probably do not refer to the historical place but rather to the ecclesiastical "Ember Days and Ember Weeks" (Imber is an accepted variant spelling for Ember). According to the eleventh edition of the *Encyclopedia Britannica,* the Ember Days and Ember Weeks refer to "the four seasons set apart by the Western Church for special prayer and fasting, and the ordination of clergy, known in the medieval church as *quatour tempora,* or *jejuna quatuor temporum.* The Ember weeks are the complete weeks following Holy Cross day (September 14), St. Lucy's day (December 13), the first Sunday in Lent and Whitsun day. The Wednesdays, Fridays and Saturdays of these weeks are the Ember days distinctively, the following Sundays being the days of ordination." It is perhaps significant that Dora's arrival at Imber occurs in early September and that the dedication of the new bell is scheduled for what may be the first Sunday after Holy Cross day. There are no precise dates in the novel but the action is clearly limited to the period between early September and late October (1957?). Murdoch's description of her fictional Imber Court and Imber Abbey, on the other hand, is very precise, though its location is also kept vague. We know only that it is fairly near Oxford and within easy driving distance of Swindon. According to Sharon Kaehele and Howard German, the topography of Imber may represent an attempt on Murdoch's part to duplicate the topography of Dante's *Inferno* (1967, 557).

just left in hurried embarrassment, she suspects they must be talking about her. Now, instead of being amused and superior, she is afraid they will be "set before her as judges." Now she realizes that what she had thought would be a pleasant but insignificant interlude might very well turn out to be "merely the prelude to some far drearier knowledge" (22).

From all this it is perhaps fair to conclude that Mr. Bennett is not quite so negligible a figure for Murdoch as he was for Woolf, and that indeed he and not just Virginia Woolf were holding tickets on the same train as Dora (he is, perhaps, the aforementioned "elderly man")—a train that leads all its passengers, even those who thought they were just riding along in order to observe their fellow travelers and listen to their talk, to destinations that they as yet know little of.[8] Sartre, too, it seems, is also seated somewhere in the same compartment, perhaps disguised as one of the "nondescript grey ladies," speculating sardonically about these goings-on, for it is only when Dora grows aware that her gaze has evoked (or perhaps even provoked) an answering gaze that she also becomes aware that she is not alone, that a whole world—the world of Imber, to be precise, inhabited by these two people and also by her husband Paul—actually *exists,* and has done so for some time already, quite apart from her own separate existence and consciousness.

And, of course, all along Dora has been accompanied by Murdoch herself or, *pace* Wayne Booth, by her occasionally visible fictional representative, the unnamed but extremely knowledgeable narrator. Though, given the predominance of the technique of "style indirect libre" (or as it is usually called in English, "free indirect discourse")[9] in the narration of the novel, it is sometimes dif-

---

8. In her book on Sartre, Murdoch finds fault with Woolf's characters for being "presented as a series of more or less discrete experiences, connected by tone and colour rather than by any thread of consistent struggle or purpose" (1974, 56).

9. In the English translation of Franz Stanzel's *Theorie des Erzählens* (1979) (*A Theory of Narrative,* 1986), the original German term "erlebte Rede" is translated as "free indirect style" (actually a literal translation of the usual French phrase for this narra-

ficult to distinguish the voice of the narrator from the thoughts of
the three characters to whose consciousnesses we are given access,
there are numerous occasions throughout the novel when it is clear
that we are in the presence of a judging, generalizing observer, rather like the even more intrusive "commentator" of E. M. Forster's
novels.[10] As with Forster, Murdoch's narrator is often ironic, as she
is, in a rather gentle way, in reminding us repeatedly of young Toby's fondness for the somewhat unusual word "rebarbative," whose
meaning he has only recently learned; or, somewhat less gently, in
her ironic treatment, especially at the beginning of the novel, of Dora's inability to make meaningful choices, either with regard to trivial matters (such as yielding her seat in the train to an obnoxious
older woman) or very serious ones (notably what to do about her
unsatisfactory marriage to Paul Greenfield).

This use of irony to govern the reader's response to character is,
however, probably not to be set down to a process of actual narrative intrusion.[11] But there can be no doubt about the narrator's delib-

---

tive device). In his section on "The Presentation of Consciousness," Stanzel argues
that "[f]rom a detailed analysis of the frequency and distribution of the presentation
of inside views among the individual characters of the novel, conclusions can sometimes be drawn about the values and attitudes in an author's deeper layers of consciousness" (1986, 128–29).

10. Though the similarity to Forsterian techniques of narration is not, I think,
deliberate, as it is in the case of Woolf, Murdoch may intend her readers to think in a
general way of Bloomsbury idealism—and Bloomsbury religious naiveté—in connection with Imber. So Dora's name, appearance, and association with the Slade, as well
as her unhappy marriage to the vaguely "foreign" and formidably jealous Paul Greenfield and her subsequent attachment to the homosexual Michael, strongly evoke aspects of Dora Carrington's life, though Murdoch's Dora (aside from her dealings with
the bell) leads a far more conventional life than Carrington did with Mark Gertler and
Lytton Strachey. Murdoch may also mean us to think of Woolf's famous essay "The
Death of a Moth" in connection with Dora's liberation of a Red Admiral butterfly
just after arriving at the railway station nearest Imber.

11. In *The Black Prince* (1973), Murdoch's principal narrator, Bradley Pearson, argues that "we may attempt to attain truth through irony. (An angel might make of
this a concise definition of the limits of human understanding.) Almost any tale of
our doings is comic. We are bottomlessly comic to each other. Even the most adored
and beloved person is comic to his lover. The novel is a comic form. Language is a
comic form, and makes jokes in its sleep. God, if he existed, would laugh at his cre-

erate interference in such instances as the introductory (and rather ominous) comment about Michael Meade's position as "unofficial leader" of the Imber community: "Those who hope, by retiring from the world, to earn a holiday from human frailty, in themselves and others, are usually disappointed" (85). Or her observation about the incipient love relationship between Michael and Nick Fawley: "The talk of lovers who have just declared their love is one of life's most sweet delights" (104). Or her sardonic generalization about how Michael's kiss has affected Toby's outlook on life: "Toby had received, though not yet digested, one of the earliest lessons of adult life: that one is never secure" (160). Or her almost immediately following comment about Toby's rushing to judgment: "Like all inexperienced people, Toby tended to make all-or-nothing judgements" (161). And so on and so forth.

The narrative strategy of the supposedly old-fashioned "Bennett" sort of novel, it should be obvious by now, is still effectively present in Murdoch's fiction. Still, despite the presence of a guiding and sometimes intrusive narrator, most of the action and much of the inner nature of the characters are perceived from the point of view (as well as via the technique of "style indirect libre") of three principal figures: Dora, Toby, and Michael. The development of these shifting perspectives does not seem to be consistent, though in general there is a progression from Dora to Toby to Michael. To appreciate just how Murdoch manages this progression, it might be useful to tabulate roughly the order and proportions she devotes to presenting the consciousness of each of these three characters. The novel begins with Dora Greenfield, who, after being briefly introduced by the narrator, becomes the initial "center of consciousness" of the novel (to use Henry James's term). Partly through direct entry into Dora's thoughts and emotions, partly through the indirect approach of free indirect discourse, Murdoch largely presents the

---

ation. Yet it is also the case that life is horrible, without metaphysical sense, wrecked by chance, pain and the close prospect of death. Out of this is born irony, our dangerous and necessary tool" (55).

initial parts (that is, most of the first three chapters) of the novel from Dora's very limited point of view. Chapters 5, 9, 14, 20, 22, and parts of the last chapter (26) are similarly narrated from Dora's perspective. In terms of the number of pages, Dora's point of view predominates in the novel, with well over a third of the book devoted to her developing consciousness. The depiction of Toby Gashe's consciousness, on the other hand, is confined to only about fifty pages, namely, chapters 4, 10, the first part of 12, 13, 17, and 21. Finally, the rendering of Michael Meade's consciousness occupies a little less than a third of the novel, beginning with chapters 6, 7, and 8, and continuing with the latter half of chapter 12, chapters 16, 18, 25, and parts of 26.

Given this striking division of the novel into three distinct and disproportionate points of view—actually four, if one also counts, as one no doubt should, the perspective of the unnamed narrator—one inevitably wonders what the point of it all might be. Part of the "point" undoubtedly—and this is true not only of Murdoch's novel but of all "center of consciousness" or so-called perspectival narration—is to show the limitations of those centers of consciousness and thereby place in question the truth of what they have perceived. Truth, in other words, ceases to be absolute insofar as it is made relative to the limited and fallible perspective of the individual perceiver. (Truth, however, still remains absolute as far as Murdoch's narrator is concerned.) Put another way, life has ceased to be secure—if it ever was—not only for Toby, but also for Dora and Michael.[12]

There may be another factor involved here too. According to Murdoch, in Sartre's view "the mode of self-awareness of the modern

12. There is an interesting analogue here to the way Mrs. Ramsay is presented in Virginia Woolf's *To the Lighthouse*. According to Auerbach, "[t]he essential characteristic of the technique represented by Virginia Woolf is that we are given not merely one person whose consciousness . . . is rendered, but many persons, with frequent shifts from one to the other. . . . The multiplicity of persons suggests that we are here after all confronted with an endeavor to investigate an objective reality . . . she is as it were encircled by the content of all the various consciousnesses directed upon her" (1971, 536).

novelist is the internal monologue [i.e., free indirect discourse]. . . . The modern novelist is not usually telling us about events as if they were past and remembered; he is presenting them, through the consciousness of his people, as if they were happening now." Murdoch goes on to point out that for Sartre, however, character cannot be revealed in this manner, since for him "'[c]haracter has no distinct existence except as an object of knowledge of other people.'" The way to resolve this difficulty, again in Sartre's view, is "'to work in a variety of outside views of each person, so that we may obtain an "objective" picture.'" Though Murdoch explicitly disagrees with Sartre's argument, it may be that it nevertheless has influenced her decision to portray "character" in *The Bell* by providing a series of different internal perspectives (1974, 53–4).

That still leaves open the question, however, as to why Murdoch should have chosen to present the consciousness of precisely these three people, and in precisely this order. If, for example, the unexplored psychological perspectives of several other important characters—Nick, James Tayper Pace, and the Abbess spring to mind—had been chosen as well as or instead of the ones Murdoch did choose, we would have been presented with a very different kind of novel. So too, for that matter, if the events of the novel had affected first the consciousness of Michael, then of Dora, and finally of Toby, instead of in the very different order in which Murdoch chose to present that impact.

To this line of inquiry one can of course simply answer: Why not? Some sort of choice, after all, has to be made, not only by the fictional Dora and the fictional Michael but also by the very real Murdoch. Still, whatever else we can or should say about Murdoch's choice, it is a significant choice, not merely a random one. The significance of her choice may be (at least if we define "significance" in the manner of E. D. Hirsch, as referring to whatever meaning an event or character has for the reader rather than for the author), in the case of deciding to begin the novel with Dora, that she thereby is able to provide, in a very natural way, some of the needed expository information about what Imber and its inhabitants are like. In this sense, Dora's introductory role is strongly reminiscent of the old and sometimes even hackneyed device (especially popular in utopian fictions) of having the outsider discover what the social institutions are like that govern the lives of the people inside. The same is true, at least initially, of Toby—another outsider who feels compelled to find out what's inside (especially inside the Abbey)—as it is true too of Dora, to find out what's inside the self. In this way the reader is allowed entry, without undue intrusion, and while no doubt sharing many of the same doubts and skeptical reactions as Dora (and to a much lesser degree, Toby), into what the "inside" is like. Also, both characters are young, attractive, and unformed; both are looking for answers—especially Dora, but also Toby later on—as to how to live their lives, which is why a good deal of the novel (particularly those parts devoted to rendering the consciousnesses of Dora and Toby) reads like a *Bildungsroman*.

But even if we grant the hypothesis that Dora and Toby are being used by Murdoch in order to introduce her readers, through their mental and emotional responses, to the world of Imber, there remains the question as to why she needs two such characters rather than just one. Is it in order to provide, even at this early stage in the novel, differing perspectives on the "same" reality, thereby achieving a more radical relativization of it? Is it in order to show how young people of different genders, life experience, and religious outlooks respond to a structured world that is both new and strange to them? Is it to show how, under the influence of Imber Court and Imber Abbey, a "guilty" outsider like Dora can eventually become innocent; and how Toby, at first innocent, can become "guilty," at least in his own eyes (as well as in those of Nick)? Dora too is initially hostile to the religious aspects of life at Imber, but is eventually won over, whereas Toby is initially sympathetic and is, for a time at least, alienated.

Perhaps more important, novelistically speaking, is the function of these two characters in preparing the way for our encounter with

Michael's consciousness. We are first made to see him through their eyes before we are allowed to see him through his own. Their eyes "see" him, to begin with, as rather ordinary. Later on he becomes the major influence in their lives during their stay at Imber. Indeed, he is already, or becomes in the progress of the narrative, the major influence on just about every one of the principal characters in the novel, including Nick and Catherine Fawley, and perhaps not even excluding James Tayper Pace.

Michael Meade is a good man, or at least he would like to be a good man, as is evident not only from his constant analysis of the motives for his own behavior with respect to the other characters but from his long-standing ambition to become a priest, that is, in his view, a kind of professionally good man. Unlike Dora and Toby, when we first meet him he is already a very complex personality; hence we fittingly know more about his past—about how he came to be the complex person he is—than about that of any other character in the novel; indeed, a whole chapter (7) is devoted to it. That is not to say, however, that he is utterly unlike the other two centers of consciousness in the novel. He especially resembles Dora in his habit of being decisively indecisive.

This characteristic is especially evident when Michael wonders how to deal with Toby—about "deciding what to do," as he puts it to himself—after having impulsively kissed him the evening before. He quickly notices that, as with a similar but more deliberate incident involving Nick some thirteen years earlier, he is now "intensely anxious to see Toby again and to speak to him about what had occurred." He then considers the possibility of playing safe by simply disregarding the matter altogether, so as not to prolong the incident or make it appear more important to Toby than it actually was. He resolves to seek enlightenment by visiting the Abbey chapel and praying. His prayers produce a certain calming effect but they also make him realize that he has in fact sinned against the boy, that is, he decides that the incident was indeed important. Now he further "decides" that it would be better to "postpone the interview till the following day," since such a delay would, he believes, induce greater coolness and calm. Later the same day, after a period of reflection and hard physical labor in the garden, he reverses that decision, concluding that it would now seem "gratuitously mystifying to Toby, to postpone the interview." He then decides that he needs to clear the air almost at once, since his current state of emotional upset has "made all other activity impossible."

Having now "decided to wait no longer," Michael "decide[s] not to interview Toby in his office or bedroom." He wants the interview to be "business-like, not intimate." He now devotes his attention to planning the interview and to "deciding what he was going to say, even with a sort of satisfaction." As usual, however, his plans don't quite work out. Though he successfully apologizes to Toby after taking him out that evening into the woods to observe and listen to the almost magical flight of the nightjars, he can't resist a final moment of intimacy. When, subsequent to his apology, Toby "forgives" him, Michael reaches out with "his hand blindly toward the boy— and as if drawn magnetically Toby's hand met his in a strong grip. They stood silently together in the darkness" (166–70).

Some, but definitely not all, of Murdoch's rendering of Michael's tortuous mental gymnastics in making up his mind and then changing it again (and again) while trying to reach a decision about how to deal with the "problem" of Toby is, as in the more obvious case of Dora, clearly intended to be comic. The serious part, however, though less obvious, is also more important, and has to do with the crucial existentialist issue of choice, especially as described by Sartre and critiqued by Murdoch. (Sartre is wrong, according to Murdoch, to describe all choice as conscious choice, rejecting the Freudian notion of the unconscious. He is, as she puts it succinctly in her title, a "romantic rationalist" [1974, 27].) Despite the evident comedy and irony here, Murdoch manages to make Michael into a sympathetic and not just a ridiculous character, since he is shown to be able to see (or at least to be able to speculate persuasively about) the possible and perhaps even probable consequences of several different courses of action.[13] Like Prufrock, but also like Hamlet, Michael is subjected to "decisions and revisions which a minute will reverse." His vacillation suggests weakness while at the same time suggesting intellectual complexity. And it also makes him into a more attractive personality, because it is "human" to vacillate and to be weak.[14]

Perfection and Reality

With Michael Meade we also confront the problem of the "brotherhood," that is, the as yet incomplete (and never to completed) realization of the "idea of making the Court [Imber Court] the home of a permanent lay community attached to the Abbey," an idea originally proposed to Michael by the Abbess (81). In her conception, the Imber community would be "an intermediary form of life" for those "many" people, including of course Michael himself, "who can live neither in the world nor out of it . . . a kind of sick people, whose desire for God makes them unsatisfactory citizens of an ordinary life, but whose strength or temperament fails them to surrender the world completely" (81). "Our duty," the Abbess tells Michael by way of justifying this halfway house of the spirit, "is not necessarily to seek the highest regardless of the realities of

13. It is the complexity with which Murdoch portrays Michael that A. S. Byatt finds "really good" about *The Bell*, specifically "the way in which the consequences of the moral decisions he must take are almost never clear to the reader in advance"—or even, one might add, to himself (1956, 86).

14. The very striking pattern of doubling in this novel is, I think, related to this important theme of choice. Most obviously there are the two bells (with their identical names but very different mottoes), the old and the new, the one that is raised and the other that is sunk; but there are also Imber Court and Imber Abbey, the spiritually "sick" and the spiritually healthy communities; there are the two contrasting leaders of the Imber community, Michael Meade and James Tayper Pace, with their two important but opposing sermons; there are the twins, Nick and Catherine Fawley; there are the repeated confessions by Michael's adolescent lovers, Nick and Toby; there is the specious "world," as represented for Dora by Noel Spens, and the unwordly "reality" of the National Gallery; there is the medieval legend of the drowned nun (and Michael's recurrent dream about it) and there is the would-be nun Catherine's attempt to drown herself; and finally there are the opposing values of secular love and spiritual love, most notably represented for Michael by Nick and the Abbess.

our spiritual life as it in fact is, but to seek that place, that task, those people, which will make our spiritual life most constantly grow and flourish" (81). The repeated "our" in the Abbess's words, to be sure, is evidently not meant to include the Abbess herself, since she has unquestionably sought to follow the "highest," for otherwise she would not be what (and where) she is; instead, the "our" refers exclusively to spiritually "sick" people like Michael whose lives consist, or so the Abbess seems to want us to believe, of continual compromises with the ideal.[15]

Michael wants to be good and may even be good, but he does not always see clearly what the good is. He hopes to seek the highest (e.g., to be a priest) but he also knows that the confused "realities" of his spiritual life may not permit him to achieve it. In this respect he also differs greatly from the other leading "brother" in the group, James Tayper Pace. This difference—and the importance of that difference for the novel—is made clear in the two contrasting sermons which James and Michael deliver to the assembled community on successive Sundays. In his sermon (the first of the two), James warns against complexity and imagination—that is, against what Sartre calls subjectivism. His opening sentence, along with the rest of his sermon, is radically anti-Sartrean, though undoubtedly since he seems not much given to reading philosophy, he is not aware of this aspect of what he is saying—and perhaps would not care if he was. (Sartre's name is never mentioned, here or anywhere else in the book.) "The chief requirement of the good life," James begins by saying, "'is to live without any image of oneself. . . . The study of personality, indeed the whole conception of personality, is,

---

15. According to Peter Conradi, Murdoch "admitted a little to identifying" with the Abbess (Conradi 2001b, 145). There may also be a connection between the unnamed fictional Abbess and Dame Magdalene Mary Euan-Smith, the "notable abbess" of the Anglican Benedictine Malling Abbey in Kent, whom Murdoch visited several times, starting in October 1946 (Conradi 2001a, 247–48). Murdoch also admitted to sympathizing with "the vision of an ideal community in which work would once again be creative and meaningful and human brotherhood be restored" (quoted in Conradi 2001b, 146).

as I see it, dangerous to goodness. We were told at school, at least I was told at school, to have ideals. This, it seems to me, is rot. Ideals are dreams. They come between us and reality—when what we need most is precisely to see reality. *And that is something outside us.* Where perfection is, reality is" (131, emphasis added).

Contrast these remarks with what Jean-Paul Sartre says in his book on existentialism (1947).[16] According to Sartre, the first principle of existentialism is "subjectivity," or in other words (his words): "Man is nothing else but what he makes of himself." For the Sartrean existentialist, furthermore, it is a fundamental tenet "that it is impossible to transcend human subjectivity." As a result, "there is not a single one of our acts which does not create an image of man as we think he ought to be." By being what I am, in other words, I have chosen what I am. Choice is implicit in everything I do, and is the basis of who I am. In choosing to be who I am I have also created "a certain image of man of my own choosing. In choosing myself, I choose man" (18–21). The search for perfection, in other words, is a search for a subjective perfection—often called an "ideal"—and that search is inescapably a function of the image we choose (whether deliberately or not) to have of our selves, an image which then becomes just as inescapably the image we implicitly ask others to have of themselves too. This image is never of something that is outside of us but always of something that is inside of us. It is a product of our consciousness, our subjectivity.

For James, on the other hand, probing "the filth of our minds or regarding ourselves as unique and interesting sinners . . . is essentially something tedious, something to be shunned and not something to be investigated. . . . We should consider not what delights us or what disgusts us, morally speaking, but what is enjoined and what is forbidden." James is not naive or stupid. He is, as we can see, fully aware of the existence of a subjective realm of experience.

16. In a 1950 BBC broadcast Murdoch describes this, somewhat patronizingly, as "a rather bad little book" (1997, 111).

He simply objects to the kind of experience which such subjectivity provides. The preoccupation with subjectivity, in his view, prevents us from pursuing the reality of perfection. Instead of delving into our consciousness, he wants us to "quite simply" follow the rules, which means, for example, that "truth is not glorious, it is just enjoined; sodomy is not disgusting, it is just forbidden. These are rules by which we should freely judge ourselves and others too" (132). James concludes his sermon by pointing to Catherine Fawley, who is soon to join the secluded order of Anglican Benedictine nuns in the nearby Abbey. He identifies her as a paragon of innocence and equates her with the (new) bell, a bell that is made, as he puts it, "to speak out," and which has no "hidden mechanism" (135).

How right or wrong is James in rejecting subjectivity in favor of rules? Or in choosing Catherine as an "image" of perfection? And do we need to be aware of Sartre's existentialist views on the matter to be able to decide if he is right or wrong? On the one hand, the answer to the last question would seem to be "quite simple": namely, a resounding no. No, because in pointing to Catherine as the emblem of external perfection, James is utterly wrong, as emerges later when it turns out that Catherine is neither innocent (she loves Michael and may have had an incestuous relationship with her twin brother Nick) nor possessed of a "mechanism" that is easily comprehended. (We are never provided with a full or even remotely satisfactory explanation of why she is as she is or acts as she does.) When the (old) bell "speaks out" at Dora's instigation, and when the (new) bell sinks into the lake because of some "hidden mechanism" devised by Catherine's brother, Imber's official mechanic, the two bells seem to pronounce her doom—or so she seems subjectively to conclude. James too, we must never forget, is like Michael and the other "full" members of the Imber community, a spiritually "sick" person—otherwise he wouldn't be there—and hence we need to wonder if his views may not also be affected (infected?) by his sickness.

On the other hand, can we fairly say that James is proved entirely wrong? Apparently not, at least not if we take at face value Dora's subsequent epiphanic experience in the National Gallery. Having, on the spur of the moment, escaped what she initially thinks of as the dreary, rule-ridden world of Imber, along with her domineering husband, for the pleasures of London and her sometime adulterous playmate, Noel Spens, she suddenly realizes that she is being just as much "organized" in Noel's world as she was in Paul's. Driven by some unconscious instinct, she makes for the National Gallery, looks at various familiar paintings, and finally stops before Gainsborough's picture of his two daughters. Here she undergoes a "revelation"—one which in part echoes James's sermon and perhaps serves to confirm it:

> It occurred to her that here at last was something real and something perfect. Who had said that about perfection and reality being in the same place? Here was something her consciousness could not wretchedly devour, and by making it a part of her fantasy make it worthless. Even Paul, she thought, only existed now as someone she dreamt about; or else as a vague external menace never really encountered and understood. But the pictures were something real outside herself, which spoke to her kindly and yet in sovereign tones, something superior and good whose presence destroyed the dreary trance-like solipsism of her earlier mood. When the world had seemed to be subjective it had seemed to be without interest or value. But now there was something else in it after all. (190–91)

Reality (great art) and perfection (also great art) do seem to be synonymous, as well as external rather than internal manifestations, not, in other words, simply products of an all-devouring subjectivity.[17] So James is perhaps right after all? Perhaps, though again Murdoch (or her otherwise intrusive narrator) does not provide us with

17. In "The Idea of Perfection," the opening chapter in *The Sovereignty of Good*, Murdoch argues that "aesthetic situations are not so much analogies of morals as cases of morals. Virtue is *au fond* the same in the artist as in the good man in that it is a selfless attention to nature" (1971, 41). And in *The Fire and the Sun* she almost explicitly confirms the rightness of Dora's response in the National Gallery when she writes that "[g]ood art, thought of as symbolic force rather than statement, provides a stirring image of a pure transcendent value, a steady visible enduring higher good, and perhaps provides for many people, in an unreligious age without prayer or sac-

conclusive evidence one way or the other, but instead seems to want us to make up our own minds on the limited evidence there is. So, only a few hours after having had her revelation about subjectivism and reality in the National Gallery, Dora proposes to Toby (who has just told her about finding what may be a huge bell in the lake) a preposterous plan to substitute the old bell for the new and thereby produce a kind of phony miracle. "James said," she tells Toby by way of feeble justification, "that the age of miracles wasn't over" (198). Here indeed Dora is, by choosing for herself, choosing also for Toby, and indeed for the rest of the community, an "image" of reality that is false and misleading. She allows her powerful imagination (her subjectivity) to overcome her sense of reality. Here surely there is no sign of perfection, and also very little sign of reality.

James's position is moreover placed in doubt by Michael's sermon, delivered the following Sunday, a sermon which is in no way overtly indebted to Sartre's views on subjectivity but is based rather on Michael's own sense of personal inadequacy. Recognizing that he is a weak man (the sermon is delivered not long after Michael has kissed Toby), his principal theme is, though he does not say so explicitly: "Where imperfection is, there reality is."[18] In Michael's view, it is the hubris of thinking that perfection is possible that makes for disaster—or for tragedy, as Aristotle, following a similar train of thought, might say. The good man, therefore, is not the man who unthinkingly obeys the rules but the fallen, flawed man who uncertainly gropes his way toward acting rightly. In reply to James's citation of Saint Paul's assertion that the "good man lives by faith (Galatians, three eleven)," Michael could very well have referred to the parable of the prodigal son, implying that the sinner who goes first

---

raments, their clearest *experience* of something grasped as separate and precious and beneficial and held quietly and unpossessively in the attention" (1977, 76–77).

18. In *Acastos* Murdoch has Socrates argue that "[w]e are not gods. What you [Plato] call the whole truth is only for them. So our truth must include, must *embrace* the idea of the second best, that all our thought will be incomplete and all our art tainted by selfishness" (1986, 62).

astray and then finds his way is a better man than the virtuous man who has never strayed at all. The claims of faith, in other words, are balanced by those of good works, or at least they traditionally have been. Should one, like James, love a cloistered virtue (in his mistaken view, a virtue embodied by Catherine) and condemn an uncloistered one, one that is, say, more genuinely embodied by Toby? Or should one, like Michael, prefer an uncloistered virtue, without at the same time condemning the cloistered one?

In the immediate proximity of the cloister, the right answer would seem to be James's rather than Michael's, but the very existence of the Imber community—of which James too is a prominent member—suggests that not all of us are able to practice or even tolerate (e.g., Dora) a cloistered virtue, or at least not all the time. Does that mean that there is no virtue outside the cloister? Surely not.

That "we" are perhaps meant to think of Michael's sermon as more applicable to "our" lives (generally lived outside the cloister) than James's is indirectly confirmed by the fact that Michael is a (the?) central character of the book, whereas James is a relatively marginal one. Subjectivity evidently matters to Murdoch, for, while Michael's consciousness is extensively explored in the course of the narrative, we are never granted access to James's. Surely James does not just consist of a robot-like "mechanism" of rules (in the way that perhaps Mrs. Mark does)? Surely he also possesses a consciousness? Why then prefer Michael's consciousness to James's? The answer to this question may be that Michael's consciousness is more interesting, novelistically speaking. Novels, at least most modern ones (and certainly Murdoch's), tend to deal, as we have seen, with subjective states—with consciousness—and Michael evidently has a great deal more (and more complex) consciousness than does James.

The Voices of Love

Paradoxically, Michael's position regarding the seeming irrelevance of cloistered virtue to the lives of the inhabitants of the Imber community is partly confirmed by the principal inhabitant of the cloister herself, the Abbess. Just before closing her unsatisfactory interview with him during the period of crisis occasioned by the raising of the bell, she delivers a kind of mini-sermon to him in which she affirms central aspects of Michael's position. She stresses, for example, the gap between intention and realization, as Michael did in implicitly equating goodness with imperfection. She goes on to define goodness as an overflow (one is reminded here that the "market garden" which is the principal economic activity of the Imber community is based on *surplus* production); and she points out that "we can only learn to love by loving." She then concludes by remarking that "[i]mperfect love must not be condemned and rejected, but made perfect. The way is always forward, never back" (235).

Here the Abbess raises, and answers affirmatively, one of the principal questions that Michael has sought in vain to answer satisfactorily for himself, namely: is his homosexual love for Nick—and for Toby—good or bad? Can sexual love—especially the kind of homosexual pedophilia that Michael is prone to—be included in what the Abbess terms "imperfect love," or is such love always too imperfect, too close to self-love, to ever be made "perfect"? The Abbess does not clarify the issue but it is surely significant that, at the close of his own sermon, Michael had thought to himself something similar when he concluded that God, after all, had made him what he was and "he did not think that God had made him a monster" (205). (In maintaining this position, Michael deviates sharply from Sartre's idea that we invariably choose who we are.) This conclusion echoes an earlier reflection made when his infatuation with Nick was at its height, namely, that "his religion and passions sprang from the same source" (105). Close to the end of the novel, while still grieving for Nick's death by his own hand, Michael finds a kind of consolation in the thought that "[s]o great a love must have contained some grain of good" (307).

But if this is so, then Paul Greenfield's possessive and sometimes fiercely aggressive love for Dora must also contain a grain of good. It too must be an imperfect love waiting to be made perfect. The

same must be true also, for that matter, of Nick's apparently incestuous love for his sister, Catherine, whom "he loved, he swore, with
a Byronic passion" (104). In fact, none of the loves expressed in the
novel seems to be anything at all close to "perfect," except possibly
for the love felt by the dog Murphy for Nick. (Ironically, the word
"dog," we should recall in this connection, is a common anagram
for God, and Nick's Christian name is sometimes, though not in the
novel, ominously preceded by the adjective "Old.")

The bell, especially the old bell, may help us understand a little
better the relationship between secular (especially sexual) love and
religious or spiritual love, a topic which is, as Murdoch indicates by
choosing to refer to the bell (which one?) in her title, centrally important. The mechanism of the bell, which both James and Michael
mention in their respective sermons, is both real and symbolic—in
both cases. We can agree with James when he states that, from a
physical as well as spiritual point of view, the bell exhibits "simplicity. There is no hidden mechanism" (135). But we can also agree with
Michael that the bell's mechanism is symbolic of much more than
mere simplicity; we can agree that, spiritually speaking, "[t]he swing
that takes it down must also take it up." This means—and here Michael is consciously contradicting James—that "[w]e must work from
inside outwards," or from inner subjectivity to outer reality, so that
"by using exactly that energy which we have, [we will] acquire more.
This is [and here Michael echoes an earlier quotation of the Abbess]
the wisdom of the serpent. This is the struggle, pleasing surely in the
sight of God, to become more fully and deeply the person that we
are" (204). How much more subjective can Michael become?

For Michael, then, the down and up movement of the bell is
symbolic of the down and up movement from imperfect to perfect
love, whereas for James the easily comprehended mechanism of the
bell is symbolic of the easily comprehended morality enjoined by
God. But neither James's nor even Michael's sermon exhausts the
symbolic potential of the bell(s). The bells themselves explicitly refer to their (different) symbolic functions. The motto inscribed on

the old bell is *Vox ego sum Amoris. Gabriel vocor* (I am the voice of love. My name is Gabriel). Here, the Archangel Gabriel who is the voice of love seems to be the same Gabriel who came to tell Mary that she was with child through the love of God. The motto written on the new bell, on the other hand, seems to refer to a very different Gabriel (the new bell is also called Gabriel), that is, the Gabriel who notoriously blows the last trumpet when the world is about to come to an end: *Defunctos ploro, vivos voco, fulmina frango . . . Gabriel vocor* (I mourn the dead, I call the living, I break the lightning bolts. My name is Gabriel).

It is surely symbolic that it is into the mouth of the old bell, the bell that is the voice of love, that Toby and Dora fall in an erotic embrace, thereby making it "speak out," soon after they have succeeded in raising it. They also thereby set in motion the events that are adumbrated in the legend of the drowned nun, her fallen lover, and the bishop's curse (events that are also partly anticipated in Michael's recurrent dream about the corpse of a drowned nun), and which find their approximation in reality in Catherine's near drowning and her brother/lover's suicide. Here extreme subjectivity and brutal reality join to produce tragic consequences. But here also, at least symbolically, erotic love and spiritual love join in a kind of continuum that is reminiscent of the Abbess's remark about the conjunction of imperfect and perfect love. The bell, after all, though on the one hand undoubtedly the traditional symbol of religious or spiritual expression—it rings to bring believers into the house of God—is also, on the other hand, an obvious and very "simple" mechanical symbol of the sexual act, with a long and hard clapper moving actively inside a hollow receptacle. Secular and spiritual love unite in the symbol of the bell.[19]

19. Critics have reacted variously to the symbolic bell. A. S. Byatt finds it unsuccessful as a symbol and James's and Michael's interpretations of it "contrived" (1965, 198). For Dorothy Winsor the old bell "is a symbol of forces which are potentially transformable but which the inhabitants of Imber Court have denied and buried" (1980, 150). According to Stephen Wall, it is "difficult to postulate for the bell a static or fixed symbolic meaning. In fact, its significance alters, according to the perspective

James's and Michael's sermons, along with the Abbess's mini-
sermon, may be the most important sermons in the novel, but there
is still one further "sermon" to discuss, a sermon which, like the Abbess's to Michael, is delivered to an audience of one: Nick's mock
"sermon" to Toby. His sermon is not really occasioned by his having witnessed the kiss between Michael and Toby, since prior to this
event he tells Toby that "I'll give you a sermon one day. . . . They
haven't asked me to spout, so I'll give you a private one." In the
event, an inebriated Nick has literally to force his sermon down the
ears of a very reluctant Toby, who by this time is very much occupied by a complex of new emotions involving Michael and Dora.

"Dearly beloved," Nick ironically addresses the trapped Toby,
"we are come of a fallen race, we are sinners one and all. Gone are
the days in the Garden, the days of our innocence when we loved
each other and were happy. Now we are set each man against his fellow and the mark of Cain is upon us, and with our sin comes grief
and hatred and shame." So much for the vaunted "brotherhood,"
at any rate as far as Nick is concerned. The only brotherhood he is
aware of, or at least that he wishes to endorse, is the brotherhood of
Cain and Abel. Nick then goes on to reveal that he knows all about
Toby's relations with Michael, including the secret meetings, as well
as his attempt to seduce a not very reluctant Dora. "'I've seen you at
it,' said Nick. 'I've seen your love life in the woods, tempting our virtuous leader to sodomy and our delightful penitent to adultery. . . .
And what about your little frolic with the bell? Oh, yes, I know all
about the bell too, and that faked-up miracle you're planning with
your female sweetheart'" (258–59).

Nick, it turns out, knows everything, though just how he has
acquired this extensive knowledge remains unclear. What is clear,
however, is that he wants to make this knowledge public, using Toby
as the means. Toby, in short, is to "confess"; he is to experience, as

---

from which it is viewed." From this it follows that the symbol of the bell "serves as a
central point round which the plot of the book is organised, but it is not the reposi-
tory of the novel's meaning" (1963, 271).

Nick apparently did himself in similar circumstances some thirteen years earlier, "the joys of repentance, the delights of confession, the delicious pleasure of writhing and grovelling in the dust. *O felix culpa!*" (257).[20] Unless Toby goes to tell James the "truth" about what has happened, Nick threatens to do so himself, suggesting ironically (and no doubt again on the basis of personal experience) that "one never paints oneself so black as the unprejudiced and unsympathetic spectator can paint one. Another of the charms of confession" (260).

It is not entirely clear what Nick's ultimate motives are in thus forcing a "confession" on Toby. It may be that he wishes another young person to experience the betrayal that he himself perpetrated on Michael years earlier, thereby proving to himself that he, too, is no "monster." Or he may simply be a troublemaker, as James had warned Michael that he would be. Perhaps by discrediting Michael and by "uncloseting" him, he hopes to break his sister Catherine's love for Michael, or at least prevent her entry into the Abbey. Or he may actually be adhering unconsciously (though there seems very little about Nick that is unconscious; he is in that sense very Sartrean) to James's advice to speak the truth no matter what the consequences; the truth (or the "truth"), it seems, is always preferable to a lie or a half-truth. In any case, this is Nick's only action which earns James's unqualified approval. Or it may be that Nick is jealous of Toby, while still retaining his affection (love?) and admiration for Michael. Significantly, while compelling Toby to repeat the act by which he himself lost Michael's love and destroyed Michael's career, he also reverses Toby's action of raising the old bell by arranging to sink the new one. Nick and Toby are at one and the same time very much alike and very dissimilar—like Cain and Abel?[21]

20. Before going on to dismiss all prior criticism on *The Bell* as "futile," David Beams proposes a rigidly allegorical reading, which he describes as new and coherent, based on the idea of the "fortunate fall" (1988, 419).

21. Dorothy Jones identifies Nick as one of two "rejected outsider[s]" in the novel, the other being Dora, and sees his motivation for forcing Toby to confess as sado-

When Michael is confronted by James after Toby has "confessed" to him, he at first, and perhaps at last too, thinks Nick did it out of revenge. By forcing Toby to play the part Nick himself had played years earlier, "[h]is revenge could not have been more perfect" (295). When Nick shortly thereafter kills himself—again the motives are unclear—Michael realizes that he had been wrong: Nick's revenge had not yet been perfect.[22] "It was perfect now" (297). Now Michael will never be able to make up for the neglect he had deliberately shown Nick—his own revenge, as it were. By now the word "perfect" carries unmistakable overtones, echoing as it does James's sermon: "Where perfection is, reality is." Reality has certainly arrived on the scene: Nick is really dead, perfectly dead. But does this newly perfected reality confirm James's thesis or not? Was it "good" that Nick confessed and thereby destroyed Michael's hopes to become a priest? Was it "good" that he made Toby confess too, with even more disastrous results? And was it, in both cases, the truth that was spoken, loudly and clearly—like a bell—in these confessions?

It is the muscularly Christian bell—the new bell invoked by that Christian soldier, James Tayper Pace—the bell that calls the living and the dead to judgment, that will finally hang in the Abbey's Norman tower, uttering its call to a vanished brotherhood and, with presumably greater efficacy, breaking the lightning bolts. Whereas the old bell—the bell that was and evidently still is the voice of love—is

---

masochistic and related to his inability to distinguish between his "private vision and the real situation" (1967, 89). According to Michael Levenson, Nick "is, in a word, Murdoch's vision of Existential Man, fully devoted to his own impossible agon" (2001, 565).

22. Nick's suicide and surname suggest that Murdoch wants us to connect him with Jude Fawley, the unhappy protagonist of Thomas Hardy's *Jude the Obscure* (1894). Juxtaposing Nick's apparent lack of religion and his position of gatekeeper at Imber with Jude's lack of faith and profession of restoring churches may be the ironic reason for Murdoch's linking of the two characters. Some of the other names may also "signify": Michael's surname "Meade" may suggest that he is "deserving." James Tayper Pace's surname means "peace" in Italian but the primary implication may be that he is able to move, morally speaking, at only a "tapered pace." Toby Gashe's surname seems to refer his being only superficially "wounded" by his experience at Imber.

hauled off to London to be studied by dry-as-dust experts like Paul. It is the new bell that speaks with James's voice that has (ironically?) triumphed, not Michael's old bell, though—who knows?—it too may one day make the leap into the lake, vanish for centuries, and be forgotten in the muddy bed of the unconscious. Stranger things have happened in Murdoch's fiction.

Though Nick's death is agonizingly real, ironically one of Michael's deep-seated problems is that he repeatedly has difficulty distinguishing between the real and the unreal, between subjective and objective reality. At the beginning of chapter 6, Michael awakens on hearing "a strange hollow booming sound" apparently coming from the lake. He gets up, goes to the window, and in the bright moonlight sees a group of nuns dragging the corpse of a drowned person out of the water. "The fantastic thought came to him suddenly that it was someone whom the nuns themselves had murdered" (78). Thoroughly frightened, he tries to cry out but finds he cannot. He also finds, a moment later, that he is still in bed and has been dreaming—a recurrent dream that is always accompanied by "an overwhelming sense of evil" and by the impression that the booming sound preceding the dream was real and not part of the dream itself.

Chapter 18 begins with the identical words as chapter 6: "Michael Meade was awakened by a strange hollow booming sound which seemed to come from the direction of the lake" (223). As in the preceding instance, he gets up, goes to the window, and looks out over the lake, which is lit up brightly by the moon. There are no nuns, no corpse, and Michael is really awake—and he has really heard the sound of the bell, which has just sounded as Toby and Dora have fallen into it, though of course at this point Michael does not know that. He also remembers vague stories "heard in childhood of noises coming out of the sea to portend disaster" (223). Significantly, Michael does not consciously "remember" the legend of the bell that Paul had earlier told Dora about and that Dora had later communicated to Toby. (Paul also mentions having told the story to Catherine.) It may be that Michael has never heard about it—in which case his dream would be either telepathic or miraculous, or both; or, alternatively, he may actually have suppressed memories of the legend, which he perhaps heard on one of his childhood visits to Imber when it was still inhabited by his relations.[23] In that case, however, the recurrent dream may in some way be a subconscious warning to Michael that his neglect of his love for Nick in favor of his religious concerns (as represented by the nuns) may be causing Nick's death. (Michael, we know, has been worried about Nick's killing himself.) Significantly, the corpse in the dream is not identified by gender, though it is in the legend, and Michael remembers that just before he awoke, when he heard the sound of the "real" bell, he had been dreaming of Nick.

It is also in connection with his other "lover," Toby, that Michael is again unable to distinguish clearly between what is happening subjectively in his imagination and what is happening in objective reality. Coming back slightly intoxicated from Swindon with Toby, Michael suddenly feels "a very distinct impulse to thrust his hand into the front of [sleeping] Toby's shirt. The next instant, as if this thought had acted as a spark, he had a very clear visual image of himself driving the Land-Rover into a ditch and seizing Toby violently in his arms." At this point Michael is still, though only with effort, able to keep his imagination under control, while at the same time he is surprised "that it could play him such a trick." He realizes, however, that he has been "blessed, or cursed, with a strong power of visualizing, but the snapshots it produced were not usually so startling" (156). As with Nick again, Michael finds it hard to believe that the love he feels welling up for Toby can be bad; and again he tries to link his sexual to his religious love. "It could not be," he thinks, "that God intended such a spring of love to be quenched utterly. There must, there must be a way in which it could be made a power for good" (157).

23. Dorothy Winsor is wrong when she claims categorically that "all of the characters involved know of the legend" (1980, 150). It may be that they all do know but, in the case of Michael, it is by no means certain.

A few moments later, after he has impulsively kissed Toby on the mouth, he isn't sure whether he has imagined the act or whether it has really occurred: "It happened so quickly that the moment after Michael was not at all sure whether it had really happened or whether it was just another thing that he had imagined" (158). Still later, back in his room, Michael reflects again on how strange it is that he should not only have thought to kiss Toby but should actually have done it; and he is tormented by thoughts—apparently with reason— that Nick may now consider him unfaithful (164).

Utopia and Its Enemies

It is Michael's inability to distinguish clearly and correctly between dreams or imaginary acts and reality that identifies him as a genuinely *utopian* man. It is only such a man who can take a dream and turn it into reality, which is no doubt why the Abbess, careful reader of human character that she is, picked him as the leader of the utopian brotherhood in the first place and insists that he remain its leader even after the arrival of the more obviously capable James Tayper Pace. The latter can evidently manage people and things very efficiently, but he lacks Michael's imagination and creativity, as well as, it must be admitted, his subjectivism. Michael possesses the eidetic imagination of the artist, without, however, being at the same time an artist.

Ultimately, of course, the utopian dream of approximating if not achieving the spiritual perfection exemplified by the Abbey fails. Oddly, however, unlike most utopias, both real and imaginary, it fails not on practical grounds but on spiritual ones, even "personal" ones. If Michael had not agreed, at Catherine's instigation and over James's strenuous objections, to admit Nick into the community, the brotherhood might very well have been a success. (Old Nick, it seems, has been at work again, doing his worst to expel a sick humanity from the utopian Garden.) But, as with Michael's sermon, we need to remember the parable of the lost son; we must take into account the claims of good works as well as the claims of faith. Can or should a utopia be founded on the denial of certain aspects of human nature and the exclusion of certain kinds of human beings? Aldous Huxley's New World State of AF 632 and George Orwell's Oceania of 1984 are both premised on a reduction/simplification of the complexities of human nature; that is also why both are dystopias, why in the former John Savage and in the latter Winston Smith are the last recognizable human beings. If the Imber community is to be genuinely utopian, then Nick must also be included, even though his inclusion may spell its destruction, as in fact it does, though perhaps not inevitably.

We must not forget, however, that there is, or at least so it would appear, another utopian community at Imber that does work, both practically and spiritually. That community is, of course, the Abbey itself.

Though almost all of the nuns in the Abbey conform to the very strict Benedictine rules of seclusion and stability of place—for example, outsiders remain behind a screen and are never able to see the nuns at mass and the Abbess grants interviews only through a small, slatted window like that of a confessional—the Abbey nevertheless gives the impression of being open to practical ideas and innovation. It was the Abbess's idea, after all, to start the Imber community and support it by means of a market garden. What is more, when called upon for help, as it is when Catherine and Dora are drowning, the Abbey is not prudish or a stickler for rules; it comes immediately to the rescue in the person of the semi-nude aquatic nun, Mother Clare. Nor are the nuns murderers, as they appear to be in Michael's dream, but saviors. There is nothing evil about them. If nothing else, this is proved by the way the nuns are able to deal kindly and sensibly with Toby when he thinks he is breaking their rules by entering their enclosed cemetery.[24]

24. When, not long after Murdoch had been diagnosed with Alzheimer's disease, a tall, urbane Irish Benedictine monk came to visit her, they discussed two of her nov-

At the same time, the Abbey is a place of very great and also very traditional religious power. Everyone comes *running* when the Abbess summons them. Everyone feels the Abbey's great spiritual power when they enter the Visitor's Chapel. The Abbess is shown to be extraordinarily wise and uncannily knowledgeable about goings on outside the Abbey, even though it is a place she rarely or perhaps never leaves. That the Abbey's spiritual power is real is indicated by the mysterious, "supernatural" phenomena associated with it, such as the booming of the bell that Michael hears in the night, as well as perhaps by the way Dora is changed for the better by being close to it. Nick, on the other hand, may be unaffected because he lives too far away in the lodge.

Why does the Abbey succeed where the brotherhood fails? Is it paradoxically the very proximity of the Abbey that produces or at least hastens the brotherhood's failure? Do the spiritually sick become even sicker when exposed to too much spirituality? Perhaps the Abbey succeeds where the brotherhood fails because it has simplified life, though admittedly rather arbitrarily and somewhat in the manner of Huxley and Orwell.[25] It has, to begin with, excluded half of humanity—there are no men. Presumably we are to conclude that the nuns have in this way solved the "problem" of sexuality— the spiritual "disease" from which, with the exception of James, all the more important "outside" characters in the novel suffer. Are we to believe that sisterhood works but brotherhood does not because

---

els, *The Book and the Brotherhood* and *The Good Apprentice,* both of which, according to the monk, had served as inspirations in "the recent setting up of the monastery, and the way they wanted it to go," though neither of these novels features an actual monastery, Benedictine or otherwise. No reference was made, apparently, to the Benedictine Abbey in *The Bell* (Bayley 1998, 127).

25. In *The Fire and the Sun,* Murdoch comments with gentle irony on the "delightful, and surely not ironic, description in the *Republic* (372) of the small natural ideal state where men live modestly upon cheese and figs and olives, and recline drinking their wine upon couches of bryony and myrtle" (1997, 15). This "ideal state," however, is founded on the exclusion of, among other things, the arts—on the exclusion, in other words, of a full humanity. Murdoch also cites Glaucon's deprecating, almost Orwellian remark on this supposedly ideal state: "'You are describing a city of pigs.'"

sexuality has become for the enclosed nuns what William Golding once called it, referring to its absence among the pubescent and pre-pubescent boys stranded in the Pacific in *Lord of the Flies,* a "relative triviality" (1965, 90)? If so, which is doubtful in any Murdoch novel but is never explicitly discussed—if, that is, the Abbey indeed self-selects people who are untroubled by sexuality—then it cannot serve as a practicable utopia for most of humanity, male or female, or at any rate not until Orwell's scientists have succeeded in eliminating the orgasm, and, along with it, most likely, the human race.

In the end, the brotherhood is dissolved and the Abbey is about to expand into Imber Court. To Michael this does not seem regret-table. Perhaps it should not seem so to us either. Still, it does mean that there is not, and perhaps cannot be, a halfway house between spirituality and worldliness. Previously there was a set of walls sep-arating Imber Court from the outside world and another from the Abbey. The Court was also linked to the outer world by three bridg-es and to the Abbey by a causeway. After a reformed and chastened Dora leaves, there will, in effect, be only one set of walls between the inner world and the outer. The dividing lines will have become clearer but not more porous. There has been a loss, an undeniable diminishment of the power of the spirit to change the world for the better. No possible beneficial effect on the life of an individual like Dora can make up for that loss.

CONCLUSION

One of the main problems in dealing with utopian literature of the modern period—that is, from, say, the late nineteenth century to the late twentieth—is that during this period utopian literature tended to be written by literary people (i.e., mostly professional novelists), whereas critiques of utopian literature have tended to be written by people interested in, and usually also trained in, the social sciences. The disjunction between these two groups has led, as I have tried to show in the foregoing analyses (*literary* analyses, let me emphasize again) of particular utopian fictions, to a misunderstanding of the aims of utopian literature in the modern period, and to a disregard for, or at least to a neglect of, the essential literary values of most contemporary utopias.

While the problem may be fairly simple to discern, its resolution unfortunately is not. Its roots lie very deep and are of ancient growth. The fact is that earlier utopias were usually written by philosophers and by what today we would call social scientists, e.g., Plato, More, Campanella, Bacon, etc. Given what they were, their aim naturally was not so much to persuade their readers of the fictional reality of their characters or even their ideal states but rather to depict the sociopolitical features of those ideal states themselves. Their utopias were (and are) social treatises in fictional guise, rather than literary fictions containing a social component. That is not to say, of course, that these earlier utopias were always lacking in literary value. Undoubtedly, the enduring power of Plato's *Republic* has a good deal to do with the fact that its author was a poet, someone, in other words, who knew that human beings were not to be persuaded by rational means alone. To his logical dialectic, therefore, Plato added myth and allegory, rather like Mozart adding melody and story to his, relatively speaking, monotonous *recitativo*. Still, the focus in a utopia like the *Republic* is on setting forth the specific requirements of an ideal state, in terms of the education of its citizens and rulers, its institutions, the nature of its governors, and its continued maintenance. These are important issues, both to us as social beings confronted daily with actual social problems and of course especially to those of us who are social scientists, but in and of themselves they are not of particular literary interest. Sir Thomas More's *Utopia*, for example, is almost devoid of literary significance except for those parts which are not explicitly "utopian," that is, those parts of the book that deal with the character of More himself or, more particularly, with his fictional protagonist and alter ego, Raphael Hythloday.

One of the chief reasons why it is precisely those apparently nonutopian elements of *Utopia* that are most literary is, I think, that those elements deal either with the psychology of the characters involved or else are primarily satirical in nature. Modern readers, as the students in my recent seminar on utopian fiction often demonstrated by their more or less enthusiastic responses, are more interested in the satiric descriptions of the follies and injustices of sixteenth-century England than they are in the supposedly splendid urban planning of unlikely utopian cities. In other words, what has happened to the genre of utopia since about the mid-eighteenth century—though, as we have seen, there were already signs of a shift in earlier works like *Utopia*—is that its function has changed. Utopia is no longer primarily a vehicle for describing in socio-political detail what an ideal state might look like, but has become chiefly a means for showing the deficiencies of existing states and institutions—and people. From Voltaire's *Candide* to Johnson's *Rasselas* to Butler's *Erewhon* and Morris's *News from Nowhere*, the aim of utopian fiction has been to attack the pretensions of contemporaneous social institutions and their human representatives, rather than to develop specific models to replace the inadequacies of those institutions and people. Utopia, in other words, has become a way of expressing satire rather than a way of positing an ideal. Its new aim is negative rather than positive. There are exceptions to the rule, of course: Bellamy's *Looking Backward*, for example.

The emphasis on satire in utopian fiction goes hand in hand with the general replacement over the last century or so of depictions of utopia with depictions of dystopia. The modern mind, in both its literary and social scientific manifestations, has found it increasingly difficult to believe in the possible establishment of ideal states. Confronted with the theories of Freud and—perhaps more to the point—with the horrors of mass slaughter in World War I and later in the Holocaust as well as in the Soviet Gulag, it has become more and more difficult to believe that either humanity itself or its institutions (or both) can be made perfect. Even in the relatively rare instances where that possibility has been qualifiedly affirmed—as it is in, say, Huxley's *Island*—the utopia is shown to be very fragile and of limited duration.

The end of utopia and the consequent disillusionment that goes with that end are issues, therefore, of greater interest to literary people than they are to social scientists. The paradoxical conflict between what could and even should be (the ideal) but what nevertheless can't be (the reality) is rich in literary potential, as is evident, for example, in Iris Murdoch's *The Bell*. But by no means only in *The Bell*, for this conflict has always been a source of literary inspiration, as it was in Shakespeare's *The Tempest*, for example, but also in his great tragedies. Ultimately, it is the people—real as well as fictional—who are driven by visions of the ideal and are therefore of the greatest interest to us, not the ideals themselves. Ideals soon tend to become outdated and, in many cases, difficult for later ages to take seriously (e.g., Plato's *Republic* or More's *Utopia*), but people's characters remain much the same over the centuries, though our understanding of their natures and motives has undoubtedly become more complex. That is why Aristophanes on Socrates remains more readable after two and a half millennia than Plato on Socrates. That is also why, to venture a concluding prediction, utopian fictions—with the emphasis on *fictions*—will continue to be read into the distant future, while mere utopias will only be read about.

WORKS CITED

Aldiss, Brian W. 1984. "The Downward Journey: Orwell's *1984*." *Extrapolation* 25, no. 1 (spring): 5–11.

Ash, Timothy Garton. 2003. "Orwell's List." *New York Review of Books*, 25 September. http://www.netcharles.com/orwell/articles/col-informer.htm.

Auerbach, Erich. 1971. *Mimesis*. Translated by W. R. Trask. Princeton: Princeton University Press. (Originally published 1946. Page citations are to the 1971 edition.)

Baker, James R. 2000. "Golding and Huxley: The Fables of Demonic Possession." *Twentieth Century Literature* 46, no. 3 (1 September): 311–28.

Ballantyne, R. M. 1990. *The Coral Island*. Oxford: Oxford University Press. (Originally published 1898. Page citations are to the 1990 edition.)

Barnes, Julian. 1990. *Flaubert's Parrot*. New York: Vintage.

Bayley, John. 1998. *Iris: A Memoir of Iris Murdoch*. London: Duckworth.

Beams, David W. 1988. "The Fortunate Fall: Three Actions in *The Bell*." *Twentieth Century Literature* 34, no. 4 (winter): 416–33.

Bellamy, Edward. 1995. *Looking Backward: 2000–1887*. Edited by Daniel H. Borus. Boston: St. Martin's Press. (Originally published 1888. Page citations are to the 1995 edition.)

Berghahn, Klaus, and Hans Ulrich Seeber. 1983. *Literarische Utopien von Morus bis zur Gegenwart*. Königstein: Athenäum.

Berlin, Isaiah. 1952. *Karl Marx: His Life and Environment*. London: Oxford University Press.

———. 1997. *The Proper Study of Mankind*. London: Chatto & Windus.

Biesterfeld, Wolfgang. 1982. *Die literarische Utopie*. 2d ed. Stuttgart: J. B. Metzleresche Verlagsbuchhandlung.

Biles, Jack I. 1971. *Talk: Conversations with William Golding*. New York: Harcourt. Quoted in *Contemporary Authors*, new rev. ser., 33: 172–78.

Bloom, Allan. 1989. "Responses to Fukuyama." *National Interest* 16 (summer): 19–21.

Borges, Jorge Luis. 1964. "The First Wells." In *Other Inquisitions, 1937–1952*, trans. Ruth L. C. Simms, 86–88. Austin: University of Texas Press.

Brook, Donald. 1944. *Writers' Gallery: Biographical Sketches of Britain's Greatest Writers, and Their Views on Reconstruction*. London: Rockcliff.

Burnham, James. 1941. *The Managerial Revolution*. New York: John Day.

Butler, Samuel. 1985. *Erewhon*. Edited by Peter Mudford. London: Penguin. (Originally published 1872. Page citations are to the 1985 edition.)

Byatt, A. S. 1965. *Degrees of Freedom*. London: Chatto & Windus.

Carlyle, Thomas. 1897. *Past and Present*. London: Chapman & Hall. (Original-ly published 1843. Page citations are to the 1897 edition.)

Carver, Judy. 2002. "William Golding: A Biographical Sketch." In *William Golding: A Critical Study of the Novels*, new ed., ed. Mark Kinkead-Weekes and Ian Gregor, 383–98. London: Faber & Faber.

Casement, William. 1989. *"Nineteen-Eighty-Four* and Philosophical Realism." *Midwest Quarterly* 30, no. 2 (winter): 215–28.

Conradi, Peter J. 2001a. *Iris Murdoch: A Life*. New York: W. W. Norton.

———. 2001b. *The Saint and the Artist: A Study in the Fiction of Iris Murdoch*. London: HarperCollins.

Crick, Bernard. 1980. *George Orwell: A Life*. London: Penguin.

———. 1989. *Essays on Politics and Literature*. Edinburgh: Edinburgh University Press.

Deery, June. 2005. "Review of George Orwell, *Nineteen Eighty-Four*." *Utopian Studies* 16, no. 1: 122–25.

Dickstein, Morris. 2004. "Hope against Hope: Orwell's Posthumous Novel." In *George Orwell into the Twenty-First Century*, ed. Thomas Cushman and John Rodden, 63–76. Boulder: Paradigm.

Draper, Michael. 1987. "Wells, Jung, and the Persona." *English Literature in Transition, 1880–1920* 30, no. 4 (winter): 437–49.

Eagleton, Terry. 1991. *Literary Theory: An Introduction*. Minneapolis: University of Minnesota Press.

Firchow, Peter. 1984. *The End of Utopia: A Study of Aldous Huxley's* Brave New World. Lewisburg: Bucknell University Press.

———. 1987. "Comparative Literature and Cultural Illiterates." *CNL/World Report*, n.s., 2: 15–24.

———. 1992. "Orwell's Fictions of the Thirties." In *Writers of the Old School*, ed. Rosemary M. Colt and Janice Rossen, 17–38. Houndsmills: Macmillan.

———. Forthcoming. "United States." In *Imagology: A Handbook of the Literary Representation of National Characters*, ed. Joep Leerssen and Manfred Beller. Amsterdam: University of Amsterdam Press.

Forster, E. M. [1966.] *Aspects of the Novel*. New York: Harcourt, Brace & World.

Fortunati, Vita. 1987. "'It Makes No Difference': A Utopia of Simulation and Transparency." In *George Orwell's* Nineteen Eighty-Four, ed. Harold Bloom, 109–20. New York: Chelsea House.

Freedman, Carl. 1986. "Antinomies of *Nineteen Eighty-Four*." In *Critical Essays on George Orwell*, ed. Bernard Oldsey and Joseph Browne, 90–109. Boston: G. K. Hall & Co.

Friedrich, Otto. 1984. "George Orwell." In Nineteen Eighty-Four *to 1984*, ed. C. J. Kuppig, 90–108. New York: Carroll & Graf.

Frye, Northrop. 1965. "Varieties of Literary Utopia." In *Utopias and Utopian Thought*, ed. Frank A. Manuel, 25–49. Boston: Houghton Mifflin.

———. 1986. "Orwell and Marxism." In *George Orwell: Modern Critical Views*, ed. Harold Bloom, 9–11. New York: Chelsea House. (Originally published 1946. Page citations are to the 1986 edition.)

Fukuyama, Francis. 1989. "'The End of History?" *National Interest* 16 (summer): 3–18.

———. 1989–90. "A Reply to My Critics." *National Interest* 18 (winter): 21–28.

———. 1992. *The End of History and the Last Man.* New York: Free Press.

———. 1994. "Reflections on the End of History, Five Years Later." In *After History? Francis Fukuyama and His Critics,* ed. Timothy Burns, 239–58. Lanham, Md.: Rowman & Littlefield. Originally published in *History and Theory* 34 (1995): 27–43.

———. 1999a. "A Big Mac, Fries--and Lasting Peace." *New Statesman* 128 (5 July): 53–54.

———. 1999b. "Second Thoughts: The Last Man in a Bottle." *National Interest* 56 (summer): 16–33.

Golding, William. 1959. *Lord of the Flies.* New York: Capricorn Books. (Originally published 1954. Page citations are to the 1959 edition.)

———. 1965. "Fable." In *The Hot Gates.* London: Faber & Faber.

Grene, Nicholas. 1984. *Bernard Shaw: A Critical View.* New York: St. Martin's Press.

Haynes, Roslynn. 1980. *H. G. Wells, Discoverer of the Future: The Influence of Science on His Thought.* London: Macmillan.

Hennies, Wilhelm. 1988. *Max Weber: Essays in Reconstruction.* Translated by Keith Tribe. London: Allan & Unwin.

Hillegas, Mark. 1974. *The Future as Nightmare: H. G. Wells and the Anti-Utopians.* Carbondale: Southern Illinois University Press.

Himmelfarb, Gertrude. 1999. "Responses to Fukuyama." *National Interest* 56 (summer): 37–38.

Holroyd, Michael. 1989. *The Pursuit of Power.* Vol. 2 of *Bernard Shaw: A Biography.* New York: Random House.

Howe, Irving. 1971. "*1984:* History as Nightmare." In *Twentieth-Century Interpretations of 1984: A Collection of Essays,* ed. Samuel Hynes, 41–53. Englewood Cliffs, N.J.: Prentice-Hall.

———. 1983. "*1984:* Enigmas of Power." In *1984 Revisited: Totalitarianism in Our Century,* ed. Irving Howe, 3–18. New York: Harper & Row.

Hueffer, Ford Madox. 1911. "High Germany--II: Utopia." *Saturday Review* 112 (7 October): 454–56.

Hughes, David. 1977. "The Garden in Wells's Early Science Fiction." In *H. G. Wells and Modern Science Fiction,* ed. Darko Suvin and Robert M. Philmus, 48–69. Lewisburg: Bucknell University Press.

Huntington, John. 1982. *The Logic of Fantasy: H. G. Wells and Science Fiction.* New York: Columbia University Press.

Huntington, Samuel. 1989. "No Exit: The Errors of Endism." *National Interest* 17 (fall): 3–11.

Huxley, Aldous. 1948. *Ape and Essence.* New York: Harper Brothers.

———. 1956. *Do What You Will.* London: Chatto & Windus. (Originally published 1929. Page citations are to the 1956 edition.)

———. 1957a. *Jesting Pilate.* London: Chatto & Windus. (Originally published 1926. Page citations are to the 1957 edition.)

———. 1957b. *Proper Studies.* London: Chatto & Windus. (Originally published 1927. Page citations are to the 1957 edition.)

———. 1958. *Brave New World Revisited.* New York: Perennial Library.

———. 1960. *The Olive Tree.* London: Chatto & Windus. (Originally published 1936. Page citations are to the 1960 edition.)

———. 1962. *Island.* London: Chatto & Windus.

———. 1969. *Letters.* Edited by Grover Smith. London: Chatto & Windus.

———. 1971. "Letter to George Orwell." In *Twentieth-Century Interpretations of 1984: A Collection of Essays,* ed. Samuel Hynes, 102–3. Englewood Cliffs, N.J.: Prentice-Hall.

———. 1989. *Brave New World.* New York: Harper Perennial. (Originally published 1932. Page citations are to the 1989 edition.)

Hynes, Samuel. 1971. "Introduction." In *Twentieth-Century Interpretations of 1984: A Collection of Essays,* ed. Samuel Hynes, 1–19. Englewood Cliffs, N.J.: Prentice-Hall.

Jacoby, Russell. 1999. *The End of Utopia: Politics and Culture in an Age of Apathy.* New York: Basic Books.

Johnson, Paul. 1992. "Review of Francis Fukuyama, *The End of History and the Last Man.*" *Commentary* 93 (March): 51–54.

Jones, Dorothy. 1967. "Love and Morality in Iris Murdoch's *The Bell.*" *Meanjin* 26: 85–90.

Kaehele, Sharon, and Howard German. 1967. "The Discovery of Reality in Iris Murdoch's *The Bell.*" *PMLA* 82, no. 7 (December): 554–63.

Karl, Frederick. 1973. "Conrad, Wells, and the Two Voices." *PMLA* 88, no. 5 (October): 1049–65.

Kateb, George. 1971. "The Road to 1984." In *Twentieth-Century Interpretations of 1984: A Collection of Essays,* ed. Samuel Hynes, 73–87. Englewood Cliffs, N.J.: Prentice-Hall.

———. 1976. *Utopia and Its Enemies.* New York: Schocken.

Kaye, Julian B. 1958. *Bernard Shaw and the Nineteenth-Century Tradition.* Norman: University of Oklahoma Press.

Kemp, Peter. 1982. *H. G. Wells and the Culminating Ape.* New York: St. Martin's Press.

Kermode, Frank. 1983. "The Meaning of It All." In *William Golding,* Lord of the Flies, ed. James R. Baker and Arthur P. Ziegler Jr., 97–202. New York: Wideview/Perigree.

Kinkead-Weekes, Mark, and Ian Gregor. 2002. *William Golding: A Critical Study of the Novels.* New ed. London: Faber & Faber.

Koppenfels, Werner von. 1984. "Orwell und die Deutschen." *Deutsche Vierteljahresschrift* 58: 658–78.

Krutch, Joseph Wood. 1956. *The Modern Temper: A Study and a Confession.* New York: Harcourt, Brace & World. (Originally published 1929. Page citations are to the 1956 edition.)

Kumar, Krishan. 1986. "Wells and 'the So-Called Science of Sociology.'" In *H. G. Wells under Revision: Proceedings of the International H. G. Wells Symposium,* ed. Patrick Parrinder and Christopher Rolfe, 192–217. Selingrove: Susquehanna University Press.

—. 1987. *Utopia and Anti-Utopia in Modern Times.* Oxford: Basil Blackwell.

—. 1993. "The End of Socialism? The End of Utopia? The End of History?" In *Utopias and the Millennium,* ed. Krishan Kumar and Stephen Bann, 63–80. London: Reaktion Books.

Kuppig, C. J., ed. 1984. Nineteen Eighty-Four *to 1984.* New York: Carroll & Graf.

Lee, Robert A. 1986. "The Uses of Form: A Reading of *Animal Farm.*" In *Critical Essays on George Orwell,* ed. Bernard Oldsey and Joseph Browne, 39–53. Boston: G. K. Hall & Co.

Levenson, Michael. 2001. "Iris Murdoch: The Philosophic Fifties and *The Bell.*" *Modern Fiction Studies* 47 (spring): 558–79.

Marcuse, Herbert. 1941. *Reason and Revolution: Hegel and the Rise of Social Theory.* London: Oxford University Press.

—. 1972. *One-Dimensional Man: Studies in the Ideology of Advanced Industrial Society.* London: Abacus. (Originally published 1964. Page citations are to the 1972 edition.)

McConnell, Frank. 1981. *The Science Fiction of H. G. Wells.* New York: Oxford University Press.

Medcalf, Stephen. 2005. "Island Skies: William Golding Reappraised." *TLS,* no. 5344 (2 September): 12–13.

Minney, R. J. 1969. *The Bogus Image of Bernard Shaw.* London: Leslie Frewin.

Monteith, Charles. 1986. "Strangers from Within." In *William Golding: The Man and His Books,* ed. John Carey, 57–63. London: Faber & Faber.

Muegge, M. A. 1914. *Friedrich Nietzsche: His Life and Work.* London: T. Fisher Unwin.

Murdoch, Iris. 1962. *The Bell.* London: Penguin Books. (Originally published 1958. Page citations are to the 1962 edition.)

—. 1971. *The Sovereignty of Good.* New York: Schocken. (Originally published 1970. Page citations are to the 1971 edition.)

—. 1973. *The Black Prince.* London: Chatto & Windus.

—. 1974. *Sartre: Romantic Rationalist.* London: Collins. (Originally published 1953. Page citations are to the 1974 edition.)

—. 1977. *The Fire and the Sun: Why Plato Banished the Artists.* Oxford: Clarendon Press.

—. 1986. *Acastos: Two Platonic Dialogues.* New York: Viking Penguin.

—. 1997. *Existentialists and Mystics.* London: Chatto & Windus.

Nietzsche, Friedrich. *The Portable Nietzsche.* Edited and translated by Walter Kaufmann. New York: Viking Press, 1971.

Orwell, George. 1954. *A Collection of Essays.* Garden City, N.Y.: Doubleday.

—. 1968a. *The Collected Essays, Journalism, and Letters of George Orwell.* Edited by Sonia Orwell and Ian Angus. Vol. 4, *In Front of Your Nose, 1945–1950.* London: Secker & Warburg.

—. 1968b. "Preface to the Ukrainian Edition of *Animal Farm.*" In *The Collected Essays, Journalism, and Letters of George Orwell.* Edited by Sonia Orwell and Ian Angus. Vol. 3, *As I Please, 1943–1945,* 402–6. London: Secker & Warburg.

———. 1983. *Nineteen Eighty-Four.* New York: Harcourt Brace. (Originally published 1949. Page citations are to the 1983 edition.)

———. 1996. *Animal Farm.* New York: Penguin Putnam. Edited and with an introduction by C. M. Woodhouse. (Originally published 1945. Page citations are to the 1996 edition.)

———. n.d. *Coming Up for Air.* New York: Harcourt, Brace & World.

Parrinder, Patrick. 1985. "Utopia and Meta-Utopia in H. G. Wells." *Science Fiction Studies* 12, no. 2 (July): 115–28.

Pearson, Hesketh. 1950. *G.B.S.: A Full Length Portrait.* New York: Harper.

Rainwater, Catherine. 1995. "Encounters with the 'White Sphinx': The Re-Vision of Poe in Wells's Early Fiction." In *The Critical Response to H. G. Wells,* ed. William Scheick, 75–88. Westport: Greenwood, 1995.

Rodden, John. 1988. "Soviet Literary Policy, 1945–1989: The Case of George Orwell." *Modern Age* (spring): 131–39.

Roppen, Georg. 1956. *Evolution and Poetic Belief.* Oslo: Oslo University Press.

Rose, Jonathan. 1992. "The Invisible Sources of *Nineteen Eighty-Four.*" *Journal of Popular Culture* 26, no. 1 (summer): 93–107.

Sanderson, Richard K. 1988. "The Two Narrators and Happy Ending of *Nineteen Eighty-Four.*" *Modern Fiction Studies* 34, no. 4 (winter): 587–95.

Sartre, Jean-Paul. 1947. *Existentialism.* Translated by Bernard Frechtman. New York: Philosophical Library.

Shaw, George Bernard. 1931. *Complete Plays.* London: Constable.

———. 1936. *The Perfect Wagnerite.* New York: Dodd, Mead.

———. 1944. *Everybody's Political What's What?* London: Constable.

———. 1949. *Sixteen Self-Sketches.* New York: Dodd, Mead.

———. 1955. *Major Critical Essays: The Quintessence of Ibsenism; The Perfect Wagnerite; The Sanity of Art.* London: Constable.

———. 1961. *Essays in Fabian Socialism.* London: Constable.

———. 1967. *Man and Superman.* New York: Bantam Books. (Originally published 1903.)

———. 2000. *Major Barbara.* London: Penguin. (Originally published 1906. Page citations are to the 2000 edition.)

Shelden, Michael. 1991. *Orwell: The Authorized Biography.* New York: HarperCollins.

Stanzel, Franz K. 1986. *A Theory of Narrative.* Cambridge: Cambridge University Press.

Steiner, George. 1983. "Killing Time." *New Yorker,* 11 December, 168–88.

Steinhoff, William. 1975. *George Orwell and the Origins of 1984.* Ann Arbor: University of Michigan Press.

Stewart, Jack F. 1980. "Dialectics in Murdoch's *The Bell.*" *Research Studies* 48, no. 4 (December): 210–17.

Stewart, Jon, ed. 1996. *The Hegel Myths and Legends.* Evanston: Northwestern University Press.

Talmon, J. L. 1952. *The Rise of Totalitarian Democracy.* Boston: Beacon Press.

Tennyson, Alfred. 1955. "Locksley Hall." In *Poetry of the Victorian Period,* ed. George Benjamin Woods and Jerome Hamilton Buckley, 45–49. Chicago: Scott, Foresman & Co.

Tolkien, J. R. R. 1984. "On Fairy-Stories." In *The Monsters and the Critics, and Other Essays,* ed. Christopher Tolkien, 109–61. Boston: Houghton Mifflin.

Toynbee, Arnold. 1957. *A Study of History.* Vol. 2. Abridged by D. C. Somervell. New York: Oxford University Press.

Travis, Alan. 2005. "Real Life 'Big Brother' Watched over George Orwell." *Globe and Mail* (Toronto), 19 July, A3.

Turco, Alfred, Jr. 1976. *Shaw's Moral Vision: The Self and Salvation.* Ithaca: Cornell University Press.

Valency, Maurice. 1973. *The Cart and the Trumpet: The Plays of George Bernard Shaw.* New York: Oxford University Press.

Wall, Stephen. 1963. "The Bell in *The Bell.*" *Essays in Criticism* 13: 265–73.

Wells, H. G. 1899. *When the Sleeper Wakes.* New York: Harper's.

———. 1900. *Tales of Space and Time.* Leipzig: Tauchnitz.

———. 1923. *Men Like Gods.* New York: Macmillan.

———. 1934. *Seven Famous Novels.* Garden City, N.Y.: Garden City Publishing Co.

———. 1942. *The Outlook for Homo Sapiens.* London: Secker & Warburg.

———. 1987. *The Definitive* Time Machine. Edited by Harry M. Geduld. Bloomington: Indiana University Press. (Originally published 1895. Page citations are to the 1987 edition.)

Wells, H. G., Julian Huxley, and G. P. Wells. 1931. *The Science of Life.* Vol. 4. Garden City, N.Y.: Doubleday.

Wilson, Colin. 1969. *Bernard Shaw: A Reassessment.* London: Hutchinson.

Winsor, Dorothy A. 1980. "Iris Murdoch and the Uncanny: Supernatural Events in *The Bell.*" *Literature and Psychology* 30, nos. 3–4: 147–54.

Wisenthal, J. L. 1974a. *The Marriage of Contraries: Bernard Shaw's Middle Plays.* Cambridge: Harvard University Press.

———. 1974b. "The Underside of Undershaft: A Wagnerian Motif in 'Major Barbara.'" *Shaw Review* 24 (May): 56–65.

Woolf, Virginia. 1961. "Mr. Bennett and Mrs. Brown." In *Approaches to the Novel,* ed. Robert Scholes. San Francisco: Chandler.

Zwerdling, Alex. 1971. "Orwell and the Techniques of Didactic Fantasy." In *Twentieth-Century Interpretations of 1984: A Collection of Essays,* ed. Samuel Hynes, 88–101. Englewood Cliffs, N.J.: Prentice-Hall.

INDEX

Animal Farm (Orwell), 98, 100–111; and defamiliarization, 104–5; difficulty of publication, 100–101; and essentialism, 105–6; moral deterioration in, 108–10; as political allegory, 102–4, 107; positive message of, 110–11; as satire, 108
Apocalypse, 6n, 26, 27, 55
Aristotle, xi, 8, 175
Atwood, Margaret, 5

Ballantyne, R. M., 11, 131, 136, 139n, 143
Barrie, James, 136, 137
Bell, The (Murdoch): and Bloomsbury, 163n; brotherhood in, 170; confession in, 181–83; ethics in, 159–68, 171–76; irony in, 163, 164n; love in, 177–78, 184; narrative technique, 157n, 158, 162, 163–64, 165n; realism in, 161n; subjectivity in, 160–70, 173–74, 176, 184; supernatural in, 183; symbolism of the bell, 178–79; utopia in, 185–88
Bellamy, Edward, 19, 57, 59, 191
Berdyaev, Nicholas, 3, 71n
Blair, Eric. *See* Orwell, George
Bloom, Allan, 71, 81n, 87n
Burnham, James, 71n, 106, 118n, 129n
Butler, Samuel, 7n, 15, 40, 190

Callanbach, Ernest, 5
Carlyle, Thomas, 37, 56, 57, 58
Conrad, Joseph, 18n, 20, 22, 23, 119n
Crick, Bernard, xvn, 102n, 106n, 117n, 118n

Darwin, Charles, 28, 29, 34, 55. *See also* Huxley, T. H.

Dostoyevsky, Fyodor, 79, 111, 125n, 157
Dystopia. 1, 14; as erstwhile utopia, 4; and fiction, 159, 186; as genre, 11, 107, 133; and Hegel, 93; and literary merit, 9n; and modernity, 191; as reversal of utopia, 10; and satire, 5, 191; and technology, 6, 7n

Eagleton, Terry, 16, 17
Empson, William, 105n

Fabian Society, 2n, 4, 33n, 42n, 65
False consciousness, 69, 83, 84, 85, 86
Fiction, 22, 104, 138, 147, 149n, 158, 160, 164; and science fiction, 6, 20; and utopia, xii–xiii, 5, 6, 10, 11, 13, 14, 15, 16, 22, 23n, 134, 159, 167, 189, 190, 191
Ford, Ford Madox, 2
Ford, Henry, 15, 68
Forster, E. M., 7
Freud, Sigmund, 24, 55, 68, 78, 79, 112, 135, 157, 169, 191
Friedman, Thomas, 73
Fukuyama, Francis, xiii, 12, 54, 68, 69, 70, 71, 72, 73, 74, 75, 76, 77, 80, 81n, 82, 83, 85, 86, 87, 88, 90, 91, 92, 96, 117

Galilei, Galileo, 118, 119
Goethe, Johann Wolgang, 37, 38
Golding, William, xiii, xv, 6, 9, 10, 11, 13, 130–53, 188; and fable, 130, 133, 142; and authenticity, 131. *See also Lord of the Flies*

Hawthorne, Nathaniel, 25
Hegel, Georg Friedrich, 65, 69, 70, 71n,